Casanova Was a Librarian

Casanova Was a Librarian

A Light-Hearted Look at the Profession

KATHLEEN LOW

McFarland & Company, Inc., Publishers
Jefferson, North Carolina, and London

LIBRARY OF CONGRESS CATALOGUING-IN-PUBLICATION DATA

Low, Kathleen.
Casanova was a librarian : a light-hearted look
at the profession / Kathleen Low.
p.   cm.
Includes bibliographical references and index.

ISBN-13: 978-0-7864-2981-3
(softcover : 50# alkaline paper) ∞

1. Library science — Miscellanea.   2. Librarians — Miscellanea.
3. Library science — Humor.   4. Librarians — Humor.
I. Title
Z665.L69   2007   020 — dc22   2007005755

British Library cataloguing data are available

On the cover: detail of *Casanova* (2005) ©Buena
Vista Pictures/Photofest; books ©2006 PhotoSpin

Manufactured in the United States of America

*McFarland & Company, Inc., Publishers
Box 611, Jefferson, North Carolina 28640
www.mcfarlandpub.com*

To my parents, who cringed when I decided to become a librarian, but who supported me in my career decision nonetheless, to my sisters who have to cope with a sister that's a librarian, and to librarians everywhere who toil at their jobs daily not for the money, but for the love of the job and their commitment to serving their community

Table of Contents

Preface

On Halloween in 1984 I pulled my hair up into a bun, put on a grey plaid skirt that fell way below my knees and a long-sleeved white cotton blouse that buttoned up to the middle of my neck, added a cameo brooch, and stepped into a pair of old black plumps with clunky one-inch block heels. I had started work as a reference librarian in a large library just two weeks earlier and I had learned many of the librarians and assistants went to work in costume on Halloween. Since I was the youngest (in my twenties at the time) and newest librarian on staff, I felt I was probably expected to participate in this holiday fun. Dressed in my librarian costume, I was ready for the workday.

The day started with the weekly staff meeting, followed by my assigned hours on the reference desk. Throughout the day my co-workers complimented one another on their costumes, which ranged from clowns to witches. But from the minute I arrived at work to the moment I left, no one commented on my costume. I was puzzled.

Many years later I asked my supervisor about my first Halloween in the department. Why didn't anyone comment on my "librarian" costume that year? She replied the staff did not know me well enough at that time to determine whether I was in costume or my attire that day was part of my style. For a moment, I stopped breathing. What type of profession had I entered?

Back then, there were librarians who wore their hair up in a bun and dressed in frumpy clothes. Back then, at parties, it was as difficult for me to admit I was a librarian as it probably is for some alcoholics to admit they've got a drinking problem. Because back then, when you said you were a librarian, partygoers immediately pegged you as a boring person, and they'd say things like, "You must like to read," or, "That's a nice quiet job." (You have to remember this was when libraries still had card catalogs and the Internet was primarily used by government agencies and academics.)

Now, after having been in the profession for more than twenty-five years, I still wonder about the profession. Recently, I started to investigate the nature of librarianship and found some interesting facts about librarians. The librarians who wore their hair up in a bun have long retired. They're been replaced by a fun and interesting group of individuals.

If you think librarians are boring ladies who read all day and like telling people to be quiet, be prepared have your opinion changed dramatically. This book, which is intended for anyone who has ever walked into a library or come into contact with a librarian, offers a peek at the interesting, humorous, and interesting side of librarians. It is not intended to be all-inclusive in any of the topics covered. Instead, it seeks to expose some intriguing facts and fancies that will whet your appetite for a closer look at the men and women who chose to become librarians.

Librarians have been famous revolutionaries, lovers, saints, and politicians. They've been immortalized in songs, poems, movies, comic strips and books. They've had action figures made in their image. They have websites and nick names like the Kung Fu Librarian, Barbarian Librarian, and Spooky Librarians. And merchandise ranging from thongs to pet collars has been designed just for librarians. Today's librarians are anything but boring — so be prepared to have your preconceptions shattered.

I want to acknowledge all the wonderful support I received for this project. I am grateful for the assistance and library services provided by the staff of the State Information and Reference Center of the California State library, especially Jocelyn Napier and Chris Spry, and for the advice and assistance I received from Vera Nicholas and Audrey Dodds. Many thanks are also extended to Kevin Guhl, Bill Barnes and Gene Ambaum for providing sample comic strips for inclusion in the book, and to my writing buddies Ron Barnes and Chris Berger for their ongoing support.

1

Famous Librarians

The stereotypical librarian is portrayed as a shy, meek individual. But in fact, many of the most memorable librarians throughout history were far from the image of librarians portrayed in the media. Many famous inventors, revolutionaries, world leaders, philosophers, composers, mathematicians, saints, popes, and individuals of notoriety have been librarians. Casanova, Golda Meir, Benjamin Franklin, and the Grimm brothers are just a few of the many famous individuals who have held the position of librarian. This chapter introduces you to a sampling of the many famous librarians throughout history.

The Infamous

Giacomo Casanova (1725–1798)

Like many other famous librarians, this infamous lover and womanizer did not choose librarianship as his initial career. Born in Venice, Casanova was a sickly child and his parents, who were actors, were frequently absent. At age nine, he was sent to Padua for his formal education. His move to Padua also marked the beginning of his amorous escapades. He studied law at the University of Padua, and received his doctor of civil and canon law degree from the university in 1742. Initially he sought a career in the church. However, the clergy was not his calling. His accomplishments, adventures, numerous imprisonments, and sexual escapades are well documented. In addition to being an adventurer, he was also a violin player in the orchestra of the San Samuele Theater at one time. But his fortune came from his role in developing the French state lottery, a fortune he eventually lost over time. Then in 1794 Casanova met Count Josef Karl Emmanuel von Waldstein, who offered him a librarian position in his castle in Dux. Needing the employment, Casanova accepted the position. His time in Dux was not pleasant, but his librarian job provided him with leisure time to focus on his writing. He remained at Dux until his death.

Hypatia (circa 370–415)

Hypatia is often referred to as the first famous female mathematician. Reputed to be a beauty, she lectured on mathematics and Neoplatonism, a philosophical system that holds that all existence consists of emanations from the one with whom the soul may be reunited. But during the period in which she lived, Hypatia's teachings were considered paganism. And in 415, an angry mob of Christians reportedly pulled her from her passing carriage, tore her from limb to limb, and then burned her broken body in the street for her pagan teachings. It's frequently written that she worked in the great Library of Alexandria, and that at some point she was librarian of Alexandria. However, many scholars and historians consider this to be a myth since few facts has been found to verify the appointment.

Sir Anthony Panizzi (1797–1879)

Born in Brescello, Italy, Panizzi fled Italy to avoid arrest as a revolutionary. Fleeing to England, he started teaching Italian, eventually becoming an Italian professor. He was then appointed assistant librarian at the British Museum, became a British citizen, and in 1856, he became the chief librarian at the British Museum. Under his leadership, significant improvements were made to the library, and the British Museum became one of the world's great cultural institutions. Who would have imagined a revolutionary becoming a famous librarian!

Scientists and Inventors

Eratosthenes (circa 276 BC–circa 194 BC)

Not a household name, Eratosthenes is best known as the man who calculated the circumference of the Earth. He also measured the tilt of the Earth's axis and developed a calendar that included leap years. An astronomer, mathematician, writer, and scientist, he served as the librarian in the great Library of Alexandria at one time.

Benjamin Franklin (1706–1790)

When you mention Benjamin Franklin, most people remember the story of how he flew a kite with a key attached to a wire string during a storm. And when lightning struck the kite and traveled down the wire to the key, Franklin had invented the lightning rod and proved that lightning was electricity. Others may remember him as one of the signers of the Declaration of Independence and the Constitution of the United States. But few remember the role he played in library history. Even fewer people know that back in 1731 only the very wealthy owned a lot of books. Franklin himself could only afford to own a couple of books. But he, and other members of Junto, a philosophical society he belonged to, realized that if they consolidated their money, they could purchase a number of books that could be accessible by all members of the society. That's exactly what they did. And the Library Company of Philadelphia, a private subscription library, the first in America, was founded. The Library Company of Philadelphia was the early predecessor of the public library, and Franklin is credited with founding the first American library. For a brief period he was also the librarian at the Library Company after the first librarian left to become a printer. He served in that role very briefly and was succeeded by a shoemaker. And yes, although librarianship is a wonderful career, throughout history it has not been a highly lucrative one.

Gottfried Wilhelm Leibniz (1646–1716)

Best known for building the first mechanical calculator that multiplied and divided numbers and for his role in the development of infinitesimal calculus, Leibniz was also a noted philosopher. He was born in Leipzig, Germany, into a Lutheran family. His father, a professor of moral philosophy, died when Gottfried was only six. Gottfried received his bachelor's degree in law from the University of Leipzig and studied for his doctorate, but was not granted his doctorate from the university. Biographers provide a number of potential reasons regarding why he was denied his doctorate. However, Leibniz persevered and subsequently received a doctorate in law from the University of Altdorf. After graduation, he held various positions, starting with secretary to a society of alchemists, then as a legal advisor, and then court councillor at Hannover under Duke Johann Friedrich of Brunswich-Luneburg. While councillor, he was also the librarian and archivist for the duke's library. At one point, Leibniz was also offered a job as librarian at the Vatican, but turned it down because he refused to convert to Catholicism.

Johann Joachim Winckelmann (1717–1768)

The son of a cobbler, Prussian-born Winckelmann is considered the founder of modern scientific archeology and a major influence in the rise of the neoclassical movement in the late 18th century. As a young man, he studied theology at the University of Halle, then medicine at the University of Jena. In 1748 Count Heinrich von Bunau appointed him the secretary of his library at Nothnitz near Dresden, the equivalent of being a librarian today. It was there Winckelmann made a name for himself writing art histories and essays. In 1754 he joined the Roman Catholic Church and served in a series of papal appointments. He was appointed librarian to Alberico Cardinal Archinto, then librarian to Cardinal Passionei, and then to Cardinal Albani. Eventually he rose to the position of prefect of antiquities. Winckelmann was murdered in Triste in 1768 by his gay lover.

World Figures

Laura Bush (1946 —)

The wife of President George W. Bush, Laura Bush was born in Midland, Texas. She was an only child. Her father was a home builder and her mother a book-keeper. She earned a bachelor's degree in education from Southern Methodist University in 1968 and subsequently taught elementary school in Dallas and Houston. Her love of reading contributed to her pursuit of a library degree, and in 1973 she earned her master's degree in library science from the University of Texas. With her new degree, she took a job at the Houston Public Library, and later she took a job as the school librarian at Dawson Elementary School in Austin. In 1977 she met George Bush and later that year married him.

Golda Meir (1898–1978)

Born in Kiev, Golda Meir moved to Milwaukee, Wisconsin, in 1906 when her family immigrated to the United States. It was in Wisconsin that Meir had a brief library career. In her memoir, *My Life*, she writes, "I left school (how strange that it had lost its great importance for me) and went to Chicago, where on the strength of my having worked briefly as a librarian in Milwaukee, I was taken on by the public library." In 1921 she moved to Tel Aviv, and ultimately served as prime minister of Israel from 1969 to 1974.

Mao Tse-Tung (1893–1976)

The former leader of the Communist Party of China, Mao Tse-Tung was the son of a peasant farmer. The oldest of four children, he served in the Hunan army during the 1911 revolution. Subsequently he graduated from the Hunan Normal School. His future father-in-law got him a job as the assistant to Li Dazhao, the head of the Peking University library. It's unclear if he held the title of librarian. Mao Tse-Tung later went on to unite China and become chairman of the Communist Party.

Popes and Saints

Saint Louis Marie Grignion de Montfort (1673–1716)

Born in Montfort, France, Louis Marie received his calling to the priesthood while attending college. He traveled to Paris to study at the seminary at Saint-Sulpice. It was there he was given the task of librarian, one he enjoyed during his seminary years due to his love of reading. He was ordained a priest in 1700. During his lifetime, he wrote several books, including *The Secret of the Rosary* and *True Devotion to Mary*. He also founded the Company of Mary, a congregation of missionaries, and The Sisters of Wisdom (also known as the Daughters of Wisdom), a congregation devoted to the teaching of poor girls and helping the sick in hospitals. Pope Pius XII canonized Louis Marie in 1947.

Pope Pius XI (1857–1939)

Born Ambrogio Damiana Achille Ratti in Desio, Italy, to a silk manufacturer, this future pope excelled in philosophy and paleography. He was named chief librarian at the Milan seminary, and later became vice prefect of the Vatican Library. Much of his lifetime was spent working as a librarian and he developed a classification system for the library. However, in 1785 he limited access to manuscripts in the Vatican Library. This prompted Spanish priest Juan Andres to accuse the pope of being in charge of "a cemetery of books not a library." In 1921 Ratti was appointed cardinal archbishop of Milan, and in 1922 he was elected pope. He is most remembered for the 30 encyclicals he published on a wide variety of topics, and for signing the Lateran Treaty with Italy (under Benito Mussolini), which created the Vatican state.

Philosophers

David Hume (1711–1776)

A historian and one of the most important philosophers during his country's Enlightenment, Hume was born in Edinburgh, Scotland, and attended the University of Edinburgh. His philosophical contributions include the problem of causation, the problem of induction, free will versus indeterminism, and many other philosophical arguments. His publications include a *Treatise of Human Nature*, *Essays Moral and Political*, and *The History of England*. At 43, he was appointed the librarian at the Advocates' Library. During his appointment, he penned several other major works.

Immanuel Kant (1724–1804)

This noted German philosopher was the son of a harness maker. Born in Konigsberg, East Prussia, he was the fourth of nine children. He started attending the University of Konigsberg in 1740, but when his father died in 1746, he was unable to pay for his education and left the university until he could find the finances. Luckily he was able to obtain a job as a private tutor and eventually returned to the university and earned his master's degree. After graduation, he worked as a non salaried professor, depending upon payment directly from his students for his teaching services. Fortunately, to supplement his income he was able to obtain the post of under-librarian at the Konigsberg Royal Library. His situation improved, and his library career ended when he was promoted to a paid professor of logic and physics at the university. His contributions to the philosophical world include the publication of his book *Critique of Pure Reason*, which addresses the fundamental question of epistemology, *Critique of Practical Reason*, *Critique of Judgment*, and other works and papers, such as "The General Natural History and Theory of the Heavens."

Gotthold Ephraim Lessing (1729–1781)

Born in Kamenz, Saxony, this famous writer and philosopher is often referred to as the most outstanding German representative of the Enlightenment. His father, a clergyman and theologian writer, had earned some local notice as well. In 1746, Gotthold began his studies in theology at the University of Leipzig. But his real love was literature and the theater. During this period he wrote several comedic plays that helped establish his place in history. But his father, disapproving of his son's involvement with the theater, forced him to return home. Gotthold then expressed an interest in studying medicine, and his father allowed him to return to Leipzig. But Gotthold's financial involvement with a failed theatre company forced him to leave Leipzig for Berlin, where he worked a variety of jobs for several years. Eventually, in 1752 he received his medical degree in Wittenberg. The following year volumes of his works were published which contained some of the comedies for which he is most noted for today, such as *Miss Sara Sampson*, considered the first major German bourgeois domestic tragedy. After working as a secretary to General Tauentzien, the military governor of Silesia, then as an advisor to the German National Theatre, he became the librarian at the Herzog-August-Bibliothek in Wolfenbuttel in 1770. In 1765 he unsuccessfully applied for the position of director of the Royal Library.

Poets

Jorge Luis Borges (1899–1986)

Born in Buenos Aires into a wealthy Argentine family, this famous poet and writer was born with a growing hereditary blindness. His family was traveling in Europe when World War I broke out, so the family decided to settle in Switzerland until the war ended. Thus, Borges was educated in Switzerland and completed his formal education at the College in Geneva. His first book of poetry, *Fervor de Buenos Aires*, was published in 1923, his first book of essays, *Inquisiciones*, in 1925, and his first book of prose, *Historia universal de la infamia*, in 1935. In 1938 he obtained a job as assistant librarian at the Miguel Cane Municipal Library in Buenos Aires, which was his primary livelihood for many years. But when Juan Peron came into power, Borges was removed from his job for disagreeing with Peron's political views and offered a job as a chicken inspector. After Peron's government was overthrown, Borges was appointed director of the National Library of Argentina in 1955. Despite being almost completely blind by that point, he successfully served as director of the library until his retirement in 1973, when Juan Peron again returned to power.

Philip Larkin (1922–1985)

Born in Coventry, England, where his father was city treasurer, Larkin is most famous for his poetry, then his prose. Some of his most well-known poems include "The Whitson Weddings," "Annus Mirabilis," "This Be the Verse," "An Arundel Tomb," with some of his best-known books being *The Less Deceived, The North Ship, The Whitsum Weddings, High Windows, Jill* (novel), and *A Girl in Winter* (novel). A common theme in his writing is isolation from a society he's unable to change. He considered himself shy both as a child and as an adult. After graduation from St. John's College, Oxford, he tried to join the military but failed the physical exam due to his poor eyesight. Then, he happened to see a newspaper ad for a librarian job. This led to a job as a librarian for the town of Wellington in 1943. The experience helped inspire the unappreciated library character in his novel *A Girl in Winter*. Three years later, in 1946, he took a job as assistant librarian at the University College, Leicester. Then, in 1950 he served as a sublibrarian at Queens University in Belfast. In 1955 he became the librarian at the University of Hull, a position he remained in for the rest of his life. A year before his death he declined the opportunity to become poet laureate, preferring to shy away from the media attention associated with the position.

Henry Wadsworth Longfellow (1807–1882)

Longfellow is a well-known poet with over 20 books to his credit, including *The Song of Hiawatha, Tales of a Wayside Inn, Hyperion, In the Harbor,* and *Voices of the Night.*

Henry W. Longfellow was born in Portland, Maine, to Stephen Longfellow, a lawyer, politician, and member of the 18th Congress of the United States, and Zilpah Longfellow, a devoutly religious woman. One of seven children, Longfellow excelled academically. His first poem was published when he was only 13. The following year he began attending Bowdoin College. After he graduated from Bowdoin, the college offered him a professor position if he also accepted the position of school librarian. He accepted the offer and from 1929 to 1935 served as both a professor of modern languages and the college librarian.

Archibald MacLeish (1892–1982)

Born in Glencoe, Illinois, MacLeish attended Yale University and began to distinguish himself. He played on the football team, served as captain of the water polo team, and was a member of the university's elite and secretive Skull and Bones Society. After Yale, he attended Harvard Law School and graduated first in his class in 1919. He was already a noted poet and Pulitzer Prize winner when President Franklin D. Roosevelt asked him to be the librarian of Congress. Although MacLeish initially refused, he ultimately accepted and served as the ninth librarian of Congress from 1939 to 1944. Upon leaving his library position, he became assistant secretary of state for cultural and public affairs. By the time he died, he had received a National Book Award, three Pulitzer Prizes, an Academy Award, and the Medal of Freedom. His many works include such accomplishments as *New Found Land*, *Tower of Ivory*, *Conquistador*, *Collected Poems 1917–1952*, *The Eleanor Roosevelt Story* (play), and *J.B.* (play).

Writers and Composers

Hector Berlioz (1803–1869)

Born in La Cote Saint-Andre, this French composer of operas, symphonies and other works authored several books on music. His symphonies include "Romeo and Juliet" and "Symphonie Fantastique," while examples of his opera credits are "Beatrice and Benedict," "The Trojans" and "Benvenuto Cellini." Other noted works include "The Damnation of Faust" and "Requiem." Shortly after his arrival in Paris in 1821, he began studying at the library in the Paris Conservatoire, although he didn't formally become a student at the conservatoire until 1826. Despite his accomplishments, the highest position he was able to obtain at the conservatoire was that of librarian starting in 1850. (Prior to that he served as assistant librarian from 1838 to 1850.) His inability to obtain a higher position at the conservatoire, and the recognition he deserved, is often contributed to his strained relations with the conservatoire, which is discussed in his *Memoirs*.

Daniel Boorstin (1914–2004)

Once a member of the Communist Party, Boorstin was born in Georgia but grew up in Oklahoma. As a youth, he showed academic excellence and at age fifteen, began studying at Harvard University. As a Rhodes scholar, he studied law at Oxford University, returning to the United States to study a year at Yale Law School where he earned his Juris Doctor. In 1938 he joined the Communist Party, but his concern over events in Europe led him to leave the party the following year. He enjoyed a brief career in law before pursuing an academic career, first at Swarthmore College, then as a professor at the University of Chicago for 25 years. In 1969 he was appointed director of the National Museum of History and Technology, followed four years later by an appointment as senior historian at the Smithsonian Institution. His writings up to this point earned him several awards, including the Pulitzer Prize, the National Book Award, the Bancroft Prize, and the Bowdoin Prize. In 1975, President Gerald Ford nominated him to serve as Librarian of Congress, a post he held from 1975 to 1987. He also possessed no formal education or training as a librarian.

John Braine (1922–1986)

This British novelist was born in Bradford, Yorkshire, into an Irish Catholic family. The son of a sewage works supervisor, Braine won a scholarship to Saint Bedes Grammar School. But at 16, he left before taking his school certificate exams and entered the workforce. He held a variety of short-term jobs, working in a furniture store, bookstore, factory, and laboratory until landing his first library job. In 1940 he began working as an assistant at the Bingley Public Library. During his time at the library, he decided to pursue library training at the Leeds School of Librarianship. After four attempts, he successfully passed his librarianship examinations and was promoted to chief assistant at the Bingley Library. But in 1951 he decided to leave that job to devote his time to writing. He ultimately authored over a dozen books and several TV scripts and screenplays. His most famous and memorable work is *Room at the Top*.

Sam Walter Foss (1858–1911)

Sam Foss proves that librarians are not without humor. The son of a New Hampshire farmer, Foss had already established himself as a poet by the time he graduated from Brown University. A year after graduation, he and a friend purchased a newspaper. Circumstances suddenly required him to write the paper's humor column himself. His humorous columns and poems brought him popularity and several ensuing editorial positions. Then in 1898, he was appointed the librarian for the Somerville Public Library in Massachusetts. Despite his lack of prior library training, he excelled in the position, significantly increasing the library's circulation of materials, and added a reference room and children's room to the library.

The Grimm Brothers: Jacob Ludwig Karl Grimm (1785–1863) and Wilhelm Karl Grimm (1786–1859)

Jacob and his brother Wilhelm were born in Hanau Hesse-Cassel, Germany. They were two of nine children (eight boys and one girl) born to Philip Wilhelm Grimm, a lawyer, who passed away when Jacob and Wilhelm were only 11 and ten respectively. Later, both brothers began studying law at the University of Marburg. With the death of their mother in 1808, Jacob was forced to take a job as librarian in the private library of King Jerome of Westphalia (a new kingdom created out of portions of territories that belonged to Hesse, Hanover, Cassel, and Prussian Brunswick). It's rumored Jacob had previously applied for a job at one of the Cassel city libraries but was not hired. Later, he was appointed auditor to the council of state. Then in 1830, he moved to Gottingen where he received an appointment as a librarian and professor of German literature at the University of Gottingen.

Wilhelm's history is similar to that of Jacob's, except Wilhelm was a sickly child who also suffered from ill health as an adult. Like his brother, Wilhelm also studied law at the University of Marburg. During a period of extreme bad health, he expanded his studies to include Norse literature. He began his library career with an appointment as assistant librarian at the University of Gottingen. Later, he, like his brother, was appointed librarian and professor of German literature at the university. He and Jacob held those jobs for several years until they were both fired for their political views.

Madeleine L'Engle (1918 —)

Born in New York, this prolific and popular writer of children's and young adult novels is the daughter of a journalist. L'Engle graduated from Smith College in 1941 and became an actress. While acting on Broadway, she wrote her first novel and met her future husband, actor Hugh Franklin (who played Dr. Tyler on the soap opera *All My Children*). L'Engle has written over five dozen books, the most well-known being *A Wrinkle in Time*, which was made into a movie. She is currently the writer in residence and librarian at the Cathedral of St. John the Divine in New York.

Marcus Terentius Varro (116 BC — 27 BC)

Varro is regarded as one of Rome's most prolific writers. Scholars estimate he wrote somewhere between 400 to 700 volumes on a wide variety of topics ranging from poetry and satire to mathematics and a broad spectrum of the sciences such as medicine, agriculture, and astronomy. Varro held several offices in Rome and fought during the civil war in support of Pompey (Julius Caesar's rival). After Pompey's death, Caesar pardoned Varro and directed him to establish a library of Greek and Latin literature. Basically, he was a librarian charged with establishing a library. But after Caesar was murdered, Mark Anthony, one of Varro's enemies, declared him an enemy of the state. His library was destroyed and his property confiscated, including his voluminous works, which is why scholars and historians can only estimate the volume of Varro's works.

Librarians Extraordinaires

James Billington (1929 —)

The current librarian of Congress was born in Bryn Mawr, Pennsylvania. A graduate of Princeton University, Billington earned a doctorate in philosophy from Oxford as a Rhodes scholar. After a brief stint in the army, he began his academic career, first with a job at Swarthmore College, then Harvard University, and then Princeton University. A well-known scholar of Russian history and literature, he was nominated in 1987 by President Reagan to be librarian of Congress, a position he has held ever since. Although Billington has no education or training as a librarian, he is not alone. Only three of the 13 individuals, all men, who have served in the position of librarian of Congress were educated and trained in librarianship.

Charles Ammi Cutter (1837–1903)

A famous historical figure within the library profession, Charles Cutter, a Boston native, graduated from Harvard University at the age of 14. Initially intending to pursue a career in the clergy, he went on to study at the Harvard Divinity School. After only a year in Divinity School, the allure of librarianship led him to pursue an assistant librarian job at Harvard. In 1868 he was elected librarian of the Boston Athen'um, a famous American proprietary library. It was there he labored for years to produce the *Catalogue of the Library of the Boston Athen'um.* His catalog drew acclaim because of its size and thoroughness and because of the difficulty of compiling such a catalog. To help himself and his colleagues, Cutter developed *Rules for a Printed Dictionary Catalogue.* It quickly became the leading manual for systematic dictionary cataloging. He subsequently developed his *Expansive Classification.* Today, many libraries still follow his rules and classification tables. If you've ever visited a library that arranges its book by Cutter number, you can thank Charles Cutter.

Melvil Dewey (1851–1931)

Melvil Dewey was the creator of the Dewey Decimal Classification System. He was the youngest of five children. His mother was a strongly religious woman, and his father a boot maker. While attending Amherst College, he obtained a job in the college library. He continued working in the library for two more years after graduation. And in 1876, he wrote *A Classification and Subject Index for Cataloging and Arranging the Books and Pamphlets of a Library.* This system, known as the Dewey Decimal Classification System, helps librarians classify and organize materials in a manner that makes it easy for both library staff and patrons to find the materials they need.

Sir Edmund William Gosse (1849–1928)

The son of naturalist Philip Henry Gosse, noted literary historian and translator, Edmund Gosse was born in London, England. He is credited with introducing English language readers to the works of Henrik Ibsen with his translation of *Hedda Gabler*, and two other Ibsen plays. The author of several literary criticisms, biographies, and histories, he also authored a book about his father, *The Life of Philip Henry Gosse*. He was raised in a strict religious household, and his access to nonreligious books was very limited. Yet, he was hired to work in the British Museum library from 1865 to 1875. He left that job to work first as a translator, then as a teacher of college English. Then from 1904 to 1914 he was librarian for the House of Lords. In 1925 he was knighted.

J(ohn) Edgar Hoover (1895–1972)

The son of a federal employee, this former director of the U.S. of Federal Bureau of Investigation, was born in Seward Square in Washington, D.C. As a child he stuttered, but he overcame that problem and even joined his high school debate team. He was a captain in ROTC and a member of the high school track team. He enrolled at George Washington University in 1913. And to qualify for a work-study program for government employees at the university, Hoover got a job working at the Library of Congress. Although it's often said he was a librarian, he, in fact, worked as a library cataloger and clerk and never served in the position of librarian. But biographers often speculate that if Hoover had remained working in the library, he ultimately would have become chief librarian. After Hoover earned his Bachelors of Law, and ultimately a Master of Law in 1917, he left his position at the Library of Congress to begin work at the U.S. Department of Justice. In 1924 he was appointed head of the Bureau of Investigation of the Justice Department (later renamed the Federal Bureau of Investigation). The FBI's arrest of Al Capone and other infamous gangsters made Hoover, and his "G-Men" household names.

2

Facts About Librarians

Everyone seems to remember his or her first encounter with a librarian. But how much do you really know about librarians? Are they really shy elderly females? Do they really spend their day walking through the library telling people to be quiet? If you want to know the answer to these and other questions, read on.

Are Librarians Really Old Maids Who Like Their Hair Pinned Up in a Bun?

Yes and no. According to the U.S. Census, librarianship is a female-dominated profession. Only 18 percent of librarians are male. But you'll have to look really hard find a librarian these days who has her hair pinned up in a bun.

The median age of librarians is 47 years old. Close to 55 percent of the profession will reach age 65 by 2009. So we can expect a wave of retirements in the near future, creating many job opportunities for new librarians.

Librarianship is also becoming a more diverse profession. Hispanics currently comprise 3.3 percent of librarians, Asian/Pacific Islanders 3.2 percent, African Americans 6 percent, and American Indian/Alaska Natives .04 percent.

Are Librarians Really Meek and Shy?

Practicing librarians have also wondered about the personalities of their fellow librarians. So they've undertaken studies to answer just that question.

Several recent studies have used the Myers-Briggs Type Indicator (MBTI) tool to profile librarians. The MBTI is a psychometric instrument commonly used to measure personality types based upon Carl Jung's psychological types. Studies using MBTI show the three most common personality types of librarians are ISFJ, INTJ, and ISTJ. All three are, no surprise, introverted personalities.

ISFJs are Introverted, Sensing, Feeling, and Judging personalities. These individuals prefer to obtain data from their five senses. They like closure. They're often described as responsible and conscientious individuals.

INTJs are Introverted, Intuitive, Thinking, and Judging personalities. They like connections and complexity between things. They're often described as having original minds, being organized, independent, and critical.

ISTJs are Introverted, Sensing, Thinking, and Judging personalities. They're often described as orderly, responsible, serious, and practical.

How Many Librarians Are There in the United States?

The U.S. Bureau of Labor Statistics reports that librarians held 159,000 jobs in 2004. To put that number in perspective, it's more than 11 times the number of professional athletes, twice the number of probation officers, slightly more than the number of physical therapists, but only half the number of mail carriers, one-sixth the number of accountants and auditors, and only one-thirteenth the number of registered nurses.

What Are the Different Types of Librarians?

Within the profession, librarians are categorized into four broad types. The library in which they are employed defines each type. The four types are: public librarian, school librarian, academic librarian, and special librarian.

Public librarians work in libraries charged with providing library services to the public at large. These are libraries funded with public dollars, such as city and county libraries. The city or county pays the librarians' salaries.

Public librarians are found in the over 16,500 public library service points throughout the nation. They're in almost every community. According to the American Library Association, there are more public libraries and branches than there are McDonald's. So it's easier to feed your mind with a good book than to satisfy your craving for a hamburger.

School librarians, also known as school media specialists, work in schools educating children in kindergarten through grade 12. These schools include public, private, and charter schools.

School librarians work on the front line of providing library services to school-age children. School librarians and libraries play an important role in the education of our youth. In fact, the American Library Association reports that students visit school library media centers some 1.7 billion times during the school year — about twice the number of visits to state and national parks.

Academic librarians work in the libraries in public and private colleges. These colleges may offer two-year or four-year degrees or additional years of academic study.

Special librarians work in all the different types of libraries not considered public, academic or school libraries. This broad spectrum includes librarians working in law firms, hospital libraries, corporate libraries, state or federal libraries, and other types of entities such as nonprofit organizations and associations.

How Many Librarians Are There by Type?*

School librarians far outnumber other types of librarians in the nation. Of the 159,000 working librarians in the nation, school librarians number 66,471. Public librarians number 45,115 and academic librarians account for 26,152.

The remaining number are presumed to be librarians working in other types of libraries serving corporations, nonprofit organizations, hospitals, law firms, etc. And unfortunately it's not possible to estimate the number of other paid staff working in special libraries.

When you walk into a library, most of the people you see working there are not librarians. In fact, in public libraries the approximate number of staff classified as librarians is only 33 percent. Of that 33 percent, only 23 percent possess a master's degree in library and information science. And in academic libraries, the number of library staff classified as librarians is even smaller, 32 percent.

And if you ever get the sense that the librarian seems overworked, he probably is. To put these numbers into perspective, nationwide in public libraries, there are only 2.7 librarians providing help and information per 25,000 people.†

What Qualifications Are Required of Librarians?

Public and Academic Librarians

The minimum requirement for most librarian positions in public and academic libraries is possession of a master's degree in library and information science from a graduate program accredited by the American Library Association. Most university libraries also require or prefer a second master's degree in an academic discipline related to the specific position.

School Librarians/Library Media Specialists

The minimum education/certification requirement for public school librarians varies from state to state. But most states require the school librarians/library

American Library Association, Library Fact Sheet #2.
†*2004 Bowker Annual.*

media specialists to be certified as teachers and to have obtained some level of library course work.

Law Librarians

Nearly all law librarian positions require a master's degree in library and information science. Approximately 30 percent of all law librarian positions also require a law degree (JD or LLB). Some graduate library school programs offer a joint course of study leading to a JD/MLIS degree.

Medical Librarians

Medical librarianship requires a master's degree in library and information science. Although an undergraduate degree in biological or medical sciences is not required, course work in these areas is highly desirable.

Other Special Librarians

The requirements for other types of special librarians vary depending upon the employer. However, a graduate degree in library and information science is always useful in these positions.

Where Do People Go to Become Librarians?

The American Library Association has accredited 56 graduate programs that grant a master's degree in library and information science. Those programs can be found in 32 states and seven Canadian provinces. A list of the programs can be found on the website of the American Library Association at www.ala.org.

Do Librarians Like Their Jobs?

Overall, librarians are indeed happy with their jobs. Several studies have been done on job satisfaction. Sixty percent of librarians are satisfied with their jobs.[*] Of librarians, reference librarians are the most satisfied with the work they do.[†] And although librarians enjoy a 60 percent satisfaction level, the overall job satisfaction for all types of library workers is even higher at 80.4 percent.[‡]

---

[*]*"Job Satisfaction in the Library Profession: Results and Implications from a Pennsylvania Survey,"* by Arvid Bloom and Christina McCawley, Library Administration and Management, v. 7, no. 2, Spring 1993, pp. 89–93.

[†]*"Job Satisfaction in Libraries: Relationships of the Work Itself, Age, Sex, Occupational Group, Tenure, Supervisory Level, Career Commitment, and Library Department,"* by Beverly Lynch and Jo Ann Verdin, Library Quarterly, v. 53, no. 4, pp. 434–447.

[‡]*"Librarians at Work: Are We as Satisfied as Other American Workers?"* by Johann A. van Reenen, Information Outlook, July 1998, 2 (7), pp. 23–28.

In Which State Do Librarians Serve the Most People?

If you guessed California or New York, try again. The answer is North Carolina. According to a 2002 report by the National Center for Education Statistics, North Carolina has 1.95 paid FTE (full-time equivalent) librarians per 25,000 persons. Following North Carolina are Georgia with 2.15 FTE librarians per 25,000 persons, Arkansas with 2.35, Nevada with 2.44, and Tennessee with 2.48.

On the opposite end is New Hampshire with 8.49 paid FTE librarians per 25,000 persons. Wyoming is close behind with 8.19, with Vermont on its tail with 8.11. So if you want to live in a state with the greatest number of librarians in proportion to its population, head to New Hampshire. And if you want to get away from as many librarians as possible, run to North Carolina!

What Do Librarians Earn?

The *Occupational Outlook Handbook* lists the median salary for all librarians in the nation as $45,900 in May 2004. Academic librarians enjoy the highest median salary of $47,830. Right behind them are school librarians with a median salary of $47,580. Public librarians trail behind with a median salary of only $42,500.

The middle 50 percent of all librarians earned between $36,980 and $56,960 a year in 2004. The lowest-paid 10 percent earned less than $28,930. The highest-paid 10 percent earned more than $70,200 a year.

Although no government data could be found on the salaries of special librarians, the Special Libraries Association's 2004 salary survey of its members showed their mean salary to be $63,151 for its American members.

Do Academic Librarians Really Get the Best Benefits?

That's a difficult question to answer. But it can be safely said that more academic libraries tend to offer their full-time employees a variety of benefits than public libraries. In 1993 the Office for Research and Statistics of the American Library Association sent out a questionnaire regarding employee benefits. The results showed that 63.8 percent of responding academic libraries offered their full-time employees health insurance, while only 57.9 percent of responding public libraries offered their full-time employees health insurance. A higher percentage of academic library respondents also offered dental, life, vision, disability, and prescription insurance to employees than their public library counterparts.

The percentages between academic and public library benefits are even greater in terms of leave. Of academic library respondents, 51.3 percent offer vacation leave to full time employees. In comparison, only 32.1 percent of public library respondents offered full-time employees vacation leave.

Do Most Librarians Only Work Part-Time?

No. Two out of ten librarians work only part-time. Libraries frequently hire part-time librarians to work evening and weekend schedules.

Do Librarians Belong to Unions?

Librarians are considered professional library staff. According to a 1997 library survey conducted by the American Library Association, 16.4 percent of libraries responded that all their professional staff is covered by a collective bargaining agreement.

Are Most Head Librarians Women?

Yes. Results of a 1999 survey conducted by the American Library Association show that in academic and public libraries combined, 61 percent of library directors were female and 39 percent male. Is this disproportionate to the gender breakdown of the profession? Absolutely, since the number of male library directors is a significantly higher percentage than their representation in the profession.

That same survey showed that the male directors earned more than their female counterparts. The average salary for male directors was $68,586, while the average salary for female directors was only $61,614.

Do Librarians Do Anything Else Besides Check Out Books?

The individuals who check out books (many libraries now have self-checkout systems) to patrons are usually not librarians, but other library workers. The list of tasks performed by librarians is almost endless. Librarians analyze the type of information a patron wants, and then they find and provide the information needed. They instruct library users in how to use the many electronic and other information sources patrons may need to use in their research. Librarians who work in technical services are responsible for selecting, acquiring, classifying and cataloging books and other materials for the library's collection. They are leaders in using technology to help preserve historical materials for future generations, while also finding ways to make the information on those materials widely accessible to the public (for example, digitizing historical photographs and making them accessible through the library's website). They plan, publicize, and present special programs, such as author talks, literary festivals, and a variety of classes for adults and children that range from how to search the Internet, to consumer legal courses. Children's librarians also do storytelling and develop special activity programs for children who visit the library.

Librarians in management positions oversee the management and operations of the library, develop and manage budgets, negotiate contracts for services and products, recruit, train, and supervise staff, and are involved in, or perform public relations and fundraising activities. They analyze the ongoing needs of their community and plan, develop, and implement programs and services to meet those needs. Some are responsible for planning and overseeing construction of new library facilities or branches, or writing grant applications to secure external funds. The list of daily activities performed by librarians is almost endless.

But one lesser-known activity engaged in by librarians is protecting your intellectual freedom. Librarians actively analyze current and past topics and provide access to library materials that provide varying viewpoints. They fight against censorship of materials. They help to protect your right to read the material of your choice.

Librarians have been at the fore of the fight to protect the public's intellectual freedom, civil liberties and privacy. They fight for your freedom to read whatever you want, and they oppose all forms of censorship. In 2001 the American Library Association (ALA) filed a lawsuit to overturn the Children's Internet Protection Act which required public libraries to use blocking technology in order obtain federal grant funding or discounts for Internet access. In a March 2001 press release, then American Library Association president Nancy Kranich explained that "forcing libraries to choose between funding and censorship means millions of library users will lose — particularly those in the most poverty-stricken and geographically isolated areas of the country ... the federal government should not be subsidizing commercial filtering companies by forcing libraries to buy technology that doesn't work."

The ALA also closely monitors the USA Patriot Act and its impact on protecting the privacy of the library records of patrons. The American Library Association issued a Resolution on the USA Patriot Act and Related Measures, of which one section reads "That the American Library Association considers sections of the USA PATRIOT Act are a present danger to the constitutional rights and privacy rights of library users and urges the United States Congress to: 1. provide active oversight of the implementation of the USA PATRIOT ACT.... 2. hold hearings to determine the extent of the surveillance on library users and their communities; and 3. amend or change the sections of these laws and the guidelines that threaten or abridge the rights of inquiry and free expression...."

Librarians also speak out on the importance of access to government information. "ALA supports equal, ready and equitable access to information collected, compiled, produced, funded and/or disseminated by the government of the United States. ALA also supports the protection of individual privacy in information collected, compiled, produced, funded and/or disseminated by the government of the United States, and the right of individuals to gain anonymous access to government information."

The duties performed by librarians cover a broad spectrum of activities. The men and women who have chosen a career in librarianship find their jobs anything but boring.

Why Do People Decide to Become Librarians?

The reasons are many and varied. But an e-mail survey conducted in the summer of 1997 by Mara Houdyshell, Patricia Robles, and Hua Yi indicated that the opportunity to be part of a service-oriented profession (95 percent of respondents) and the intellectual challenge (82 percent of respondents) were the predominant motivating factors. That same survey showed a large number of librarians had worked in libraries prior to pursuing their master's degree in library and information science.

Beyond this and other surveys, the reasons why people chose to become a librarian ranges from altruistic, to sheer circumstance. To read the stories of why a select group of individuals chose to become librarians, go to www.becomealibrarian.org.

Do Librarians Just Work in Dusty Old Library Buildings?

The nature of the job usually requires most public, academic and school librarians to work all or part of their time in a physical space known as the library. But special libraries are located in many places. Some work in hospitals, museums, movie studios, prisons, banks, churches, and news agencies. A few librarians work literally in castles. Some librarians even work in the libraries found on cruise ships and even battleships. And I'm still waiting for the day I can apply for a librarian job aboard the space station!

Are There Nonlibrary Jobs for Librarians?

Definitely. Recruiters and employers value the analytical, organizational and technical skills possessed by today's librarians. Individuals with a Master of Library and Information Science degree frequently hold jobs in private industry with titles that often include systems analyst, information analyst, database designer, website designer, webmaster, content resource manager, technical writer, competitive intelligence researcher, indexer, software designer, and trainer. Some are self-employed as information brokers and consultants.

Now That We Can Search the Web, Do Librarians Have a Future?

Definitely. Librarians play a key role in helping and teaching individuals the best strategies to efficiently find information on the web and how to evaluate the information for reliability and accuracy. And librarians are still vital resources in helping the public locate information in the volumes of historical information not accessible on the Internet. The U.S. Bureau of Labor expects jobs for librarians to grow as fast as the average for all occupations in the future.

What Do Librarians Dress Up as on Halloween?

Although no formal surveys have been conducted on this, past discussions on various library listservs indicate that in the past, many female librarians have donned grey hair pulled up into a bun and dressed like the stereotypical librarian. Many male librarians have costumed themselves as Melvil Dewey, the founder of the Dewey Decimal System. (I don't know about you, but this veteran librarian author hasn't a clue what Melvil Dewey looks like!)

3

Librarian Recreation, Fun, and Health

You see them standing at the reference desk, reading stories to children, or doing a variety of other library tasks. But what do librarians do after the library closes? There are as many answers as there are librarians. However, some librarians participate in fun activities fairly specific to the profession.

This chapter peeks into some forms of librarian recreation and then takes a serious look at health issues and hazardous conditions affecting librarians. Working in libraries does pose hazards to librarians, not the same type of hazards facing police officers or firemen, but serious health hazards nonetheless. And these hazards have nothing to do with books falling off shelves.

Librarian Recreation and Fun

Outdoor Exercise for Librarians:
Book Cart Drill Teams

If you're a librarian who wants to participate in a team activity, or someone who enjoys watching librarian team events, start thinking about book cart drill teams. This is both a creative and precision sports activity. And yes, it is a competitive sport.

Pushing around book carts, especially when they're loaded with books, is physically demanding and helps build muscle and stamina. Pushing a book cart while running and trying to execute precision movements in tandem with others proves a good aerobic workout. No slouchers are allowed on the drill team.

Book cart drill teams are also wonderful opportunities for librarians to promote themselves in the community while showcasing the fun side of librarians. Drill teams create their own personalities. For example, one drill team decorated their carts as horses with the librarians dressed up as cowboys and cowgirls. Themes and cart decorations have ranged from baby buggies and race cars to cats and dinosaurs, with team members dressed accordingly.

The first ever Book Cart Drill Team World Championship was held in 2005 in Chicago in conjunction with the American Library Association's annual conference. Teams consisting of 12 or fewer members were eligible to compete. Each team was limited to a four-minute performance. Besides bragging rights and making history, the winning team also received a prize — a shiny new book cart! Demco, Inc., which coincidentally sells book carts as part of its product line, sponsored the first championship.

Who won the first championship title? "Dewey, et al for My Baby," the University of Wisconsin library school students' team, grabbed first place with a score of 60. Just .1 point behind, in second place, was the "Cartwheelers Precision Book Card Drill Team" from the Thousand Oaks Library in California. Third place was grabbed by the "Readin' & Rollin'" team from Batavia, Ohio.

The second championship was held during the ALA's conference in New Orleans in the summer of 2006. The team from Tulane University, "Booked on New Orleans" won the championship. Some of the other teams competing for the title included "The Bookie Monsters" from the School of Library and Information Studies at the University of Wisconsin, and "The Bookineers" from the Seattle Public Library.

If you think book cart drill teams are not serious stuff, think again. If you're thinking of participating in a drill team, or starting one, be sure to check out *The Library Book Cart Precision Drill Team Manual* by Linda McCracken and Lynne Zeiher (McFarland, 2002). The book helps you plan, equip, recruit and train members, decorate the carts, and costume the team members. It even includes choreographed routines.

Meditations for Librarians

If you've ever worked in a job where you dealt with the public, you know how stressful it can be. So it should be no surprise that librarians, especially those that work in a public-service capacity in the library, find their jobs stressful at times. One way many of them dispel that stress is through meditation. Two books by Michael Gorman, 2005 president elect of the American Library Association, contain meditations just for librarians. In *Our Singular Strengths: Meditations for Librarians*, Gorman presents readers with 144 meditations. Each takes the form of a quotation, an essay, and then a resolution. The meditations are divided into 12 sections ranging from "Practicalities" to "Eternal Promises." In the preface, Gorman states that his "aim is to present a topic, thought, or story that encapsulates some aspect of libraries and learning as an aid to understanding or reassessment." He goes on to say he wants "to provide aid and comfort" to fellow librarians.

If you ever wondered what librarians meditate about, looking at this book will give you a good idea. Take for example the meditation on page 121. The title at the top of the page reads "Ssshh!" The resolution at the bottom of the page reads, "I will provide quiet places in the library." Or take a look at page 14 with the title "Your Pornography, My Erotica." The resolution at the bottom of the page reads, "I will avoid personal value judgments in defending free access."

Published in 1998 by the American Library Association, *Our Singular Strengths* was followed by *Our Own Selves: More Meditations for Librarians.* Published in 2005, this second book has 100 new meditations grouped in ten sections.

Online Diversions

Like every worker, librarians are not immune to enjoying an online game or other diversion on the web from time to time.

AM I GEEKY ENOUGH TO BE A LIBRARIAN?

Whether or not you agree that librarians are geeky, here's a quick quiz to determine if you're a geek. Accessible on the Librarian Avenger website, the quiz (http://librarianavengers.org/?p=90) consists of 20 yes/no questions. The questions include: "When confronted with a pile of books I think 'Hmmm ... first I would sort by author, then by title." "I possess a useless graduate degree." "I know the first line of *A Tale of Two Cities.*" It only takes a couple of minutes to take the test and find out if you're geeky enough to be a librarian!

LIBRARY SCIENCE JEOPARDY

How do some librarians in training enjoy a challenge? By playing Library Science Jeopardy of course! If you think Jeopardy is too easy, and you're not a librarian, give Library Science Jeopardy a try. If you're a librarian, test your recall of what you learned in library school. Library Science Jeopardy is online at www.wam.umd. edu/~aubrycp/project/jeopardy.html.

Developed in 1998 by three graduate students in library and information science at the University of Maryland, Library Science Jeopardy is patterned after the popular television series. There are six categories: Pioneers, Machinery & Technology, Buildings, Systems of Organization, In the Arts, and History. Each category has five questions with ascending ranges of difficulty. The lowest point value in each category starts at fifty, with the highest being 250. You earn the point value for the question chosen if you answer it correctly. But you deduct the point value for a wrong answer.

When you click on a point value in a category, you're presented with an answer and a set of questions. You must select the question that matches the answer. If you answer the question correctly, you're provided with more information about the answer.

To give you an example, under the History category at the one hundred point value, you're provided with the answer "Credited with having built the first public library in his own country, this person contributed to the preservation of classic learning." You're then prompted to select the question that matches the answer: "a. Who was Abbasid caliph Harun al-Ma'mun? b. Who was Alcuin? c. Who was Flavius Magnus Cassiodorus? d. Who was Charlemagne?" If you're stumped by this example, the game does offer more widely known subjects. For example, in the Arts category, one answer presented is "This movie featured ghosts floating through a library." The questions presented are: "a. What is *Ghostbusters*? b. What is *Casper*? c. What is *Beetlejuice*? d. What is *Ghost Catchers*?" If you want to know what the correct questions are, you'll just have to play the game!

No More Questions

This online diversion from Bibliozine.com, an electronic magazine for librarians not currently being produced, is similar to a skeet shoot game. If you work at a busy library reference desk, or are in retail or any type of stressful customer service position, this game is a fun way to unwind at the end of the day.

Part of the introduction reads "People are firing questions at you. What do you do? Fight back." Using your mouse, you get to take aim at and shoot down the people firing questions at you. There's even a second level to this game if you stay above the target amount. Enjoy the fun at www.bibliozine.com/lighterside/wastern/wastern.shtml.

Reshelving Shuffle

If you're in the mood for a word guessing game, give Reshelving Shuffle a try. Also brought to you by Bibliozine.com, the game features a graphic of a young man, probably a library page, balancing a tall stack of books in his arms. Like the word game Hangman, your goal is to guess the word before the young man drops the books. As you build in wrong guesses, you begin to see him drop one or more books. If you want to try your hand at saving those books from falling, go to www.bibliozine.com/lighterside/hangman/hangman.shtml.

The Test of Librarianship

Do you think you have what it takes to be a librarian? Or if you are a librarian, do you think you really chose the right career? If so, you may want to check out "The Test of Librarianship" at http://web.archive.org/web/20011020190416/www.vuw.ac.nz/~rigbyfi/librarian_test.htm. At the top of the test it states "Not the School of Communications and Information Management," and "Not the Master of Library and Information Studies." So that should put you in the right mind to take the test.

The test is comprised of seventy yes/no" questions, such as "Do you love that 'new book' smell? Have you entered a borrower called James Tiberius Kirk into your library system? Do you organize your pantry alphabetically?"

At the end of the test, you tally up all your yes answers. Depending on your score, the test will tell you if you are well suited to the profession, if you have some librarian traits and "if you work hard you may be able to repress the non-librarian side of your nature." Or, if you score really low and are not suited for librarianship, you should "try and get a job away from the public gaze, say, coal mining."

Board Games

I have to admit the following two board games were not designed specifically for librarians. But I wanted to mention them because they are perfect for librarians and anyone who loves to read. And only avid readers will truly appreciate these games.

BOOKTASTIC!

A review in *Publishers Weekly* described Booktastic! as "Cozy, family-oriented entertainment that expands our minds and our hearts." Developed by Laine Keneller of Granite Bay, California, this board game is for players age ten and above. In the game, players choose a reading list then move around a board designed as a town square full of bookstores. As they move around the board, the players must answer questions to earn money. The object of the game is to buy, sell and trade books until you've obtained all four books on your reading list.

The game is available in bookstores across the nation. For more information on the game, go to www.booktasticgame.com.

LIEBRARY

As the title implies, the ability to lie, and a knowledge of books both factor into this game. The game is played with one player reading the title, author, and synopsis of an actual book. The other players then write down the first line of that book. All the first lines submitted by players, plus the real first line of the book are read to the players. Players get points when other players select their submission for the first line of the book, or for selecting the real first line.

For players age 12 and older, this game was created by actress Daryl Hannah and Hilary Shepard. For more information on the game, go to www.liebrary.com.

B. Librarian Health

The stereotypical librarian works in a cavernous old library filled with floor to ceiling wood bookcases of dusty old books. If you think librarians work in a safe profession, think again. Librarian's Lung and Sick Library Building Syndrome are just two of many occupational health hazards faced by librarians. Many of these health hazards are associated with the dust, fungus and bacteria found in library books and the poor air quality in some library buildings.

Librarian's Lung and Mold

Yes, there is a disease known as Librarian's Lung officially recognized by OSHA. Similar to Farmer's Lung, Librarian's Lung is also associated with the inhalation of mold spores over an extended period of time. Causing respiratory problems, the disease tends to afflict librarians who regularly handle old or rare books that are prone to contain mold spores. Librarian's Lung is not an allergy or an infection, but a condition brought on by exposure to certain mold spores. The mycotoxins produced by moldy books can also cause irreversible cellular damage, particularly in the kidneys and liver.

Although outbreaks of Librarian's Lung are fairly rare, they can be costly. In 1994 the *Canadian Occupational Safety* magazine reported an outbreak of Librarian's Lung at the New York Museum of Contemporary Art in a $400 million lawsuit filed by workers there. The lawsuit was settled out of court. But other outbreaks have been recorded, including a recent one at the Knox Presbyterian College at the University of Toronto.

Mold outbreaks in libraries are definitely not uncommon. Any quick search of newspapers across the nation will yield several reports of libraries being shut down for the cleanup of a toxic mold outbreak. The effects of toxic mold have been widely documented in the health and medical literature. The exposure of library staff to toxic mold is a serious health concern, which is why libraries are generally closed to staff and patrons during the removal of toxic mold.

Fungi

The presence of fungi in libraries is a hazard faced by a number of librarians worldwide. A study conducted in the 28 libraries at the University of Sao Paulo, Brazil, showed high concentrations of fungi in the air, resulting in 49 percent of the librarians suffering from asthmatic or rhinitic symptoms. The study, reported in the *Journal of Investigational Allergology & Clinical Immunology* (January/February 1993, vol. 3, no. 1, pp. 45–50), is just one of many medical articles on the topic.

Dust

Dust is a more prevalent health hazard to librarians across the globe. A number of medical studies have been conducted on the presence of *Dermatophagoides pteronyssinus* and other dust mites in libraries and their impact on the health of librarians. Dust inevitably accumulates on the sides of books. According to a paper presented by Hassan Bolourchi at the 2004 Indoor Air Quality Meeting in Padova, Italy, "when you open a dusty book, an air current is created which pushes up the dust accumulated on and in the books directly to your nose. There are no other normal cases that you blow dust in your nose by yourself."

Extended exposure to dust has been linked to asthma, allergies, skin problems and other medical conditions. Any library worker or avid library user knows that dust is unavoidable in many libraries.

Sick Building Syndrome

Health problems caused by poor indoor air quality are generally categorized as Sick Building Syndrome. In 1983 the World Health Organization published a list of eight noninclusive symptoms that characterize this syndrome. The symptoms include irritation of the eyes, nose and throat; dry mucous membranes and skin; erythema; mental fatigue and headache; respiratory infections and cough; hoarseness of voice and wheezing; hypersensitivity reactions; and nausea and dizziness. In general, the symptoms are generally contributed to an unidentified source, contaminant, or a combination of contaminants.

During the past ten years, incidents of sick library syndrome have been reported in library and medical literature, as well as in newspapers. Occurrences have been reported in libraries throughout the nation, from San Jose, California, to Broward County, Florida. The syndrome has also occurred in all types of libraries both in the United States and in other countries. In a survey of Sick Building Syndrome in Great Britain libraries that was reported in *Library Management* (1995, v. 16, no. 3), the authors note that the evidence suggests "air-conditioned libraries are more likely to be affected than those which are naturally ventilated." Now there's a good reason why many of us like library buildings with windows you can actually open!

For an interesting perspective on the syndrome, check out the article "Sick Library Syndrome" by R.J. Hay in the December 16, 1995, issue of *Lancet*. Near the end of his commentary, he notes that some classes of fungal metabolites potentially found in libraries have properties that could cause hallucinations upon inhalation of these spores. He writes, "the source of inspiration for many great literary figures may have been nothing more than a quick sniff of the bouquet of mouldy books." So if you suddenly see a flow of teens sniffing some library books, you may want to check those books for mold!

Headaches

Until I began working as a librarian, I seldom ever had headaches. I just attributed most of the workday headaches to good old-fashioned stress. I never imagined they were related to my specific occupation. I was wrong.

In 2002 Excedrin, a Bristol-Myers Squibb company, sponsored a survey to discover which professions are likely to trigger headache pain. The survey, known as the Excedrin@Work Headache-by-Profession Index, revealed that as a profession, librarianship ranked as the second highest profession most likely to trigger headache pain among its members. Only accountants ranked higher with 49 percent reporting weekday headaches.

According to the survey results, 43 percent of librarians reported workday headaches. Bus drivers and truck drivers closely followed librarians with 42 percent reporting workday headaches. At 38 percent were construction workers.

In the survey, librarians reported that patrons "who have 'no clue' how to use research resources cause the most headaches (56 percent) for them." Somehow these survey results don't exactly help the profession portray itself as a nonjudgmental service-focused profession. Information on the number of survey respondents was not available.

Neck Pain and Stiffness

The nature of librarians' work makes them susceptible to neck pain and stiffness. Spending hours hunched over a keyboard, leaning across a reference desk listening to patrons' questions, and straining to read the call numbers on bookshelves can all lead to potential neck pain and other problems.

In her article, "Don't Stick Your Neck Out, Librarian" (*American Libraries*, July/August, 1995), physical therapist and librarian Suzanne DeLong discusses "forward head posture" or "the turkey position." It's the position where the head and shoulders hunch forward, accentuating the spine. This repeated position can cause neck stiffness and pain, as well as tingling, pain, and numbness in the shoulders, arms, and hands. So librarians and everyone would do well to mind what our mothers told us about good posture and sitting up straight!

Exercise (or lack thereof)

Over the years I've heard a rumor about librarians dying quicker than the rest of the population. Unfortunately, this rumor has a basis in truth. As reported in the December 1, 1983, issue of *Library Journal*, a survey done at the Public Library of Columbus and Franklin County found that the average staff member dies nine years sooner than the optimal life expectancy. Lack of exercise was the major contributor to this lower life expectancy, along with excess weight, smoking, not using seat belts and other contributors. If you thought librarians lived extraordinarily long lives due to their profession, guess again!

Cancer and Librarians

An interesting article regarding Swedish librarians appeared in the October 2005 issue of the *American Journal of Industrial Medicine*. Titled "Cutaneous

Melanoma in Swedish Women," the authors sought to identify occupations with a higher risk of cutaneous melanoma in Swedish female workers. The authors followed up on employed Swedish women from 1971 to 1989, using the death/cancer registers. What they observed were high risks of cutaneous melanoma among librarians/archivists/curators, educators, bank tellers, dental nurses, horticultural workers, and hatmarkers/milliners.

In 1993 an American study looked at occupation as a risk identifier for breast cancer. The study, conducted by Carol Hogfoss Rubin, Carol A. Burnett, William E. Halperin, and Paul J. Seligman of the National Institute for Occupational Safety and Health, was reported in the September 1993 issue of *American Journal of Public Health*. In the study, the researchers' "analyses involved mortality data from 23 states that contribute to a database maintained by the National Institute for Occupational Safety and Health.... These data span the years 1979 through 1987 and represent more than 2.9 million death certificates coded for usual occupation and industry of the decedent according to the 1980 Bureau of the Census classification system."

They found that the breast cancer mortality ratios in white women was higher in female executives, including administrators and managers, professionals, and administrative support workers. The breast cancer mortality ratios for black women were also higher in those three occupation categories as well. The study also looked at selected occupations within the grouping that had elevated mortality ratios. And white librarians, teachers and clergywomen had more than 50 percent higher breast cancer mortality rates than expected for all white women. The study showed black librarians also had similarly higher mortality ratios.

But in 1998, the American Cancer Society conducted a study that suggested a woman's occupation had little effect on breast cancer mortality. The study, reported in the *American Journal of Epidemiology* (July 15, 1998), looked at the risk of breast cancer by occupation by analyzing data on more than 563,395 women who participated in the Cancer Prevention Study II (a mortality study of approximately 1.2 million women that began in 1982). According to the study, there was no significant increase in breast cancer mortality for librarians and teachers, and that women in administrative positions were only at a small increased risk.

But the research doesn't end there. An article titled "A Case-Control Study of Occupation and Breast-Cancer Risk in Connecticut" appeared in 2002 in the *Journal of Cancer Epidemiology and Prevention* (vol. 7, no. 1, pp. 3–11). Noting the inconsistencies in the results of studies relating breast cancer to occupation, the authors analyzed data from a case-control study of breast cancer conducted from 1994 to 1997 in Connecticut. They examined 608 breast cancer cases and obtained information about occupations from in-person interviews conducted by trained interviewers. They found that "a significantly increased risk of breast cancer was observed for teachers and librarians...." But unlike the 1993 study, "a significantly reduced risk, on the other hand, was observed for technicians and related supports.... No other occupational groups showed a significant association with breast-cancer risk."

Are female librarians at greatest risk for certain types of cancer? You be the judge.

Are Books Harmful to the Health of Librarians?

Numerous individuals handle library books in a library. Although studies have shown the books hold the same amount of germs as household books, the concept of disinfecting library books dates back at least 100 years. Have you ever wondered how they used to disinfect library books? If so, read on. The following method was described in the October 1911 issue of the British journal *the Librarian* (v. 2, no. 3, pp. 110–111).

The Disinfection of Books

The Sanitary Inspector of Tottenham, Mr. Shillito, describes a method of disinfecting books, in very general use in his country. Books for disinfection are opened and their covers clipped together; this opens all the leaves and permits the book to be stood endwise on a shelf in the disinfecting cabinet, which is simply a wooden cupboard lined with zinc standing on four feet. A formalin lamp is placed beneath cupboard, and fumes enter the cupboard through hole in the bottom. After suitable period, a slide door seals the hole, and the books are left in the gaseous disinfectant for an hour.

Any number of books may be treated at one time, and any gaseous disinfectant may be used.

This method strikes us as much less tedious than, while being as efficient as, the plan in use in parts of America and described some time since in "The Scientific American": although it is true that there school books and school library books were disinfected periodically — a practice that might be followed in this country....

Other Illnesses

Up to this point we've looked at some of the medical and scientific studies on illnesses affecting librarians. But what about those other causes of ill health among librarians, those times when librarians just simply feel "under the weather" or not at their peak performance? Back in 1903, Mary MacMillan offered some possible causes of these maladies in an article that appears below.

"Some Causes of Ill Health Among Library Workers"
by Mary MacMillan, assistant, Brooklyn Public Library
(*From Public Libraries*, v. 8, no. 9, November 1903, pp. 412–414)

Last winter was a very trying one to most libraries; an unusual number of assistants were absent on account of illness, and, as a consequence, we began to ask ourselves if the pity often stowed upon us by friends outside the library field had some foundations, whereas before this we had scorned their prophecies of an early grave. We questioned one another as to the various causes that might lead to illness. Some said long hours; others, night work, irregular meals, not enough people to share the work, Sunday work in addition to the rest of the week, great responsibility and not enough pay, the constant strain of being before an unappreciative public; and all agreed that we do not get fresh air enough. Some thought too much study was required of us outside library hours; some reprehensibly light-hearted, or light-headed, ones thought we had not enough time for amusement.

Very likely there is absolutely nothing new to be said on any of these subjects for discontent. Certain it is that for eight years I have heard them vigorously discussed wherever two or three librarians were gathered together; but, occasionally, it has occurred to me that perhaps there is another cause. In suggesting this cause, let me be clearly understood as having no library or librarian in view, but a composite picture of the conditions in very many libraries. Briefly, then, is it not lack of harmony between the assistants and the librarian? This inharmonious feeling is undoubtedly produced by misunderstanding, and what is harder to explain than a misunderstanding? I confess I can only try.

When a woman applied to be admitted into a library school, an apprentice class, or a library, no effort should be spared to impress upon her the unpleasant features of the work, to bring home to her what it means to stay till nine o'clock three evenings a week, to have only half a day a week, perhaps not that, when she may go to see her acquaintances or have them visit her, etc.; instead of which, if the applicant is prepossessing, we strive to encourage her to enter, tell her how enthusiastic we are, how we love our work, and all the rest of it. Not unnaturally, she takes our praise liberally, thinks we are "so nice," and comes among us. Then she finds many odd arrangements about hours, meals, time off, and distribution of work and often I have heard girls say, if I had known so and so, I would never have come into the library, but now I can't afford to leave. But, I say, were you not told all this? Yes, only I did not realize; it was not told as a hardship. We may say that the woman is heedless, she should have thought things over more thoroughly. Perfectly true; but we should have presented things more clearly.

Presenting library work as it is would probably discourage the majority of applicants, and from various experiences of my own, and those related to others, this is, possibly, what would be best. One thing we may be sure of; if a woman is determined to become a librarian nothing will discourage her, and she is the kind we want. However, we do encourage them, they do come, and when they are with us they sometimes find things not quite as they were led to expect, so there is a feeling of disappointment.

Then, all applicants are asked to fill out forms with certain questions printed thereon. One is, Have you any physical infirmity that would hinder you in your work? Every one promptly writes No. Of course they would be — well, not of this world — if they said yes. Besides, they probably do not consider their weak backs, delicate stomachs, headaches, heart trouble, and a dozen other ills that feminine flesh is heir to, as disabilities. Maybe these things are not disabilities, but if the library authorities would require a physician's certificate, the applicants would have no excuse for saying that the questions were so general that it was impossible to answer them in any way but by saying yes or no, and as they did not want to say yes, they said no. You can't turn a girl out just because she faints occasionally, generally when she is getting a much-deserved reproof; or, when she is constantly obliged to ask for leave because she has worked beyond her strength, and you know that she has not worked any harder than the rest of the staff. Therefore, is it not better to make sure of a woman's good health before you engage her?

Having, however, a staff of ordinary, healthy women, there are a few things to be taken into consideration regarding them. The first is that those at the top must remember the days when they themselves were at the bottom, either in libraries or in other business, and how dearly they loved to feel themselves "one of the firm." No sane, sensible and competent woman likes to be obliged to do things in the dark; she feels that if she is considered capable of holding her position she is worthy to be told why a certain rule was made, why the things she asks for cannot be given. Nor does she like to find out the policy of the library from the newspapers. She also likes to be confident that she can go to her chief in a perfectly free and frank fashion and tell him her troubles and perplexities, and that he will listen in a friendly way and not think that she is a fault-finding, discontented female. I know this will make some librarians hold up their hands in horror — Why, we should never have time for anything but listening to complaints! That is a great mistake. Women make very few complaints, and are quite capable of saying their say in a few pleasant words and going away. But it is not that they would want to be always talking; the very fact of there being such a feeling of good will between the head and the assistants of a library would do away with most of the causes for complaint. Again, a library staff likes to feel that the librarian thinks his staff the most competent, most courteous, most altogether nice staff in these United States of America. And when it hears that its librarian does not feel this way it gets discouraged; it dreams about its work by night, and makes mistakes by day, out of sheer wondering if the head will or will not be pleased. Not, understand me, because the staff is composed of toadies–a woman who toadies is such an impossible person that she should not be mentioned — but we all know how easy it is to forget a hard day's work if, at the end of it, there is a pleasant "well done." I know that a librarian has often a hard road to travel. He has a host of people to worry him — people who want him to do what he ought not to do and who do not want him to do what he ought to do. But if he only has the faculty of making respectful, loyal, frank-spoken friends of his staff, half of his battles will be fought for him; no disagreeable people will be referred to him, and he will have neither indigestion nor insomnia.

I quite sorrowfully argue that women are queer — they have "nerves." It is the masculine fashion to scorn nerves, but no man ever scorned them as much as the sensible woman who has been found to acknowledge that she has them. How, you ask, can a sensible woman have the nerves? I am sure I don't know. She does, though, and this is one of the things to be considered about a staff of women.

To be sure the state of mind, which produces visible nerves, is usually the result of ill health. Not always, however. If there were X-rays for the mind, you would find 12 out of 14 women worrying about somebody else. The trouble is that when a woman becomes a librarian she does not cease to become a home-maker. Of course, the librarian has nothing to do with this, and cannot be expected to consider the private woes of his assistants, but he can be expected to consider that women in this day carry quite as heavy a financial burden as men, and need quite as large salaries.

In a library where there are a hundred and more women there are not 20 who can spend all their salaries on themselves; they are not infrequently the support of several members of their families, yet they ought to be always handsomely dressed, and in the style that women know costs the most money — the severely plain, well-groomed style; they must not do any work beyond the seven or eight hours a day library work; if they attempt to assist at home they are not fit to do a day's work at the library, so they have to pay a servant. They need outdoor air, and out-door air costs money. They ought to go to library clubs and conventions, and these cost money. They ought to attend courses of study, and teachers are not teaching librarians because they believe in cooperation but because of the money in it. They need amusements, and goodness knows it is very expensive to be amused. Now, if you see a worried look on an assistant's face that is not labeled "library worry," you may be sure it *is* labeled "want of a larger salary." And here is a place where the librarians do not always understand their assistants. A librarian has been known to condemn a bright assistant because she was shabby.

One might go on for a long time pointing out the various ways in which there is lack of an understanding between the librarian and the assistants of a library, but it is not wise to do so. I only suggest that it might be well if all librarians would put themselves in the places of assistants, and try to feel as they feel, to see both sides of any questions at issue, to believe in their assistants and be confident that they were doing the best that circumstances permitted. Perfect frankness, and a kindly manner; unwavering justice tempered with mercy from those who are in authority, will cause a relaxation of the nervous strain under which most assistants work; and will surely make for a more healthy condition of life in a public library.

4

Librarian Jokes, Riddles, and Other Humor

Every profession has its jokes and riddles. Librarianship is no exception. For a good laugh, this chapter starts off with librarian jokes and riddles, then continues on to bumper stickers for librarians, and then pickup lines used to pick up librarians, and lines used by librarians. (I can't guarantee that some of them won't earn you a slap on the face!) And to round out this chapter are humorous sketches and stories about librarians.

Riddles and Jokes

Where do librarians always slip and fall in the library?
    ANSWER: In the nonfriction section.

Where does a librarian sleep?
    ANSWER: Between the covers.

What do librarians use as bait when they go fishing?
    ANSWER: A bookworm.

What does a librarian eat from?
    ANSWER: A bookplate.

What do librarians use to catalog melted marshmallows?
    ANSWER: The Gooey Decimal System.

Why do single librarians travel to Prague?
    ANSWER: In hopes of being Czech'd out.

What do you get when you cross a librarian with a mobster?
    ANSWER: Organized crime.

Why was the librarian in jail?

ANSWER: She was booked.

What do you get when you cross a librarian with a card dealer?

ANSWER: A card catalog.

What do you get when you cross a librarian with a stripper?

ANSWER: Just the bare facts.

What do you get when you cross a librarian with a policeman?

ANSWER: A law librarian who throws you in jail if your book is overdue.

How many librarians does it take to change a light bulb?

ANSWER: Three. One to see if there's a book in the library on how to change a light bulb, one to check the book out, and one to find the information in the book.

Why do librarians work in the tallest buildings?

ANSWER: Because libraries always have the most stories.

At 10:00 a.m. on Tuesday morning at the Discount Ladies Shop a middle-aged homeless woman robbed the store for an undisclosed amount of money. At 11:23 Detective Booker brought Ms. Smith, the town librarian into the police station for questioning.

"Why are you interrogating the librarian?" asked the puzzled police chief.

"She matches the suspect's description to a tee," replied the detective. "Middle-aged, frumpy shoes, and worn, out-of-style loose clothing."

A woman goes into the library and walks up to the librarian.

"Can I help you?" asks the librarian.

"I'm trying to find my accountant."

"What's his name?"

"Mr. Newman."

The librarian pages Mr. Newman to come to the Information Desk.

Ten minutes later the librarian says to the blonde, "I'm sorry, but he hasn't come to the desk so he must not be here."

"But he has to be here," replied the woman.

"Why do you think he's here right now?" queried the librarian.

"Because he said he was working on the books and isn't this where all the books are?"

Phrases Often Appearing on Librarians' Bumper Stickers

Librarians are novel lovers.	Librarians do it between the covers.
Librarian. Check Me Out.	Librarians do it on the shelf.
Librarians do it by the book.	Librarians do it quietly.

Old but in mint condition. Previously
   owned by a librarian.
Long Overdue Librarian.

Happy Booker.
I Brake for Books.

Pickup Lines Used on Librarians

You're a librarian? I need to visit the library more often.
I'm a bookworm. Can I get between your covers?
Knowing you're the librarian just increased my circulation.
Mind if I check you out?
Would you like to check me out?
Can I have your phone number so you can check me out later?
Come to my room and check me out so I can get checked in to you.
Meeting you made me realize I was long overdue!
Have you heard the one about the librarian with more stacks than she could handle?
You're stacked better than the public library.
I couldn't help noticing what a great book bag you have.
You have the tightest bun in the place.
Mind if I work with your stacks?
I'd like to use my "Dewey" on you.
Want to come back to my room and play cataloger? I brought my own Dewey.
Let's get Dewey.
I reshelve my own books and I bet I can find a place to fit you in.
Let's play shelf reading, you be the shelf and I'll jump in.
Care to slip between the covers with me?
Let's play closing time at the library. Stand by the door and I'll slam you!
As a public librarian aren't you supposed to let me in?
So is it true academic librarians only let scholars in?
Are you a librarian who believes in open access to your stacks?
So when's the last time you were "on the desk"?
What's your call number?
I'd love to be a page in your section.
I like your shelves. Can I get a closer look?
You can classify me in your fantasy collection.
When I'm through, you'll need to get your bun tightened.
Are you on interlibrary loan? Because, baby, you're outta this library!
I'll deliver positive results to the right question.

Pickup Lines Used by Librarians

I'm a librarian and we're novel lovers.

Did you know librarians do it by the book?

I'm a librarian, so I do it quietly.

I'd catalog you under "sex tools."

I'd sure like to get you under a plastic cover!

What's your Cutter number baby?

I'm out of bibliographic control. So I need authority control.

You won't be disappointed. I've got great authority control!

I'm a librarian. I believe in open access to my stacks.

Care to do a little shelf reading?

As a librarian, I've got experience working with women.

Nothing gets filtered in my library.

I drive the bookmobile so I always deliver.

I do both checkouts and returns.

Many of these lines appeared on the LISNews Librarian Pick Up Lines posting of September 30, 2005. Used by permission of Blake Carver.

Other Humor

The following appeared in *Library Journal*, v. 9, no. 5, May 1884, p. 88.

The library in F. has in its employ several boys and a number of young ladies, occupied at the registering desks and in the repair room.

Borrower to one of the boys–"Have you *Ten Old Maids*?"

Boy (looking toward the young ladies) "Don't know! Some of them are up-stairs."

Another borrower put his question more laconically: "*Hoosier Schoolmaster*?"

Same boy. "Didn't have any. My teacher was a woman."

That boy soon after graduated into the grocery business.

     - J.E.

Ten Commandments for Library Patrons

The following commandments appeared in *Library Jokes and Jottings* by Henry T. Coutts, H.W. Wilson Company, 1914.

TEN COMMANDMENTS FOR BORROWERS OF BOOKS

Who goeth a-borrowing goeth a-sorrowing

1. Thou shalt not buy what thou canst borrow.
2. Thou shalt take care of thine own books, for thy babies and thy puppies will find as much delight in borrowed books as playthings.
3. Thou shalt not cut the leaves of a book with a butter-knife, nor decorate the margins with jam in imitation of the old illuminated manuscripts.

4. Remember that the most artistic form of appreciation is to repair the torn leaves of a book with postage stamp edging, and to arrange the red and green lines alternately.

5. Honour the opinions of an author as expressed in his book, but shouldst thou disagree with his views, pencil thine own notes in the margins. By so doing thou wilt not only give evidence of thy vast learning, but will irritate subsequent readers who will, unmindful of thy superior knowledge, regard thee as a conceited ass.

6. Thou shalt choose thy books from amongst those most worn. Shouldst thou be dissatisfied with their contents thou wilt have the pleasure of knowing that many of thy neighbours have been "had" likewise.

7. Thou shalt consult the librarian when thou knowest not what thou requirest. Should he be unable to assist thee, substitute "in" for "con."

8. Thou shalt not pay fines on principle (current cash is much to be preferred).

9. Thou shalt not bear false witness against the library assistant, saying: "He taketh the best books and reserveth them for his friends."

10. Thou shalt not covet the books that thy neighbour hath appreciated.

Don't Harm Those Library Books!

Have you ever made pencil or pen marks in a library book? Or have you dog-eared the pages? If so, beware, and continue reading. You may be the subject of a librarian's dream. After reading librarian and author Edmund Lester Pearson's story "Their Just Reward," you may think twice before defacing a library book. The story is from *The Librarian at Play*, originally published in Boston in 1911 by Small, Maynard and Company.

"Their Just Reward"
by Edmund Lester Pearson

I looked and beheld, and there were a vast number of girls standing in rows. Many of them wore pigtails, and most of them chewed gum.

"Who are they?" I asked my guide.

And he said: "They are the girls who wrote 'Lovely' or 'Perfectly sweet' or 'Horrid old thing!' on the fly-leaves of library books. Some of them used to put comments on the margins of the pages — such as 'Served him right!' or 'There! You mean old cat!'"

"What will happen to them?" I inquired.

"They are to stand up to the neck in a lake of ice cream soda for ten years," he answered.

"That will not be much of a punishment to them," I suggested.

But he told me that I had never tried it, and I could not dispute him.

"The ones over there," he remarked, pointing to a detachment of the girls who were chewing gum more vigorously than the others, "are sentenced for fifteen years in the ice cream soda lake, and moreover they will have hot molasses candy dropped on them at intervals. They are the ones who wrote:

> If my name you wish to see
> Look on page 93,

and then when you had turned to page 93, cursing yourself for a fool as you did it, you only found:

> If my name you would discover
> Look upon the inside cover,

and so on, and so on, until you were ready to drop from weariness and exasperation. Hang me!" He suddenly exploded, "if I had the say of it, I'd bury 'em alive in coconut taffy — I told the Boss so, myself."

I agreed with him that they were getting off easy.

"A lot of them are named Gerty, too," he added, as though that matters worse.

Then he showed me a great crowd of older people. They were mostly men, though there were one or two women here and there.

"These are the annotators," he said, "the people who work off their idiotic opinions on the margins and fly-leaves of books. They dispute the author's statements, call him a liar and abuse him generally. The one on the end used to get all the biographies of Shakespeare he could find and cover every bit of blank paper in them with pencil-writing signed "A Baconian." He usually began with the statement: "The author of this book is a pig-headed fool." They caught him and put him in jail for six months, but he will have to take his medicine here just the same. There are two religious cranks standing just behind him. At least, they were cranks about religion. One of them was an atheist and he used to write blasphemy all over religious books. The other suffered from too much religion. He would jot down texts and pious mottoes in every book he got hold of. He would cross out, or scratch out all the oaths and cuss words in a book; draw a pencil line through any reference to wine, or strong drink, and call special attention to any passage or phrase he thought improper by scrawling over it. He is tied to the atheist, you notice. The woman in the second row used to write "How true!" after any passage or sentence that pleased her. She gets only six years. Most of the others will have to keep it up for eight.

"Keep what up?" I asked.

"Climbing barbed-wire fences," was the answer; "they don't have to hurry, but they must keep moving. They begin tomorrow at half-past seven."

We walked down the hill toward a group of infamous looking people. My guide stopped and pointed toward them.

"These are snippers, cutters, clippers, gougers and extra-illustrators. They vary all the way from men who cut want ads out of the newspapers in the reading-rooms, to those who go into the alcoves and lift valuable plates by the set-string method. You see they come from all classes of society — and there are men and women, girls and boys. You notice they are all a little round-shouldered, and they keep glancing suspiciously right and left. This is because they got into the habit of sinking down in their chairs to get behind a newspaper, and watching to see if anyone was looking. There is one man who was interested in heraldry. He extended his operations over five or six libraries, public and private. When they found him out and visited his room it looked like the College of Heralds. He had a couple of years in prison, but here he is now, just the same. The man next to him is — well, no need to mention names, — you recognize him. Famous millionaire and politician. Never went into a library but once in his life. Then he went to see an article in a London newspaper, decided he wanted to keep it, and tore out half the page. Library attendant saw him, called a policeman, and tried to have him arrested. You see, the attendant didn't know who he was."

"Did anything come of it?" I asked.

"Yes," replied the guide, "there did. The library attendant was discharged. Blank simply told the Board of Trustees that he had been insulted by a whippersnapper who didn't look as if he had ever had a square meal in his life. One or two of the board wanted to investigate, but the majority would have jumped through hoops if Blank had told them to. He is in this section for five years, but he has over eight hundred to work off in other departments. The men on the end of the line, five or six dozen of them, used to cut plates out of the art magazines, a common habit. Woman standing next, used to steal sermons. Man next but one to her was a minister. He was writing a book on the Holy Land, and he cut maps out of every atlas in a library. Said he didn't mean to keep them long."

This group interested me, and I wondered what was to be done with them.

"You will see in a minute," said the guide; "they are going to begin work right away."

As he spoke, a number of officials came down the hill with enormous sheets of sticky fly-paper. These were distributed among the "snippers, cutters, clippers, gougers and extra-illustrators," who there-upon set to work with penknives, cutting small bits out of the fly-paper. In a few minutes the wretched creatures were covered from head to foot with pieces of the horrible stuff; pulling it off one hand to have it stick on the other, getting it in their hair, on their eyebrows, and plastering themselves completely.

"That is not very painful," I observed.

"No," said my companion, "perhaps not. Gets somewhat monotonous after four years, though. Come over to the end of this valley. I want you to see a dinner party that is taking place."

We left the sticky fly-paper folks behind us, and proceeded through the valley. On the side of the hill I noticed a small body of people, mostly men.

The guide pointed over his shoulder at them, remarking: "Reformed Spellers."

They were busily engaged in clipping one another's ears off with large scissors. There was a sign on the hill beside them. It read: Ears are unnecessary. Why not get rid of them? Leave enuf to hear with. Don't stop til you are thru.

At the end of the valley there was a large level space. Something like a picnic was going on. People were eating at hundreds of little tables, and some were dancing, or strolling about on the grass. The guide stopped.

"The Boss is prouder of this than of anything else in the whole place," he said. "The people who are giving this party are the genealogists. Nearly all women, you notice. These are the folks who have driven librarians to profanity and gray hairs. Some of them wanted ancestors for public and social reasons; some of them for historical or financial purposes; some merely to gratify personal pride or private curiosity. But they all wanted ancestors for one reason or another, and ancestors they *would* have. For years they charged into libraries demanding ancestors. Over there, you see that big crowd? They are the two hundred and fifty thousand lineal descendants of William Brewster. Next to them are six thousand rightful Lords Baltimore. That vast mob beginning at the big tree, and extending for six miles to the northeast are the John Smith and Pocahontas crowd — some descended from one and some from the other — we haven't got them sorted out yet."

"How many of them are there?" I demanded.

"According to our best estimates," he replied, "in the neighborhood of eight million at present; but of course we are receiving fresh additions all the time. Thirty-five hundred came in last month. There is no time to count them, however."

I laughed at this.

"Time!" I exclaimed, "why, you've got eternity!"

But he merely waved his hand and went on.

"They are the largest crowd here, anyway, with the possible exception of the Mayflower descendants. They have a whole valley to themselves, beyond the second hill. Some say there are twelve million of them, but no one knows. Recently they applied for another valley, for theirs is full. You see it is so thickly planted with family trees that they have to live in deep shade all the time, and it is very damp and chilly. Then there are upwards of three hundred thousand tons of grandfather's clocks, brass warming-pans, cradles, chairs and tables, so they hardly can find standing room."

We walked down amongst the people who were giving a picnic. I wanted to see what was the object of this lawn party, for it struck me that it looked more like the Elysian Fields than any other place.

I soon discovered my mistake. Near the first group of tables was a sign with the inscription: "Grand Dames of the Pequot War," and at one of the tables sat Mrs. Cornelia Crumpet. I remembered the hours I spent hunting up two ancestors to enable Mrs. Crumpet to join the Grand Dames. I had found them at last, and so, apparently, had Mrs. Crumpet, for there could be no doubt that the pair of sorry-looking rascals whom she was entertaining at luncheon were the long-lost ancestors. One of them was the most completely soiled individual I have ever seen. He was eating something or other, and he did not waste time with forks or any other implements. The other had finished his meal, and was leaning negligently back in his chair. He was smoking a large pipe, and he had his feet on the table.

Mrs. Crumpet wore an expression that showed that her past desire to discover these ancestors was as a passing whim, compared with her present deep, overpowering anxiety to be rid of them. I felt sorry for the poor lady; but she was not alone in her misery. All about her were Grand Dames of the Pequot War, engaged in entertaining their ancestors. Some of the ancestors were more agreeable, some far more distasteful to their descendants than Mrs. Crumpet's pair. None of the Grand Dames seemed to be having what could be called a jolly time.

My guide at last led me through the maze of tables and out into the open.

"We have a good many Japanese visitors in this section," said he. "They come to get some points from the Americans on ancestor-worship."

"What do they say?" I asked him.

"They just giggle and go away," he replied.

Beyond the genealogists we found a large group of people, who, the guide said, were the persons who borrow books and never return them. The complainants, in their case, were mainly private individuals rather than public libraries.

"They are not particularly interesting," remarked the guide, "but their punishment will appeal to you."

As we passed them I shuddered to see that they were all engaged in filing catalogue cards in alphabetical order.

"How long do they have to keep that up?" was my question, and I was horrified to learn that the terms varied from twenty to thirty-five years.

"Why, that is the most damnable thing I ever heard," I said — "the sticky fly-paper folks were nothing to this!"

The guide shrugged his shoulders — "It's the rule," he said.

The next lot of people we came on were curiously engaged. Long lines of bookshelves were set up about them, and they wandered up and down, forever taking a book from the shelf, only to sigh and put it back again. As we came amongst them I could see the cause of their weariness. The shelves seemed to be lined with the most brilliant looking books in handsome bindings. They were lettered in gold: "Complete Works of Charles Dickens," "Works of Dumas, Edition de Luxe," "Works of Scott," and so on. Yet when I took one of the books in my hand to look at it, it was no book at all, but just a wooden dummy, painted on the back, but absolutely blank everywhere else. They were like the things used by furniture dealers to put in a bookcase to make it look as if it were full of books, or those used on the stage, when a library setting is required. There were many cords of wood, but there was not a real book in any of the cases.

I asked one of the sufferers why he was doing this, and he stopped for a moment his patron, and turned his weary eyes upon me.

"We are all alike," he said, indicating his associates. "We are the literary bluffers. Most of us were rich — I was, myself," and he groaned heavily. "We bought books by the yard — expensive ones, always editions deluxe, limited editions — limited to then thousand sets and each set numbered, of which this is No. 94," he added in a dull, mechanical fashion, as though he were repeating a lesson. "We were easy marks for all the dealers and agents. Especially illustrated editions, with extra copies of the engravings in a portfolio; bindings in white kid, or any other tomfool nonsense was what we were always looking for. And they saw that we got them. Whispered information that this set of Paul de Kock or Balzac was complete and unexpurgated, and that if we would buy it for $125, the publishers would throw in an extra volume, privately printed, and given away to purchasers, since it was against the law to sell it — this was the sort of bait we always bit at — cheerily! And now here we are!"

And he began again his tramp up and down, taking down the wooden dummies and putting them back again, with dolorous groans.

I could not stand this dismal spectacle very long, we so hurried on to a crowd of men bent nearly double over desks. They were pale and emaciated, which my guide told me was due to the fact that they had nothing to eat but paper.

"They are bibliomaniacs," he exclaimed, "collectors of unopened copies, seekers after misprints, measurers by the millimetre of the height of books. They are kept busy here reading the Seaside novels in paper covers. Next to them are the bibliographers — compilers of lists and counters of fly leaves. They cared more for a list of books then for books themselves, and they searched out unimportant errors in books and rejoiced mightily when they found one. Exactitude was their god, so here we let them split hairs with a razor and dissect the legs of fleas."

In a large troop of school children — a few hundred yards beyond, I came across a boy about fifteen years old. I seemed to know him. When he came nearer he proved to have two books tied around this neck. The sickly, yellowish-brown covers of them were disgustingly familiar to me — somebody's geometry and somebody else's algebra. The boy was blubbering when he got up to me, and the sight of him with those noxious books around his neck made me sob aloud. I was still crying when I awoke.

Perverted Proverbs, by Henry Coutts

These first appeared in 1914 in *Library Jokes and Jottings* (H.W. Wilson, 1914).
A book in the hand is worth two on the shelf.
It is an ill book that does nobody any good.
Select books in haste and repent at your leisure.
Be slow in choosing a book and slower in reading it.
A book should not be judged by its binding.
Two books are better than one.
Returned in time saves "fine."
Fine books make "fined" borrowers.
A library book is better out than in.
It is easier to criticise a book than to write one.
Better ill-fed than ill-read.
It is a poor book that is not worth the candle.
Many hands make dirty books.
Spare the puppy and spoil the book.
Never buy to-morrow the book you can borrow today.
The reader proposes, the library disposes.
It's a long tale that has no ending.

Librarian's Correspondence

Over the years some things never really change. The sentiments in the following letters, which initially appeared in Henry Coutts' 1914 *Library Jokes and Jottings*, could easily have been written today.

The following letter is typical of many that librarians receive, but the phraseology is original:

"DEAR SIR, — I regret to report an accident to Library Book No. 13,693. Our dog has unfortunately developed a taste for learning and digested a few of the leaves. Will you kindly let me know the cost of same, and oblige."

An illustration of the need for supernatural powers among librarians is shown in the following:

"DEAR SIR, — Please renew the book that I took out about two weeks ago, or it might be three. I forgot the author and title, but it was bound in blue with a picture of a dolphin on the back."

In reply to an advertisement for an assistant librarian, a pseudonymous wit, doubtless impressed by the disparity between the numerous qualifications required and the meager salary offered, submitted an application as follows:

"GENTLEMEN, — I beg to apply for the post of assistant librarian in your library.

"From my earliest years I have had a pronounced taste for literature. Before I could talk, or walk with any degree of accuracy or precision, I devoured Bunyan, Thackeray, Dickens, the Family Bible, and sundry picture books with an eagerness that would have put many an older 'bookwork' to shame. In looking through my father's diary recently, I came across the following entry, written when I was quite a small child; 'The boy combines the taste of a literary connoisseur with the digestion of an ostrich; I wish he would choose a less expensive hobby.'

"Through my own unaided efforts a great impetus was given to the publishing trade, and, were it not for the fact that a restraining hand fell rather heavily on me at times, the output of books from the publishing houses of this country would have been much greater.

"During my schooldays this love of books did not forsake me. I kept my books very near to my person — generally stowed away under an accommodating cost or jersey. I even hesitated to pry into the mysteries contained within their covers, until compelled to do so by an unsympathetic teacher who willfully misunderstood my motives.

"I relate these facts simply to show how natural it is that I, having now come to years of discretion, should seek to enter the profession of librarianship.

"Although I am not a university graduate, I possess several educational certificates, and am learned in nearly every 'ology' and 'ography' known to man. Classification, cataloguing, and research work would, therefore, present no difficulties to me, and, without being unduly modest, I think I could safely say that I could paste a label in a book, or use a dating stamp the right side up.

"It is love of work rather than money that induces me to make this application, which I trust will receive the consideration it deserves."

Telephone Reference

Following is a humorous account of the implementation of reference assistance over the telephone from the early 1900s. Although you will find it humorous reading, many of the situations described are very similar to real life situations faced by librarians today. The only difference being besides receiving such requests over the telephone, today's librarians also receive reference questions over the Internet. Enjoy this inside look at some of the types situations librarians deal with on a daily basis.

"By Telephone," by Edmund Lester Pearson
(From Pearson, *The Librarian at Play* [Boston: Small, Maynard, 1911]).

"On January 14th," so announced a circular issued last month by the Ezra Beesly Free Public Library of Baxter, "we shall install a telephone service at the library. Telephone your inquiries to the library, and they will be answered over the wire."

Now, January 14th was last Saturday, and this is undoubtedly the first account of the innovation at Baxter.

Miss Pansy Patterson, assistant reference librarian, took her seat at the telephone promptly at nine o'clock, ready to answer all questions. She had, near her, a small revolving bookcase containing an encyclopedia, a dictionary, the Statesman's Year Book, Who's Who in America, Mulhall's Dictionary of Statistics, The Old Librarian's Almanack, the Catalogue of the Boston Athenaeum, Baedeker's guide book to the United States, Cruden's Concordance, and a few other of the most valuable reference books, in daily use among librarians.

Should this stock fail her she could send the stenographer, Miss Parkinson, on a hurry call to the reading-room, where Miss Bixby, the head reference librarian, would be able to draw on a larger collection of books to find the necessary information.

Mr. Amos Vanhoff, the new librarian of Baxter, stood over the telephone, rubbing his hands in pleasant anticipation of the workings of the new system which he had installed.

The bell rang almost immediately, and Miss Patterson took the receiver from its hook.

"Is this the library?"

"Yes."

"This is Mrs. Humphrey Mayo. I understand that you answer inquiries by telephone? Yes! Thank you. Have you any books about birds?"

"Oh, yes — a great many. Which —"

"Well; I am so much interested in a large bird that has been perching on a syringa bush on our front lawn for the last half hour. It is a very extraordinary looking bird — I have never seen one like it. I cannot make it out clearly through the opera glass, and I do not dare to go nearer than the piazza for fear of startling it. I only discovered it as I was eating breakfast, and I do not know how long it has been there. None of the bird books I own seem to tell anything about such a bird. Now, if I should describe it to you do you think you could look it up in some of your books?"

"Why, I think so."

"Well, it's a very large bird — like an eagle or a large hawk. And it is nearly all black; but its feathers are very much ruffled up. It has a collar or ruff around its neck, and on its head there is a splash of bright crimson or scarlet. I think it must be some tropical bird that has lost its way. Perhaps it is hurt. Now, what do you suppose it is?"

"You see, I haven't any bird books right at hand — I'll send in to the reading room. Will you hold the line please?"

Miss Patterson turned to the stenographer and repeated Mrs. Mayo's description of the strange bird.

"Will you please ask Miss Bixby to look it up, and let me know as soon as possible?"

During the interval that followed, the operator at central asked three times:

"Did you get them?" and three times Mrs. Mayo and Miss Patterson chanted in unison: "Yes; hold the line, please!"

Finally the messenger returned, remarking timidly: "He says it's a crow."

"A crow!" exclaimed Miss Patterson.

"A crow!" echoed Mrs. Mayo, at the other end of the wire, "oh, that is impossible. I know *crows* when I see them. Why, this has a ruff, and a magnificent red coloring about its head. Oh, it's no crow!"

"Whom did you see in there?" inquired Miss Patterson. "Miss Bixby?"

"No," replied the young and timid stenographer, "it was that young man — I don't know his name."

She had entered the library service only the week before.

"Oh, Edgar! He doesn't know anything about anything. Miss Bixby must have left the room for a moment, and I suppose he had brought in a book for a reader. He is only a page — you mustn't ask him any questions. Do go back and see if Miss Bixby isn't there now, and ask her."

A long wait ensued, and as Mrs. Mayo's next-door neighbor insisted on using the telephone to order her dinner from the marketmen, the line had to be abandoned. In ten or fifteen minutes, however, the assistant reference librarian was once more in communication with Mrs. Mayo.

"We think the bird might possibly be a California grebe — but we cannot say for sure. It is either that or else Hawkins's giant kingfisher — unless it has a tuft back of each ear. If it has the tufts, it might be the white-legged hoopoo. But Mr. Reginald Kookle is in the library, and we have asked him about it. You know of Mr. Kookle, of course?"

"What, the author of 'Winged Warblers of Waltham' and 'Common or Garden Birds'?"

"Yes; and of 'Birds I Have Seen Between Temple Place and Boylston Street' and 'The Chicadee and His Children.'"

"Yes, indeed — I know his books very well. I own several of them. What does he think?"

"He is not sure. But Miss Bixby described this bird to him, and he is very much interested. He has started for your house already, because he wants to see the bird."

"Oh, that will be perfectly lovely. Thank you so much. It will be fine to have Mr. Kookle's opinion. Good-by."

"Good-by."

And the conference was ended. It may not be out of place to relate that Mr. Kookle, the eminent bird author, arrived at Mrs. Mayo's a few minutes later. As he heard that the mysterious stranger was on the front lawn, he approached the house carefully from the rear, and climbed over the back fence. He walked around the piazza to the front door, where Mrs. Mayo awaited him.

Mr. Kookle was dressed in his famous brown suit, worn in order that he might be in perfect harmony with the color of dead grass, and hence, as nearly as possible, unseen on the snowless, winter landscape. He had his field glasses already leveled on the syringa bush when Mrs. Mayo greeted him. She carried an opera glass.

"Right, there — do you see, Mr. Kookle?"

"Yes, I see him all right."

They both looked intently at the bird. The weather was a little unfavorable for close observation, for, as it may be remembered, Saturday morning was by turns foggy and rainy. A light mist hung over the wet grass now, but the tropical visitor, or whatever he was, could be described without much difficulty.

He sat, or stood, either on the lower branches of the bush, or amongst them, on the ground. His feathers were decidedly ruffled, and he turned his back toward his observers. His shoulders were a little drawn up, in the attitude usually ascribed by artists to Napoleon, looking out over the ocean from St. Helena's rocky isle. But it was possible, even at that distance, to see its magnificent crimson crest.

Mr. Kookle took a deep breath. "Yes," he said, "I suspected it."

"What?" inquired Mrs. Mayo, eagerly, "What is it?"

"Madam," returned the bird author, impressively, "you have my sincerest congratulations. I envy you. You have the distinction of having been the first observer, to the best of my knowledge, of the only specimen of the Bulbus Claristicus Giganticus ever known to come north of the fourteenth parallel of latitude."

Mrs. Mayo was moved nearly to tears. Never in all her career as a bird enthusiast, not even when she addressed the Twenty Minute Culture Club on "Sparrows I Have Known" — never had she felt the solemn joy that filled her at this minute.

"Are you sure that is what it is?" she asked in hushed tones.

"Absolutely positive," replied the authority, "at least — if I could only get a nearer view of his feet, I could speak with certainty. Now, if we could surround the bush, so to speak, you creeping up from one side and I from the other, we might get nearer to him. I will make a detour to your driveway, and so get on the other side of him. You approach him from the house."

"Just let me get my rubbers," said Mrs. Mayo.

"Please hurry," the other returned.

When the rubbers were procured they commenced their strategic movement. "If I could only be sure that it is the Bulbus!" ejaculated Mr. Kookle.

Mrs. Mayo turned toward him.

"Do you suppose," she whispered, that it is the great condor of the Andes?"

Mr. Kookle shook his head.

Then they both started again on their stealthy errand. Slowly, quietly, they proceeded until they stood opposite each other, with the syringa and its strange visitant half-way between them. Then Mr. Kookle raised his hand as a signal, and they began to approach the bush. The bird seemed to hear them, for he immediately took interest in the proceedings. He raised his head, hopped out from the bush, and uttered a peculiar, hoarse note that sounded like:

"Craw-w-w-w!"

Mr. Kookle and Mrs. Mayo stopped in their tracks, electrified. Then the bird put its other foot on the ground and gave vent to this remarkable song:

"Cut, cut, cut, cut, cut, ker-dar-cut! Ker-dar-cut! Ker-dar-cut!"

Then it gave two or three more raucous squawks, ran toward the fence, flew over it, ran across the street, under Mr. Higgins's fence, and joined his other Black Minorca fowls that were seeking their breakfast in the side yard

Then Mrs. Mayo returned to the house, and Mr. Reginald Kookle, the author of "Winged Warblers of Waltham" and "The Chickadee and His Children," returned his field glasses to their case, turned up the collar of his famous brown suit, and walked rapidly down the street.

But Miss Patterson had been busy at the library telephone all this time. Scarcely had she ended her conversation with Mrs. Mayo when someone called her to have her repeat "Curfew Shall Not Ring To-night" over the telephone. This was only finished when the bell rang again.

"Hello! This is the library?"

"Yes."

"Well, I wish you'd tell me the answer to this. There's a prize offered in the 'Morning Howl' for the first correct answer. 'I am only half as old as my uncle,' said the man, 'but if I were twice as old as he is, I should only be three years older than my grandfather, who was born at the age of sixteen. How old was the man?' Now, would you let x equal the age of the uncle, or the man?"

Miss Patterson could not think of any immediate answer to this, nor of any book of reference that would tell her instantly. So she appealed to Mr. Vanhoff, who had returned to the room.

"What was that?" inquired Mr. Vanhoff; "get him to repeat it."

She did so, and the librarian struggled with it for a moment. "Why, it is all nonsense. Tell him that we cannot solve any newspaper puzzles over the telephone, He will have to come to the library."

Then Mrs. Pomfret Smith announced herself on the telephone.

"That the library? Who is this? Miss Patterson? Oh, how do you do? This is so nice of Mr. Vanhoff. I was coming down to the library this morning, but the weather is so horrid that I thought I would telephone instead. Now, my cousin is visiting me, and I have told her about a novel I read last summer, and she is just crazy to read it, too. But I can't for the life of me recall the name of it. Now, do you remember what it was?"

"Why—I'm afraid I don't. Who was the author?"

"That's just the trouble. I can't remember his name to save my life! I'm not even sure that I noticed his name—or her name—whoever it was. I never care much who wrote them—I just look them through, and if they're illustrated by Howard Chandler Christy or anybody like that, I just take them, because I know then they'll be all right. This one had pictures by Christy or Wenzell or one of those men. It was a lovely book—oh, I do wish you could tell me what it was! Where is Miss Anderson? She would know. Isn't she there?"

"No—I am sorry, she will not be here till afternoon. If you could tell me something about the novel—the plot, and so forth, I might have read it myself."

"Oh, of course you've read it. Why, you read all the books that come into the library, don't you?"

"Not quite all."

"You don't? How funny! Why, whatever do you find to do with yourselves down there? You're sure you don't remember the one I want?"

"Why, Mrs. Smith, you haven't told me about the plot of it yet."

"Oh, no, so I haven't. Well—let me see—Um! Say, it was about—now, what in the world *was* it about? Oh dear, I never can think, with this thing up to my ear! What's that, Central? Yes, I got them all right—hold the line, please. Oh dear, I'll have to ring off and think it over, and as soon as I remember, I'll call you up again. Thank you, so much! Good-by."

The next was a man who spoke in a deep voice. "Hello! Is this the library? Have you a history of Peru? You have? Now, that is very fortunate. I do not know how many places I have inquired. I only want a few facts—only a paragraph or two. You can tell them to me over the 'phone, can you not, and I will take them down?"

Miss Patterson had her finger on an article about Peru in the encyclopedia. "'Peru,'" she began to read, "'the ancient kingdom of the Incas—'"

"Of the whichers?" interrupted the man.

"The Incas," she repeated.

"Spell it," he commanded.

"Incas," she spelled.

"Oh, Lord!" said the man, "that's South America. I've been hearing about them all day. The principal of the High School gave me a song and dance about the Incas. I mean Peru, Indiana. Here, I'll come down to the library—this telephone booth is so hot I can't get my breath. Good-by."

Mrs. Pomfret Smith, unlike Jeffries, had come back. She greeted Miss Patterson with enthusiasm.

"Oh, Miss Patterson, I've remembered all about it now. You see, it starts this way. There is a girl, a New York girl, who has married an English lord, or, rather, she is just going to marry him—the brother of the first man she was engaged to steps in, and tells her that the lord isn't genuine, and he presents her maid with a jeweled pin which his mother, the countess, received from her husband—her first husband, that is—three days after the battle of— oh, I don't know the name of the battle—the 'Charge of the Light Brigade,' it was, and he was in that—no, his uncle was, and he said to his tent-mate, the night before the battle: 'Charley, I'm not coming out of this alive, and my cousin will be the lawful heir, but I want you to take this and dig with it underneath the floor of the old summer house, and the papers that you will find there will make Gerald a rich man.' And so he took it and when he got to Washington he handed it to the old family servant who hadn't seen him for sixty years, and then dropped dead, so they never knew whether he was the real one or only the impostor, and so just as the wedding was about to take place the uncle — he was a senator — said to the bishop, who was going to marry them: *Please get off this line, I am using it!* And so it never took place, after all. Now, can you tell me what the name of the book is, Miss Patterson?"

"Why, I am afraid I do not recognize it. It sounds a little like Mrs. Humphry Ward and Ouida and Frances Hodgson Burnett, and someone else, all at once. Was it by any of them, Mrs. Smith?"

"Oh, no, I am sure it was not. Why, I am surprised — I thought you would know it now, without any hesitation!"

"I am sorry."

The last in a tone as acid and cold as lemon ice. It seemed to express Mrs. Smith's opinion of all librarians. Miss Patterson was much grieved, but the telephone bell rang again before she had time to reflect.

"Is this the library? Oh, yes. I wonder if you have a life of Mrs. Browning?"

"Yes — I think so. What would you like to know about her?"

"Well, there — I am certainly glad. This is Miss Crumpet, you know! Miss Hortense Crumpet. I have had such a time. Have you the book right there? I do wish you would —"

"If you will wait just a minute, I will send for the book — I haven't it here."

"Oh, thank you so much."

The book was fetched, and Miss Patterson informed Miss Crumpet that she now held the volume ready.

"Have you it right there?"

"Yes."

"Well, I want to see a picture of Mrs. Browning. We have a portrait here, and my aunt says it is George Elliot, and I know it is Mrs. Browning. Now, if you could just hold up the book — why, how perfectly ridiculous of me! I can't see it over the telephone, can I? Why, how absolutely absurd! I never thought at all! I was going to come to the library for it, only it is so horrid and rainy, and then I remembered that I saw in the paper about your answering questions by telephone, and I thought, why, how nice, I'll just call them up on the 'phone — and now it won't do me any good at all, will it?"

"I'm afraid not."

"And I'll have to come to the library after all. Oh, dear! Good-by."

"Good-by."

The bell rang again as soon as the receiver had been replaced.

"Hello! How are you for pigs' feet to-day?"

"I beg your pardon?"

"Pigs' feet! How many yer got?"

"This is the public library. Did you call for us?"

"Who? The what? No; I'm trying to get Packer and Pickleums. I don't want no public library. What's the matter with that girl at central? This is the third time —"

His conversation ended abruptly as the receiver was hung up. Miss Patterson was soon called again. Mrs. Pomfret Smith was one more unto the breach.

"Miss Patterson? I've remembered some more about that book, now. It had a bright red cover and the name of it was printed in gilt letters. It was about so high — oh, I forgot, you can't see over the telephone, can you? Well, it was about as big as books usually are, you know, and it was quite thick — oh, it must have had a hundred or two hundred pages — perhaps more than that, I am not sure. And the front picture was of a girl — the heroine, I guess, and a man, and he had his arms around her and she was looking up into his face. Now, you can remember what book it was, can't you, Miss Patterson?"

51

Librarian at Play

The following is excerpted from *In the Name of the Bodleian and Other Essays*, by Augustine Birrell, Charles Scribner's Sons, 1905.

No man of feeling will grudge the librarians of the universe their annual outing. Their pursuits are not indeed entirely sedentary, since at times they have to climb tall ladders, but of exercise they must always stand in need, and as for air, the exclusively bookish atmosphere is as bad for the lungs as it is for the intellectuals. In 1897 the Second International Library Conference met in London, attended several concerts, was entertained by the Marchioness of Bute and Lady Lubbock; visited Lambeth Palace and Stafford and Apsley Houses; witnessed a special performance of Irving's *Merchant of Venice*; were elected honorary members of the City Liberal, Junior Athenaeum, National Liberal, and Savage Clubs; and, generally speaking, enjoyed themselves after the methods current during that period. They also read forty-six papers, which now alone remain a stately record of their proceedings.

I have lately spent a pleasant afternoon musing over these papers. Their variety is endless, and the dispositions of mind displayed by these librarians are wide as the poles asunder. Some of them babble like babies, others are evidently austere scholars; some are gravely bent on the best methods of classifying catalogues, economizing space, and sorting borrowers' cards; others, scorning such mechanical details, bid us regard libraries, and consequently librarians, as the primary factors in human evolution. "Where," asks Mr. Ernest Cushing Richardson, the librarian of Princeton University, New Jersey, U.S.A., "lies the germ of the library?" He answers his own question after the following convincing fashion: "At the point where a definitely formed concept from another's mind is placed beside one's own idea for integration, the result being a definite new form, including the substance of both." The pointsman who presides over this junction is the librarian.

The young woman of whom Mr. Matthews, the well-known librarian of Bristol, tells us, who, being a candidate for the post of assistant librarian, boldly pronounced Rider Haggard to be the author of the *Idylls of the King*, Southey of *The Mill on the Floss*, and Mark Twain of *Modern Painters*, undoubtedly placed her own ideas at the service of Bristol alongside the preconceived conceptions of Mr. Matthews; but she was rejected all the same.

To speak seriously, who are librarians, and whence come they in such numbers? Of Bodley's librarian we have heard, and all the lettered world honours the name of Richard Garnett, late keeper of the printed books at the British Museum. But beyond these and half a dozen others a great darkness prevails. This ignorance is well illustrated by a pleasing anecdote told at the Conference by Mr. MacAlister:

"Only the day before yesterday, on the Calais boat, I was introduced to a world famed military officer who, when he understood I had some connection with the Library Association, exclaimed: 'Why, you're just the man I want! I have been anxious of late about my man, old Atkins. You see the old boy, with a stoop, sheltering behind the funnel. Poor old beggar! Quite past his work, but as faithful as a dog. It has just occurred to me that if you could shove him into some snug library in the country, I'd be awfully grateful to you. His one fault is a fondness for reading, and so a library would be just the thing.'"

The usual titled lady also turned up at the Conference. This time she was recommending her late cook for the post of librarian, alleging on her behalf the same strange trait of character — her fondness for reading. Here, of course, one recalls Mark Pattison's famous dictum, "The librarian who reads is lost," about which there is much to be said, both *pro* and *con*; but we must not be put off our inquiry, which is: Who are these librarians, and whence come they?...

The British nation is still savage under the skin. It has no real love for books, libraries, or librarians. In its hidden heart it deems them all superfluous. Anger it, and it may in a fit of temper sweep you all away. The loss of our free librarians would indeed by grievous. Never again could they meet in conference and read papers full of quaint things and odd memories. What, for example, can be more amusing than Mr. Cowell's reminiscences of forty years library work in Liverpool, of the primitive days when a youthful Dicky Sam (for so do the inhabitants of that city call themselves) mistook the *Flora of Liverpool* for a book either about a ship or a heroine? He knows better now. And what shall we say of the Liverpool brushmaker who, at a meeting of the library committee, recited a poem in praise of woman, containing the following really magnificent line? "The heart that beats fondest is found in the stays." There is nothing in Roscoe or Mrs. Hermans (local bards) one half so fine. Long may librarians live and flourish! May their salaries increase, if not by leaps and bounds, yet in steady proportions. Yet will they do well to remember that books are not everything.

Cranks and Crotches

The following is excerpted from "Cranks and Crotches," by Henry Coutts, which appeared in *Library Jokes and Jottings*, 1914.

When Crank meets Crank then comes a tug of war.

Persons with "bees in their bonnets" either retire from society and live like hermits, or remain in the company of their fellow-men in order to demonstrate to the world at large, and their little circle in particular, that something is wrong somewhere and they are the persons appointed to put it right. Many in the latter class find in religious and social institutions a convenient medium for advertising their idiosyncrasies. It is, therefore, not surprising that a large number of cranks gravitate towards the public library.

The library crank is an interesting study; he ranges from the milder type whose eccentricity takes the form of a particular whim, to the more dangerous — though at times less irritating — class that must be placed in the category of insanity.

First in order comes the theological crank. Usually he is attached to some obscure minor sect, and endeavours to use the public library as a means of propagating his religious doctrines. In his mistaken zeal he trys to obtain publicity for his cause by placing tracts and bills in books and other convenient receptacles. How shocked he would be if he knew how quickly his missionary efforts are discounted through the medium of the wastepaper basket, or in providing shaving papers for the male members of the staff.

One of the patrons of a Scottish library was in the habit of adding to the formal application for books a Scriptural text. There is no evidence that the staff benefited thereby, although it is to be hoped that they did so.

The zeal of the religious enthusiast often consumes his sense of propriety. An illustration of this is afforded in the following case: A certain book was donated to a library in North London, and shortly afterwards handbills were circulated in the district, as follows:–

Read "Christendom Astray" in — Free Library

The Bible True

"Man Mortral. Immortality a Gift to be bestowed in the Near Future!"

The above address will be given in the _____ HALL on Sunday, May 15, at 7 p.m.

A similar, but more advanced, type of fanatic is the "out-and-out" religious maniac. In a town in Yorkshire a man returned a library book that his wife had borrowed, and gave the following explanation: "Knowing that Our Lord is soon coming again, I desire to be ready, and would not like a borrowed book in the house, especially as the Scriptures are sufficient."

Another instance is provided in a letter that was sent several years ago to a well known librarian in South London:

"I return you a book which my boy has had from your library. He joined it without telling me, and I have forbid him borrowing. I am a believer in the second coming of our Lord (see 2 Peter iii. 10–12), and think it likely that he will do so shortly. How could I meet Him with a clear conscience whilst I had borrowed books in my house? May I respectfully urge upon you to read 1 Thessalonians v. 2, and flee from the wrath to come, for, sir, our business is sinful. Better he than a doorkeeper in the House of the Lord, than dwell in the tents of wickedness. (Psalm, lxxxiv. 10)."

Next in order is the faddist with a pet theory. If the library does not contain all the books on this particular subject he writes it down as a rubbish heap. Generally the subject is a very specialized one, often theological, and quite out of the way of the ordinary reader's study; but this is not taken into account by the faddist; he is too self-centered in his pet theory. The correspondence of the same librarian affords a good illustration of this type.

"Sir,— I beg to suggest the following books for the Reference Department ... as I, and I have no doubt others, want very badly to refer to these books, namely: Maskell's (W.) *Monumenta Ritualia*, last and previous editions.

"Now that is a most useful if not necessary book for compiling a new Liturgy, as I am doing at present, and indeed for everyone wishing to study and understand his prayer-book properly.

"Also as ye have only the old edition of the companion work, viz. *Ancient Liturgy*, I would suggest the last edition should be obtained...

"Also, as ye have only the old edition of H. Blunt's *Annotated Book of Common Prayer*, I would strongly suggest that ye should get the last edition also...

"I would strongly recommend that ye should get a most important liturgical work by a theologian in the Established Presbyterian Church of Scotland, called *The Church and her Services*. I forget the name of the author, but it is in the Liturgies Catalogue of the British Museum, under the head of 'Scotland.'

"I would also suggest that ye should get... *The Book of Common Order of the Presbyterian Church of England*. I saw it last Thursday.

"I would suggest that ye should get duplicates of all the above works, and of Daniel on the Prayer-Book, of which ye have only one copy, and that ye should put the latter in the same press with the other so that it could be obtained for reading upon Sundays. I often have a great difficulty in getting it, especially as it is often lent out.

"I think it most inconvenient and injurious that such books should be lent out, when there are not duplicates for reference, especially as there is such a plenty of useless and injurious novels which only truckle to the vitiated taste of the idle and the silly, and encourage and pander to their frivolity; whilst the best and most useful works in the Greek and Latin classics and their translations, in Medicine, Theology and Law are nearly altogether excluded...

"There is not so much use in having a fine building when most of the books which the sensible and educated part of the public specially require are not to be found there... Social Science is not there, nor translations of the classics and modern languages ... nor many Unitarian and Free Thought works. Excluding these is religious persecution.

"Surely it is most strange and surprising that ye have not all these books in the library, and carried out the other suggestions I have given...

Yours faithfully,
A Clergyman

"P.S.— Surely ye ought to heat the library more during this cold weather. It is cruel treatment of the readers to leave them nearly frozen ... I think the Sanatory Authorities should compel you to heat them properly."

The librarian to whom this letter was addressed, states that it is only one of many similar epistles received by him from the same correspondent.

As is indicated in the postscript for the foregoing letter, the man with a pet theory does not always concern himself with books; sometimes his crochet takes a more general form, such as heating or ventilation. The ventilation crank is well known in public reading-rooms. If the windows are open he feels a draught; if they are closed the room is stuffy; the thermometer is quite useless in such cases. When, as it sometimes happens, an open air faddist comes in contact with a crank who feels a draught, then comes a tug-of-war with a library official acting as umpire.

There is more truth than literary merit in the following plaint of a worried librarian:

> I surely am distracted. What is a man to do?
> I have just received a letter from Mrs. Timbuctoo;
> She writes to say the reading-room is quite devoid of air,
> And really, as a ratepayer, she will not languish there.
> But Mr. Fad, who read *The Times* till nearly half-past one,
> Is very much annoyed because the windows are undone.
> Against this gross injustice he protests with all high might,
> And thinks that he, a ratepayer, should have them closed up tight.
> Now there are those who want no air, and side with Mr. Fad,
> And say an open window is enough to drive them mad;
> But there again are many more like Mrs. Timbuctoo,
> Who want the windows open; well, what is a man to do?

Very innocent, but disfiguring from the bibliographical point of view, is the pastime of the faddist who presses ferns, flowers, and botanical specimens generally between the leaves of a volume. Most libraries have among their readers a crank of this order, and, unfortunately, he generally uses as his instrument a very heavy and expensive type of book that is seldom asked for by other readers, and so the damage is not traced to its source without much difficulty.

The bibliographical treasure crank is an interesting type. He has discovered an old book in the penny box of a second-hand bookseller, and he brings it to the librarian for valuation. He is surrounded by an air of mystery as he approaches the librarian, and carefully draws forth, from a capacious pocket, a very dilapidated volume. Usually the book, judged from a bibliographical or literary aspect, is worth about what he gave for it — sometimes less. The librarian takes to break the truth gently, but it is a dismal failure. "Look at the date," he will say triumphantly, "1785." The librarian explains that the old book is not valuable necessarily; that it needs some special bibliographical characteristic to give it a market value. "But look," he continues, "the *s* is printed like *f*." At last the librarian gives it up in despair and, if humorously inclined, refers the treasure-hunter to a fellow librarian or bibliophile.

Somewhat similar is the crank with an inventive mind. He creates the same atmosphere of mystery as he produces from an old bag a piece of very ordinary rubber tubing. He explains to the librarian, in strict confidence, that this particular tube, if affixed to a gas point, will reduce the gas bill by 75 percent; if fitted to a water tap it will filter the water; if laid on a carpet it will absorb the dust; and if fastened to the insides of pneumatic tyres it will prevent punctures. He is certain there is a fortune in the so-called invention, but that is not his main object; he is striving to benefit humanity. He treats the librarian as a confidant, and the latter promises not to divulge the secret until either the inventor makes his fortune, or dies. (The particular inventive genius the present writer has in mind is dead.)

Another who is striving to benefit humanity is the person who has discovered some cure, unknown to the medical profession, for a specific malady. Does the librarian suffer from the effects of indigestion? He thought so. Well, he will tell him a little secret. And being a secret, he whispers into the librarian's ear: "Take cold water baths winter and summer, and eat an apple morning and night."

The well-worn joke relating to young unmarried curates, infatuated lady members of congregations, and embroidered slippers is not without its parallel in the library world. An assistant librarian — unmarried, endowed with good looks and a distinguished bearing — unconsciously sowed the seeds of the tender passion in the heart of a lady who frequented the library. The gentleman, much against his will, was the recipient of numerous neckties, etc. Seeing that her feelings were not reciprocated, the lady's love turned to hatred, but the infatuation remained, and, like the foolish moth, she continued to flutter near the candle. She declared that the gentleman in question possessed the "evil eye" and had cast a spell over her. Finally, she ordered him to remove his evil influence from her, and threatened him with sundry penalties if he failed to do so. Of course, the poor lady's mind was quite unhinged.

It was the custom of a regular reader at a certain library to check the periodicals systematically, with a view to reporting any that were overdue or missing from their places. On one or two occasions he reported that the *ABC Railway Guide* was missing. This being a peculiar circumstance, the members of the staff were instructed to keep a strict watch on the readers, and in due time the thief was discovered — he was none other than the crank himself.

Some years ago a reader amused himself with a pair of scissors by snipping at this fellow-readers. On a junior assistant remonstrating with him, he straightway snipped the assistant's fingers, causing blood to flow. The humour of the situation lay in the fact that the janitor was off duty at the time, and it fell to the lot of the present writer to eject the maniac.

On another occasion a librarian was called to a man who sat in the reading room, muttering audibly, and who refused to keep quiet or leave the premises. The librarian insisted on the man leaving the building, and the following remarkable dialogue took place:

READER: Don't be hard on me because I've only got one eye.

LIBRARIAN: *(noticing the truth of the statement)*. I'm sorry, but I must ask you to step outside.

READER: I've been a soldier. Don't be hard on an old soldier.

LIBRARIAN: Will you step outside, please?

READER: All right. Am I to take the sack, or leave the sack?

LIBRARIAN: *(who sees a canvas sack under the table and is now convinced of the man's insanity)*. Bring the sack outside by all means.

READER: But I've come for my grandfather's clock!

The librarian ultimately pacified the man and persuaded him to leave the building without the clock.

A man strolled into the reading-room, sat down, pulled out his pipe, and lit it for a quiet smoke. He was at once told that this was quite contrary to all rules and regulations. He sat quietly for a time, but finding it rather dull commenced to talk loudly. Again the assistant interfered by directing his attention to the "Silence is Requested" notice. Goaded beyond endurance, the man sprang up, and exclaimed, "They won't let you smoke, and they won't let you talk, but I suppose they can't prevent you from pulling your eye out," and, suiting the action to the word, he took out one of his eyes and waved it aloft in the air. It was glass!

The Old Librarian's Almanack

Just as every farmer should be familiar with the *Farmer's Almanac*, every librarian should be familiar with Edmund Lester Pearson's humorous *Old Librarian's Almanack*. It was first published in 1909 by Elm Tree Press. The almanac is included here for your enjoyment and reference.

January hath 31 days 1774

The librarian may be justly compar'd with him who keeps an Armoury of Weapons; for as the Keeper doth neither forge the implements of War, nor employ them on the field of Battle, so neither doth the Librarian compose the learn'd Works which are under his charge, nor use their wisdom in his own especial interest.

But like that other Keeper, it is his Duty to see that his Armoury (which is the Library) be well stock'd with the fittest Weapons, and that they be put into the hands of such as can use them at the proper time.

The Metaphor need not stop at this, neither, for even as the Weapons of the Armoury are unfitted for the hands of all, so the Books (the Weapons over which the Librarian is Custodian) are ofttimes dangerous & harmful if they come to the hands of persons ill-fitted to peruse them.

Mr. Pope (an able poet, tho' a Papist) warns us that:

A little learning is a dangerous thing!
Drink deep, or taste not the Pierian spring.

The wisdom of such advice, & the folly of not observing it may be seen now-a-days, when Demagogues and others of shallow intellect seek to stir up sedition & revolt. Whence, it appears that it is as Custos Librorum (as the Ancients call'd him) or Guardian of the Books, that the Librarian exercises his true function.

I am sensible that there will be some who will enquire as to what qualities should be possess'd by him who stands thus as Guardian of the Books. These may think (if perchance the hasty and frivolous workings of their ill-taught minds may be so dignified as to term it thinking) that it matters little what the character of the Librarian be.

Such as these cannot too soon become aware of their error. For how can it be possible that a man can act as Warder of the accumulated record of the world's wisdom, piety, learning & experience, and hold the same in necessary reverence, if he be not a person of sober and Godly life, learn'd, virtuous, chaste, moral, frugal and temperate?

This should be the character of the Librarian, and it is such as he that I would extol, as through these pages, I offer for your benefit, the results of twenty years of labour in our Honourable Profession.

February hath 28 days

You shall chuse your Books with Care and Circumspection. When you have determin'd that it is Prudent to purchase a certain Work do so cautiously and make a Shrewd Bargain with the Vendor. It will then be your Duty to Peruse the Volume, even if (as doubtless will be the Fact) you have scan'd it before Buying.

Do not let the Importunities of Persons who come to the library hasten you in the Performance of this Task. They should be Content to wait for the Book until you have Satisfied yourself of its Contents.

There will then remain the Necessity of recording its Acquisition in your Ledgers of Record. As for the Entry of its Style and Title in the Catalogue, many counsel that this is not needful, since you may be expected to remember that the Book has been Purchas'd for the Library. It may, however, occupy your leisure moments. Some would advise that if it be a Volume of Sermons it be placed on the Shelves with others of its like; or if it be a work of Natural Philosophy it stand near the Volumes of that class. This is a waste of Labour.

Assign it a Number which shall correspond to its Position on the Shelf, and shall be the next in Sequence from the latest Book which you have added, and so let them stand in the Order in which they are Receiv'd. For, surely, if you desire to find a number of volumes of Sermons, it will be an easy matter for you, recalling when they were Purchas'd, to pluck them from their several resting-places.

Keep your Books behind stout Gratings, and in no wise let any Person come at them to take them from the Shelf except yourself.

Have in Mind the Counsel of Master Enoch Sneed (that most Worthy Librarian) who says: It were better that no Person enter the Library (save the Librarian Himself) and that the Books be kept in Safety, than that one Book be lost, or others Misplac'd. Guard well your Books,— this is always your foremost Duty.

March hath 31 days

ARS BIBLIOTHECARII

> First of all matters, 'tis your greatest need
> To read unceasing & unceasing read;
> When one Book's ended, with a mind unvext
> Turn then your whole Attention to the Next.
> Let naught intrude; to all the World be blind,
> And chase each vain allurement from your Mind.
> Be also deaf; 'tis well to turn the Lock,
> And let who will the outer portal knock.
> Behold in Books your Raiment & your Bread,
> So, lacking Books, you're neither warm'd nor fed;
> Chuse then with care, repudiate the Chaff,
> Or see corruption spoil the better half;
> For one base volume spread the Poison through,—
> A single Traitor can a Host undo.
> As Books, like Men, got better neatly drest,
> Let Paper, Print, & Binding be the Best.
> Your Books obtain'd, behold the Problem rise
> How best secure them from unworthy eyes;
> Or, graver yet, to guard lest you're bereft
> By Fire, Worms, or (absit omen!) Theft.
> Remember this: they're safe upon the shelf,
> When none has access thither but yourself.
> As you to guard them best are qualifi'd,
> So you to read them, clearly 'tis impli'd.
> Be vigilant your Treasury to keep,
> In watchful care know neither rest nor sleep;
> All other Readers better far keep out
> Then put the safety of your Books in doubt.
> And first, or last, this Precept ever heed;
> To read unceasing, and unceasing read.
>   J.B.

April hath 30 days

Toward the Persons who frequent your Librarian maintain a courteous Demeanour, but the utmost Vigilance. For as it is your duty to guard well the Books which are the Riches of your Treasury, so you cannot afford to relax those Restrictions which may save you from Despoilment and the most grievous Loss. The Biblioklept or Thief of Books is your eternal Foe.

John Milton truly wrote: "For books are not absolutely dead things, but do contain a potency of Life in them to be as active as that Soul was whose Progeny they are; nay, they do preserve as in Violl the purest efficacy and extraction of that living Intellect that bred them."

This, then, is the Value of a Book in the Mind of that great Poet. How far beyond mere Gold or Silver is the worth of a Book, & how Filthy & Base the Act of one who steals a Book! But there be sneeking unutterable Villains who will enter a Library, and in their furtive & Detestable fashion carry from it one of its Treasures!

And what Condemnation shall befit the accurst Wretch (for he cannot justly claim the title of Man) who pilfers and purloins for his own selfish ends such a precious article as a Book? I am minded of the Warning display'd in the Library of the Popish Monastery of San Pedro at Barcelona. This is the version English'd by Sir Matthew Mahan, who saw it writ in Latin in the Monastery, as he himself describes in his learn'd Book, "Travels in Spanish Countries, 1712."

The Warning reads thus: "For him that stealeth a Book from this Library, let it change to a Serpent in his hand and rend him. Let him be struck with Palsy, and all his Members blasted. Let him languish in Pain, crying aloud for Mercy and let there be no surcease to his Agony till he sink to Dissolution. Let Book-worms gnaw his Entrails in token of the Worm that dieth not, and when at last he goeth to his final Punishment let the Flames of Hell consume him for ever and aye."

May hath 31 days

On the Enemies of Books I especially esteem the Cockroach. That worthy Librarian, Master Enoch Sneed (for whom I profess my reverent Admiration), would have it that the Domestic Mouse, building her Nest, as she will, 'mid the Tatters of our most precious Volumes, more fairly merits the name of Chief Destroyer. But though it be true that the Ravage wrought be the Mouse is compleat, yet she & her Kind may be exterminated, & the Library rid of her Presence with no great Ado.

But the cockroach, more elusive in his Habits, & not less insidious in his Character, spreads destruction wherever his footsteps may wander, & he is grater Bother to remove, in view of the Celebrity of his Movements, & the amazing Fecundity with which he reproduces his Kind.

Some may question if the Nature of the Destruction wrought by this Pestilential Insect be of serious import, but I do earnestly Assure all such that I have witnessed with my own eyes appalling Injuries inflicted on the most Precious Books in my Custody, & these Injuries, I am convinc'd, were justly chargeable to this hardshelled Rogue who Scuttles about the Book Shelves, & owns no restraint upon his ungovernable Appetite. For the Cockroach will so gnaw & devour the Bindings, so prey upon the leaves of old Books that I have been Moved nearly to an access of Tears when I have gaz'd upon the Ruin which he has left after him. With devilish Cunning he will come at only the rare and costly Volumes, picking them out, it would seem, as by the leadership of Satan, & visiting upon them his own foul Mutilation.

I have found the following Preparation to be highly serviceable: To three minims of distilled Hen-Bane, add four drops of the Tincture of Saffron. Take this Mixture & combine it with half a gill of the Liquor which comes from boyling a peck of common Tansy. After allowing it to cool, allow four great spoonfuls of pure Vinegar, a pinch of powdered Rhubarb, &

the Juice of a score of Mulberries, heated well. The resulting Compound should be kept in a Jar, tightly seal'd, & sprinkled on the Book Shelves, or wherever the Enemy are seen.

June hath 30 days

So far as your Authority will permit of it, exercise great Discrimination as to which Person shall be admitted to the use of the Library. For the Treasure House of Literature to the use of the Library. For the Treasure House of Literature is no more to be thrown open to the ravages of the unreasoning Mob, than is a fair Garden to be laid unprotected at the Mercy of a Swarm of Beasts.

Question each Applicant closely. See that he be a Person of good Reputation, scholarly Habits, sober and courteous Demeanour. Any mere Trifer, a Person that would Dallhy with Books, or seek in them shallow Amusement, may be Dismiss'd without delay.

No Person younger than 20 years (save if he be a Student, of more than 18 years, and vouched by his Tutor) is on any pretext to enter the Library. Be suspicious of Women. They are given to the Reading of frivolous Romances, and at all events, their presence in a Library adds a little to (if it does not, indeed, detract from) that aspect of Gravity, Seriousness and Learning which is its greatest Glory. You will make no error in excluding them altogether, even though by that Act it befall that you should prohibit from entering some one of those Excellent Females who are distinguished by their Wit and Learning. There is little Chance that You or I, Sir, will ever see such an One.

Let no Politician be in your Library, nor no man who Talks overmuch. It will be difficult for him to observe Silence, and he is objectionable otherwise, as well. No Astrologer, Necromancer, Charlatan, Quack, nor Humbug; no Vendor of Nostrums, nor Teacher of false Knowledge, no fanatic Preacher no Refugee. Admit no one of loose or evil Life; prohibit the Gamestar, the Gypsy, the Vagrant. Allow none who suffers from an infectious Disease; and none whose Apparel is so Gaudy or Eccentrick as to attract the Eye. Keep out the Light-witted, the Shallow, the Base and Obscene. See to it that none enter who are Senile, and none who are immature in their Minds, even tho' they have reach'd the requir'd Age.

July hath 31 days

About this Time prepare for the Annual Examination. Close your Library not later than August 1, having given due Notice that all Books must be returned under Pain of Expulsion. See that every Book the Library owns is in its proper place on the Shelf by the first Day of the Month. It will perchance be necessary for you to seek some of them Yourself, taking care, at the same time, to administer a Reproof to the delinquent Ones.

Covers should be examined, and all those worn and tattered should be replaced. Never let a Book leave the Library without a stout paper Cover to protect it against the Abuses of the careless.

Paste is to be preferred to Glue in affixing these. To one cupful of Flour add nine spoonfuls of Water, and a little Vinegar. A half-ounce of Oil of Spearmint will be found an admirable Preservative.

Look to it that each Book is numbered in accordance with its corresponding place on the shelf. During the six Weeks that the Library remains closed to all but Yourself there is an excellent Opportunity to compile your Catalogue.

Examine your Books with great care to see that none have crept in which have an immoral or debasing Character, or which contain Pernicious and unsound Theology. A few Books of Moral tendency may be included for the Young. Their Elders will choose these, for surely children are not to be permitted in the Library themselves, to the disturbance of all others.

Cast out and destroy any book which is merely frivolous and empty of all serious meaning, for the true object of Literature is to instill Wisdom and to lead to Habits of grave Meditation, and there always are those whose vapid Minds will feed, if it be allowed, on nothing but that which amuses for the Moment. Such must not be abetted.

Make the most of every Moment during the period of the Annual Examination, for you can then be assured that the Books are safe and well cared for, rather than spread abroad and distributed Hither and Thither.

August hath 31 days

Your Library is now closed, and so it will remain for six Weeks, or perchance, two Months. These be Halcyon Days. The Annoyances to which you are subjected throughout all the Year vanish away, and there is naught to Disturb you.

Master Enoch Sneed (for whom I am ever ready to Testify my Reverence) has written: I am so be-pestered and bothered by persons insinuating themselves into the Library to get Books that frequently I am near to my Wit's end. There have been days when I was scarce able to read for two Hours consecutive without some Donkey breaking in upon my Peace. Only the thought of the Annual Examination sustains me. Then, forsooth, I can defy them all and read in some Security.

The necessary Tasks of the Examination (which I described last month) are easily performed in a Week, or less. Indeed, if you omit the preparation of the Catalogue (and worthy Master Enoch Sneed deems it better not to compile a Catalogue, both as an unavailing Bother and moreover as the absence of it makes you more Secure in your Office) then, in this case, you have a goodly season for the Relishment of your Books.

How agreeable, on these sultry Days, is the Library! The rays of the Sun, which descend so fierce outdoors, are tempered inside its walls, and your Footsteps, as you walk hither and yon among the Alcoves, echo loudly. A lonely Sound, say you? Not so, the Lover of Books is not affected by Loneliness when he is encompassed by his Friends. On every Shelf they stand, none missing (I hope truly) and all at your service.

Parents of Children are said to be more delighted in the possession when the offspring are in their Beds, than at any other time. Tho' I trust I may be pardoned for making a seeming Comparison between Books and such a subject as Children, yet it may be said that it is true of the Librarian that he is most content when all his Books are in the Library under his protection. For he can be no lover of books if he be at ease when his books are absent from the Library.

Matrimony, so maintain'd worthy Master Peleg Gudger, is no fit Diversion for the Librarian, and in truth, I commend his Wisdom in the Matter. The dissipations of Time, the vain, Emptinesses of Amusement, the general be-pesterment that follows embarkation on this doubtful Sea (doubtful, if not in fact, Perilus) all these concomitants of the Married State so conspire and agree to harass the Librarian and woo him to his legitimate tasks as to behoove him to take a great Oath never to allow himself to be entrapped. Tis the only safe course. Otherwise will he find himself badger'd when he desires to read in Peace; led forth to Domestic Duties when he should be marshalling his Books; and at all times Distract'd & Annoy'd, to the detriment of his Profession.

It is true, there be some who hold to the Contrary. Dr. Simon Bagley writes: I have not found Wives to be altogether a too heavy Encumberance. They can dust Books, and at times, they may be trusted to arrange the volumes properly in their places. Beyond this, it would perchance, be rash to go with them. I am far from advising Librarians to marry without weighing the Question soberly, and considering it discreetly, but this I do affirm: that a Wife may be train'd to partake in a Librarian's labours in such a way as not altogether to act as a Millstone about his Neck. It is scarce necessary to comment on Dr. Bagley's words. Truly he impeaches his own Contention, by the apologetick fashion of his phrases. Most willingly do I mention the Opinion of that diligent Librarian, Master Enoch Sneed, with whom on this (as on every point in our Profession) I am rejoiced to own myself at one. Steer a straight course, he says, away from feminine Blandishments. These Females are as Leeches or Bloodsuckers, hardly to be torn off. They would make you take your Victuals at certain fix'd seasons to conform to their rules of Housekeeping, regarding not that you may wish to read at those Hours; while again they will Babble & Complain should it chance that after a hard night's reading you ask that a hot Supper be served at Daybreak. Shun them as you would the Devil.

October hath 31 days

Master Caleb Pingree's Book tells of Dr. Matthew Gully who set out one Dah to dust the Books in his Library. But the first Volume which he pluck'd from the shelf was the works of Herodotus, which we had long desir'd to read yet again, and at leisure, and so entrall'd did the worthy Dr. Gully become in the writings of the Greek historian, that starting in to peruse the Book, he set it not down till he had read it from Beginning to End.

Thus it happen'd with the next Book, and the next, the excellent Doctor standing before his Book Shelves, holding in one hand the Cloth, wherewith he had purpos'd to wipe off the Dust from the Books, and in the other the Volume which he could no lay aside until he had read it.

So he abode standing, and return'd each Day to his task, yet each Day reading more of the Books, till at last full eighteen Months had pass'd, and Dr. Gully had read every book in the Library. But at that time the Dust lay as thick on the Books whereat he had commenc'd, as ever it had been in the Beginning.

Also there is related an Incident concerning Master Timothy Mason, the same who had his Bed fitted up in the Library, that he might sleep near his Books and thereby not suffer Annoyance when he should be wakeful at Night, and find not the Books at hand.

Master Timothy, being in Charge of a Publick Library, was one day reading diligently when a Member of the Library entered, and presenting his Subscription Ticket begged the Librarian to fetch him a certain Book. Master Timothy being inces'd at this Interruption of his Reading, and Chancing at that Moment to see the Constable passing the Library, did put out his Head from the Window and Bawl loudly for the Constable to come in.

When the latter had enter'd he gave the Member into custody of the Officer, preferring against him a charge of Disturbance of the Peace.

November hath 30 days

The admirable Timothy Mason (of whom we read last Month) was wont to Walk with a Book held before his Nose, reading as he pass'd along the Street. He looked neither up nor down as he Walk'd, but fixt his Attention upon the Page before him, being somewhat short of Vision, tho' wearing powerful Lenses in his Spectacles. It was his Custom to leave the Library when it lack'd a few Minutes of 6 o'clock in the Evening, he had found that his walk brought him to his Dwelling at the Moment that the Town Clock struck the Hour.

One Evening, in Midsummer, the worthy Librarian set out for his Home, holding before him & reading with Earnestness the Ecclesiastical Polity of the learn'd Hooker. Now, it chanc'd that the Town Clock had become damag'd, the Librarian, hearing not the customary Tinging, strode past his Door (despite the loud cries of his Housekeeper), continu'd down the Street, never for an instant relaxing his Zeal for Reading. At 7 o'clock the Excellent man was still walking in the direction of the neighboring Town, and only at a quarter after 8, when the failing Light caus'd him to glance up, did he perceive that he had travell'd over 6 miles & arriv'd in the Market place of the next Town, having perus'd the greater part of the Ecclesiastical Polity on the journey.

The Librarian was sore perplex'd, for at first he failed to recognize his surroundings, & he was unable to account for the hooting Rabble that dogg'd his Footsteps, in the Custom of such Vulgar Persons when they discover a Stranger of unusual Aspect. He was also at a loss to understand how his Shoes & Hose had become so be-fouled & be-mired, for he was unaware that he had crossed divers Brooks, & forded sundry Watercourses during his journey. It might have fared ill with Master Timothy, had not Master Caleb Perkins, a Brother Librarian, chanc'd to encounter him at that Moment. Through the good offices of this Friend, Master Timothy was provided with comfortable Lodgings for the Night & on the Morrow suitably convey'd to his own Home.

December hath 31 days

There is none so Felicitous as the Librarian, and none with so small a cause of Ill-Content, Jealousy or Rancour. No other Profession is like his; no other so Happy. Of the Clergy, I speak not, their Calling is sacred and not of this World. The Physician & Lawyer administer to the ills and evils of Mankind. The Merchant's happiness is conditioned upon his pecuniary Success.

But the Librarian, so far removed from any of these, ministers to the Wisdom and Light of Mankind, increases his own Knowledge, lives surrounded by the Noble thoughts of great Minds, and can take no Concern of pecuniary Success, forasmuch as such a thing is not within the boundaries of Possibility.

If any may rival him in good Fortune, it is the Author, who produces some great Work of which the Librarian shall stand as humble Guardian. But even here, again, a little reading suffices to show that Authors have frequently lived in Turmoil or Penury, dying Destitute or wretched, because that Publick Esteem which was necessary to their Contentment had been withheld until long after they had quitted this Earth.

The Librarian, as he cannot hope for Wealth (nor fret his Mind about it), so he cannot expect to achieve Fame. Where is the Monument erected to a Librarian? Great Monarchs and Warriors have theirs; in ancient times it was even a custom thus to honour the Poet. But the Librarian lives and dies unknown to Fame; the durable results of his Labours are not visible to the Eye, and if at all he receiveth Honour it is for his private Character as a Man. His Brother Librarians may know and Esteem him as an Ornament to their Profession, and that it his sufficient Reward.

He lives protected, avaricious neither of Money nor Worldly Fame, and happy in the good-liest of all Occupations, the pursuit of Wisdom.

This is the Ending of The Old Librarian's Almanack for Anno Domini 1774. To my learn'd Brethren, I wish all Health and Joy.

5

Librarians in Politics, Porn, Movies, and Books

Librarians, both real and fictitious, have infiltrated all areas of culture and society. Real life librarians have been elected to political office. While fictitious librarians have made their way onto the big screen. This chapter takes a look at some librarians, both fictitious and real, in politics, porn, movies, and books.

Librarians in Politics

They're analytical, inquisitive, and some of the most intelligent people in the world. They're known for being quiet individuals, always in the background of society. But throughout time they've also played a role in shaping society. From Lewis Arthur Larson (1910–1993), who once served as the librarian of the Oxford University Political Union and a speechwriter for President Eisenhower, to Ruth Ann Minner (1935–), former agricultural statistician and librarian for the state of Delaware and current governor of Delaware, librarians have played a role in politics at all levels of government. In most cases, a library career came first, then the move into a political career. Let's take a look at a few librarians who have ventured into politics.

Congress

At the Congressional level, at least three librarians have held the honor of serving in Congress, all in the House of Representatives. Of the three, only one was academically educated as a librarian. And of the three, one enjoyed a political career before serving as a librarian.

MAJOR R. OWENS

Born in 1936 in Tennessee, Major Owens received his master's degree in library science from Atlanta University and began his library career with the Brooklyn

Public Library in 1958. But by the mid–sixties he was very involved in politics, starting at the local level, and serving on a number of local councils. He successfully moved up to state level politics in 1974 when he was elected to the New York State Senate, an office he served in until 1982. In 1983 he was successfully elected to the U.S. House of Representatives. He is the first professionally educated librarian to be elected to Congress.

To further dispel any of those old stereotypical notions you still posses about librarians, Representative Owens also writes rap lyrics. Many of them appear in the *Congressional Record*. Below are two songs printed here with Representative Owen's permission.

Towers of Flowers
(a memorial to the heroes of September 11th that
appeared in the October 12, 2001 *Congressional Record*)

Pyramid for our age
Funeral pyre
Souls on fire;
Monumental Massacre
Mound of morning
Futures burning
Desperate yearning
Excruciating churning;
For all the hijacked years
Cry rivers,
Feel the death chill
Iceberg of frozen
Bloody tears;
Defiant orations of Pericles
Must now rise
Out of the ashes
Jefferson's profound principles
Will outlive the crashes.
Funeral pyre
Souls on fire
Lincoln's steel will
In the fiery furnace;

Mount of morning
Futures burning
Desperate yearning;
Thousands of honored dead
Perished in pain
But not in vain,
Martin Luther King's courage
Will scrub the stain;
A new nation
Will overcome its rage
And for peace
March forever fully engaged.
Souls in fire
Funeral pyre
Pyramid for our age;
O say can you see
The monument of towers
Ashes hot with anger
Mountain of sacred flowers
Under God
Booming with new powers.

Crowd the Children In
(appeared in the February 5, 2003 *Congressional Record*)

No Child Left Behind
Crowd them in,
Construction dollars
Never win.
No Child Left Behind
The budget is unkind
An increase of billions
They promised–

A bold elephant fable,
A decrease by millions
Placed on the table.
Under funding catastrophe
Lurking in the wind,
Carefully covered sin,
Regally wrapped spin,
Cutbacks cover the table.

On the made in White House label	No Child Left Behind,
Read progress,	Crowd them in,
Camouflage the big mess,	Construction dollars
Public relations success.	Never Win.

CHARLES RUFUS SKINNER

For former representative Charles Skinner, his political career began before his library career. Born in 1844, Skinner worked as a teacher and editor before beginning his political career at the local, then state level. His political career included serving in the Assembly of the New York State Legislature from 1877 to 1881, and then in the U.S. House of Representatives from 1881 to 1885. When his term of office ended, he went on to hold various education offices, including that of the state superintendent of public instruction from 1895 to 1904. From 1913 to 1914 he returned to the legislature to serve as the librarian for the state assembly, then as the legislative librarian from 1915 to 1925. He died in 1928.

FOSTER WATERMAN STEARNS

Born in 1881, Mr. Stearns served as the librarian of the Museum of Fine Arts in Boston, Massachusetts from 1913 to 1917. In 1917, he served as the state librarian of Massachusetts. Twenty years later as a resident of New Hampshire, he was elected to serve in the New Hampshire House of Representatives from 1937 to 1938. He subsequently served as a representative in the U.S. Congress from 1939 to 1945. He passed away in 1956.

State Legislature

Since public libraries are government agencies, their annual budgets are frequently at the mercy of elected and appointed officials. Library managers and directors must be adept at maneuvering the politics of government in order to be successful in protecting and increasing their library budgets. So it seems only natural that many librarians would eventually decide to run for elected office. Through the years, many librarians have been elected to their state legislatures, or to local government positions. Here's a sample of individuals who have taken their leadership abilities beyond the library.

HANNAH D. ATKINS

Born in 1923, Ms. Atkins received her bachelor's degree in library science from the University of Chicago and subsequently held positions in public, school, academic and state libraries. In 1969, she was elected to the Oklahoma State Legislature where she also earned the distinction of being the first African American woman in the legislature.

MATTHEW SIMPSON DUDGEON

A lawyer, Mr. Dudgeon was elected to the Wisconsin State Assembly and served there from 1903 to 1904. Later, he served as the director of the Wisconsin

Library School, and director of the Milwaukee Public Library. During his lifetime, he also served as secretary of the Wisconsin Free Library Commission. While serving in that position during World War I, he, as a story on the Madison Public Library's website reports "advised librarians to withdraw all books from the shelves 'as to the patriotic character of which there is any doubt.'" His advice can be viewed as either patriotic, or a form of censorship depending upon your point of view.

Cynthia Jenkins

Born in 1924, Ms. Jenkins received her master's degree in library science from Pratt University and went on to work in two large New York public libraries. In 1982 she was elected to the New York State Assembly where she served for six terms until 1994. She subsequently made a run for a Senate seat. Ms. Jenkins died in 2001.

Wayne H. Johnson

Born in 1942, Mr. Johnson served in the Coast Guard before pursing his academic degrees. He received his Master of Public Administration degree from the University of Colorado in 1970, and his Master of Library Science degree from the University of Oklahoma in 1972. He served as the state librarian of Wyoming from 1978 to 1989. In 1993 he was elected to serve in the House of Representatives in the Wyoming State Legislature where he served until 2004. In 2005 he was elected as a Senator in the Wyoming State Legislature.

What motivates a librarian to run for office? In an interview that appeared in the December 19, 2004, *Wyoming Tribune-Eagle*, Mr. Johnson answered "I consider myself a middle-class person and feel that Wyoming working men and women, small-business owners and their families are under-represented in the state Legislature. People from Senate District 6 need an advocate who will take their concerns to the Legislature."

David J. Panciera

Born in 1944, Mr. Panciera received his master's degree in library and information science from State University of New York in 1969. He is the former director of the Westerly Public Library in Rhode Island. In 1993 he was elected to the Rhode Island House of Representatives, where he served for three terms before retiring from the legislature. He went on to work as the librarian of the Langworthy Public Library in Hopkins, Rhode Island.

Mayor

If librarians were wallflowers, they'd never get elected to office. These days the skills and abilities of librarians are more widely recognized. The following examples of librarians who have been elected to the office of mayor demonstrate that librarians are "people-persons." Far from being timid, they have leadership abilities that extend beyond the library and into general government. The residents of their communities have recognized their abilities. I applaud these librarians who decided to have greater impact upon society by moving from librarian to mayor.

JEROME CONLEY

A graduate of Indiana University's School of Library and Information Science, Mr. Conley received his MLS in 1990. He is currently the head of special libraries at Miami University of Ohio and he is also the mayor of Oxford, Ohio. He was first elected to office in 2003, holding the distinction of being the first black mayor of Oxford, and he was re-elected in 2005. Prior to becoming mayor, he served on the city council.

SAMUEL A. GREEN

Born in 1830 in Massachusetts, Mr. Green studied medicine at Harvard. After serving as a doctor in the military, he served as mayor of Boston in 1882. Later, he served as the librarian for the Massachusetts Historical Society. He died in 1878. Given the salaries of physicians in comparison to librarians, we know he served as a librarian out of love for the job, not the money!

PATRICIA MACDONALD KURAN

Born in 1928 in New Jersey, Ms. Kuran was educated at Rutgers University in the early sixties. She later worked as a teacher and librarian in the Plainfield school system before embarking into politics. In 1978 she was elected councilwoman in the Borough of Fanwood, New Jersey, serving in that post until 1982. She made local history in 1984 when she was elected the first woman mayor of Fanwood, serving in the office for two terms. Ms. Kuran is deceased.

City Treasurer/Secretary

GERALDINE R. DAVID

Born in 1938, Ms. David previously held positions as librarian assistant at Elaine Junior High School and Lake View Elementary and as treasurer of the City of Lake View, Arkansas.

Librarians in Pornography

Books and Film

It's hard to say if it's because librarians are known for being moral, intelligent individuals, or if it's because they're thought of as being prim and proper, but librarians often appear as characters in pornographic books and films. Two fairly extensive lists of librarians in pornography can be found online. One is "The Image of Librarians in Pornography," by Dan Lester, which lists 49 books published between

1978 and 1988 (www.riverofdata.com/librarian/porn). Another is "Sex in the Stacks" by Candi Strecker (www.chiprow.com/articles/library.html).

To give you a sample of what's available, following are two books in this genre featuring librarians.

THE LIBRARIAN'S NAUGHTY HABIT

(By Heather Brown, Olympia Press Books, 2006.) On the back cover of the book, which sports a plain pink front cover, it states "Only the second installment from Greenleaf's legendary series of librarian porn, published when the ex–Rogues faced prison in Michigan." Yes, you read this right. This is book two of a series of librarian porn.

Starting with the first sentence in this book there's no doubt it's pornography. The book focuses on Samantha, a young librarian who works at the library's circulation desk. (In real life few, if any, librarians are assigned to working the circulation desk.) One day her boss asks her to review *The Joy of Lust* for possible addition to the library's sex manual collection. From here on you can use your imagination as to the direction the story takes. Or, as a sentence from the back cover reads, "*The Librarian's Naughty Habit* is easily the first account of sex and the circulation desk, that we at the Olympia Press can legally do." Don't expect to find a whole lot of realism about librarians or libraries in this book.

JANET, LIBRARIAN

(By Raphael Mello, Blue Moon Books, 2000.) This book focuses on a librarian named Janet Westwood. Janet is lured into a desert cabin by four individuals where she finds carnal knowledge and, of course, sex. Because most of the action takes place not in the library, but in a cabin, the focus is less on libraries and librarians and more on Janet's adventures in the cabin. And this is about as much as I'm willing to write about the contents of this book.

Librarian characters are no stranger to pornographic film. The concept of the inhibited female spinster librarian being sexually released seems to be a common theme in many of the movies. And since the pornographic film industry is such a huge industry, there's no shortage of adult films with librarian characters in them.

Pornographic films with librarian characters can be found by using a variety of film guides both in print and online. Performing a web search with words such as "XXX film guide" provides a number of search results and links to sites where adult films can be searched for librarian characters.

ON THE WEB

Yes, soft librarian porn sites can also be found on the web. One site is Jessamyn's Naked Librarians site. Accessible at http://Jessamyn.com/naked/links.html, the opening page reads "naked photos of real live women (with a librarian theme)."

The photos run the gamut. Some are provocative images of librarians from ads or book covers. Others are photographs of naked librarians from a variety of sources.

PAINT BY NUMBERS

If you're tired of thinking about librarians in pornography, skip to the next section. But if you just can't get enough and have an artistic leaning, you can also get a paint-by-number kit of a supposedly naked librarian from the Scarlet Librarian. The heading on the opening webpage (www.scarletlibrarian.com) reads "the scarlet librarian: because everyone loves naked librarians?" On the website you can view and order a paint-by-number kit of the unclothed woman you choose, or even a T-shirt.

Librarians in Movies

The librarian as a character has appeared in literally hundreds movies from the silent film era to today. In most of the early movies they fit the typical image of the librarian of that time. In their book *The Image of Librarians in Cinema, 1917–1999* (McFarland, 2005), Ray and Brenda Tevis actually analyzed the stereotypical/non-stereotypical images of librarians in the cinema.

Numerous lists of movies that contain a library scene, library worker, or librarian character abound on the Internet, and in various reference publications. In most of the movies appearing on these lists, the librarian is only a minor character. But in the past 20 years, a number of movie scripts have librarians as major characters. Many of these movies have the librarians shedding their stereotypical image and morphing into action roles, taking charge of the situation or conquering problems. These are entertaining movies to be enjoyed by librarians and library lovers. Let's take a look at some of the comedies and action films with librarians playing a major role.

Shorts

THE LIBRARIAN DIALOGUES (2005)

This humorous short (approximately three minutes) film looks at what transpires during a staff meeting of librarians. Some of the topics discussed at the meeting include the problem of theft of library materials and the beeping noise of the checkout machine. Yes, there are some stereotypes being promoted so some librarians may take offense at it. But for all of us who can laugh at our own profession, the film provides a couple minutes of levity.

The Librarian Dialogues was written, directed and produced by Sam Logan Khaleghi. In the credits, the four librarian characters have names even though in the film they are not referred to by name. I love the fact that one of them is named Spike.

At the time of this writing, the film can be viewed on the Internet at www.fatkidstudios.com/librariandialogues. The website states the film will be available for purchase on DVD soon.

LIBRARY STAFF NOTICE (2005)

In this funny short film, a library user is talking on her cell phone while she searches for books in the book stacks. As she pulls books off the shelf in her search, she drops them onto the floor rather than reshelving them. Her actions prompt a ghost to begin stalking her.

The film was produced by a team of ten students at Emory University and shown during Campus MovieFest. You can view the film online at http://video.google.com/videoplay?docid=-3672196227600735115&q=library+staff+notice.

Feature Films: Action

THE BLACK MASK

If you don't like martial arts films but love the idea of a librarian kicking butt, then you need to take the time to see this film. Set in Hong Kong, it stars martial art star Jet Li (*The One* and *Kiss of the Dragon*). Li is part of a biologically enhanced commando force with superhuman strength and immunity to pain. When some of the members become unstable, the government decides to terminate the commando force. But Li escapes and assumes a new identity. Taking the name Simon, he's now a librarian in Hong Kong.

The library is the perfect hiding place for him. He says "I like it here. It's quiet. Nobody ever bothers a librarian." But things drastically change. He dons a black mask to protect his identity as he battles criminals and members of his old commando force. And of course, throughout the action a romance forms between Li and a loopy part-time library worker.

Because of Li's small build, his appearance as a librarian is believable. He looks right at home pushing a book cart as he reshelves library books. But this librarian can effortlessly defeat an army of bad guys while maintaining a calm appearance.

The movie deserves its "R" rating. It has lots of blood, guts, bodies, and body parts. This is definitely not a film for children.

The version of the movie I watched was dubbed in English. But many of the DVDs for sale note that they contain English subtitles.

(Live/Artisan, Initially released in Hong Kong in 1996 and in the United States in 1999. Running time: 1 hour, 42 minutes.)

THE LIBRARIAN: QUEST FOR THE SPEAR

For a less bloody librarian superhero film, don't miss *The Librarian: Quest for the Spear*. Originally airing on the TNT cable network, this is an action movie for the entire family to watch. Although the movie was harshly criticized and panned by real librarians, the movie is intended to be fun, not factual. And it definitely provides some fun entertainment.

Noah Wyle stars as Flynn Carsen, who seeks a job at the Metropolitan Library as a librarian. During the interview, Jane Curtin, playing a library administrator, asks him, "What makes you think you could be the librarian?"

"Well, I've read a lot of books," he replies with a laugh.

"Don't try to be funny. I don't do funny. What makes you think you could be the librarian?" she asks again.

"I know the Dewey Decimal System, Library of Congress, research paper, web searching. I can set up an RSS feed."

"Everyone knows that," replies Curtin. "They're librarians."

Carsen ultimately gets the job as the librarian. (Don't we wish all male librarians were as cute as Wyle!)

Bob Newhart, playing a mysterious library administrator and ex–Marine, shows Carsen some of the secret treasures kept in the library, treasures such as the Ark of the Covenant and Pandora's Box. But shortly after Carsen starts his new job, the Serpent Brotherhood breaks into the library and steals the library's piece of the Spear of Destiny (broken up into three pieces and at one time Hitler had a piece of the spear, and so did Napoleon). The leader of the brotherhood seeks to retrieve and unite all three pieces of the spear to use its power to rule the world.

As the new librarian, Carsen is sent by the library administrators to retrieve the Spear of Destiny and prevent the bad guys from reuniting the spear, a task he very reluctantly undertakes. Nicole Noone (played by Sonja Walger), a fellow Metropolitan Library employee skilled in combat and martial arts, joins Carsen as he pursues the spear. She provides the brawn while Carsen provides the brains.

This *Raiders of the Lost Ark* type movie takes the viewer from the recesses of the Metropolitan Library to the Amazon and high into the Himalayas. Besides the action and scenery, the plot is bound to make you smile. Both the hero and the head bad guy are librarians! This is a must-see movie for anyone who wants to see a librarian as an adventure hero who uses his brain to defeat evil forces.

The screenplay was written by David Titcher, who also wrote the screenplay for *Around the World in 80 Days* (2004). He was also a writer for the TV series *Who's the Boss*. Titcher's sense of humor also continues to display itself in *The Librarian: Quest for the Spear.*

(TNT, distributed by Warner Home Video, released 2005. Running time: 106 minutes.)

THE MUMMY

For a fun action film with a female librarian heroine, be sure to watch *The Librarian* starring Brendan Fraser (*Bedazzled, George of the Jungle*) and Academy Award–winner Rachel Weisz (*The Constant Gardener*) as the librarian. Not your typical librarian, Weisz' character works in the library at the Museum of Antiquities in Cairo. How'd she get her job? The answer appears about 13 minutes into the film. There's a scene in the library where Weisz' character creates a domino-like accident on a ladder that causes all the bookcases to topple over. Upon seeing the mess, the curator asks in a fit of anger, "Why do I put up with you?!" Weisz replies, "Well you put up with me because I can read and write ancient Egyptian and I can … I can decipher hieroglyphics and Heratic, and I am the only person within a thousand miles who knows how to properly code and catalog this library, that's why."

Fraser plays an adventurer and treasure hunter who teams up with Weisz and others in search of the lost city of Hamunaptra. About 50 minutes into the film, they find the ruins of the lost city. That evening, after some drinking, Fraser's character asked Weisz, "What are you doing here?" She replies, "I may not be an explorer, or an adventurer, or a treasure seeker, or a gunfighter Mr. O'Connell, but I am proud of what I am." "And what is that?" he asks. She replies, "I am a librarian."

The next evening Weisz's curiosity leads her to secretly "borrowing" the *Book of the Dead* found by a competing member of the archeological dig party. When she's about to open the book, Fraser asks "are you sure you want to be playing around with this thing?" She replies, "It's just a book. No harm ever came from reading a book." So she reads from the book aloud and accidentally revives the Mummy who begins to bring ten plagues upon the earth.

The remainder of the film focuses on the efforts of many to defeat the Mummy. Weisz uses her brain to find a way for Fraser to ultimately defeat the Mummy. By the end of the film you are so impressed with the librarian you forget she was the one who accidentally brought the Mummy back to life! But in the end the Mummy is defeated and Weisz ends up with hunky Fraser.

But the fun doesn't stop there. A sequel to the film (*The Mummy Returns*) picks up the story several years later. Weisz and Fraser are happily married with a son about ten years old. Their son puts on the bracelet of Anubis, which in seven days, will awaken the Scorpion King. Through holographic images, the bracelet shows the way to the Scorpion King's kingdom. Only when the bracelet reaches the home of the Scorpion King can it be removed.

Dark forces have once again raised the Mummy. This time he kidnaps the boy to find the way to the Scorpion King. The Mummy seeks to defeat the Scorpion King, command the invincible army of Anubis, and rule over the world. But Weisz and Fraser are determined to get their son back and send the Mummy back to the underworld.

Surprisingly, this sequel is just as much fun as the initial movie. Weisz' librarian character is a confident, assertive woman in love who kicks some butt. As the film progresses, we find she is the reincarnation of Nefertiti and possesses her memories and skills. So we see her in swordplay skillfully battling the bad guys.

The wonderful thing about these movies is that when we first meet Weisz as the librarian, she's a well-organized meek looking woman. But as the two movies progress, she demonstrates her intellect, knowledge, and confidence. She gains combat skills and fearlessly fights to save the world, and the ones she loves. She's definitely a librarian superhero without the fame!

(*The Mummy*; Universal, released 1999. Running time: 125 minutes. *The Mummy Returns*; Universal, released 2001. Running time: 130 minutes.)

Feature Films: Comedies

THE GUN IN BETTY LOU'S HANDBAG

This film is a real hoot. Penelope Ann Miller (*The Relic, Kindergarten Cop*) plays Betty Lou Perkins, a young timid librarian married to a cop. She never seems to be able to get the head librarian to go along with her ideas, or to get her husband to pay more attention to her and her needs. One day she finds a gun that was used in a gangland murder. She places the gun in her handbag and runs to call her husband to tell him about the gun. But he's busy and brushes her off before she can tell him about the gun. So she embarks on trying to tell others about her find, but can't hold their attention long enough to tell them about the gun. Frustrated, she accidentally fires the gun in a restroom. When she's arrested, she suddenly loves the attention finally being paid to her, so she confesses to owning the gun and to committing the murder. This is when the fun really starts to kick in.

While in jail, she meets a prostitute who helps her describe her murderous actions more believably. The prostitute also gives her fashion pointers, helping her cut her long red hair and get rid of her homely ankle-length dress and her comfy boots. The next day when Betty Lou walks into the courtroom, she's sporting noticeable makeup, a chic short hairstyle, a sexy short black dress, black nylons, high heels, and bright red jacket. When the judge sees her, he whispers to the bailiff, "That's Betty Lou Perkins?"

"Uh huh," replies the bailiff.

"Hell, I don't go to the library enough," he replies.

But my favorite scene, and a favorite of many librarians, is about 48 minutes into the film. A standing room only crowd of people shows up at the Tettley Public Library's fundraiser organized by Betty Lou and the other librarian. Betty Lou is asked to speak to the crowd.

"Well, a funny thing happened on the way to the fundraiser," she says. "It's so great so many lovers of the library showed up. And I don't want to disappoint any of you so I'm going to give you what you want."

The crowd is silent, anticipating her next words, which are "Sex. Crime. Mystery. Romance." She continues with "I have something to show you."

She slowly opens her purse and reaches her hand into it. The silent crowd waits in fearful anticipation that she may pull out a gun. But instead, she pulls out her library card.

You'll have to see the film to truly appreciate how effective this was as a library card promotion.

(Touchstone Pictures, released 1992. Running time: 89 minutes)

FOUL PLAY

Goldie Hawn is hardly a boring and frumpy librarian in this madcap movie from the seventies. Yet, she plays Gloria Mundy, a single librarian who seldom ever takes any chances, at least until she picks up an attractive man stranded by the side of the road. Then the fun begins. I don't want to spoil any surprises if you haven't seen the movie. But I'll tell you there's a menacing Albino, a pet snake, the pope, Chevy Chase (his first starring role in a motion picture) as a detective, a hilarious Dudley Moore, Burgess Meredith as a neighbor, and wonderful San Francisco scenery. (But don't be fooled into thinking that's really the San Francisco Public Library. The scenes inside the library were actually shot at the Pasadena Public Library in Southern California.)

Don't we wish all librarians were as funny as Goldie Hawn? And despite some scenes showing her wearing big-framed glasses and one outfit with a long-sleeved white blouse buttoned up to her neck, her outfits are far from frumpy. The movie begins with her dressed in a black evening dress, and near the end of the film she fights off bad guys with a bright yellow umbrella while dressed in a short, sheer, low-cut bridesmaid/cocktail dress and high heels.

(Paramount, released 1978. Running time: 116 minutes.)

Feature Films: Musicals

GOOD NEWS

I'm a big fan of musicals. They're fun and have great music and happy endings. And best of all, they're easy to watch while multitasking during the evenings. So I was thrilled to discover *Good News* while doing the research for this book.

This 1947 MGM film features a young Peter Lawford and June Allyson. Allyson is a student and assistant librarian at the campus library who tutors the college football hero, played by Lawford. Watch the sparks fly when you add in a sexy vixen who also desires Lawford.

June Allyson is no ugly duckling. So it's amusing in one scene where Allyson is dressed up for a date with Lawford and a friend sees her and says, "You sure don't look like a librarian." Allyson is an attractive actress and throughout this film she's dressed like other students on campus. There are definitely no frumpy clothes in this movie. But you'll be treated to lots of toe tapping music and heel kicking dance numbers.

But what really earns this film a gold star is Allyson as an attractive and interesting librarian. She uses her brains instead of her looks to ultimately land the guy. She wonderfully demonstrates the intelligence of librarians.

(MGM, released 1947. Running time: 93 minutes.)

THE MUSIC MAN

If you haven't heard of Conan the Librarian, you've probably heard of Marian the Librarian. In the 1962 musical *The Music Man*, Robert Preston plays Harold Hill, a charming con man who drifts into River City and convinces the residents that they need a boy's marching band. He promises to equip the band with instruments and teach the boys how to play, all the while intending to take their money and run. But what he doesn't count on is slowly falling in love with Marian, the town librarian. Marian the Librarian is immortalized in one of the movie's most memorable songs. Played by Shirley Jones, Marian uses her reference skills to discover Harold Hill is a fraud. But being a musical, don't worry. This movie has a happy ending.

(Warner Brothers, released 1962. Running time: 151 minutes.)

A made-for-TV remake of *The Music Man* was made in 2003. Featuring Matthew Broderick in the role of Harold Hill and Kristin Chenoweth as Marian the Librarian, this version includes two songs that weren't included in the 1962 movie.

(Walt Disney Pictures, released 2003. Running time: 150 minutes.)

Feature Films: Dramas

LAST LIFE IN THE UNIVERSE

This foreign film centers on Kenji, a suicidal librarian. This of course changes when he meets an attractive young woman. They become an odd couple with him being a clean freak and her being a slob. The film was an official selection at the Sundance Film Festival, Toronto Film Festival, and Venice Film Festival. It received wonderful reviews by a variety of noted film critics and has been called a masterpiece, poetic, and haunting. But despite its excellent reviews, I couldn't get past the first 20 minutes of the film. As a librarian, a movie about a strange suicidal librarian just doesn't appeal to me.

The movie opens with Kenji imagining himself hanging from a noose. This is definitely not a film to watch with the family. It's loaded with adult language and subject matter, including drug abuse and violence.

The film is in Thai and Japanese with English subtitles. But there's verbal commentary in English on various aspects of the film while the film is playing — which I found very annoying.

(Palm Pictures, released 2003. Running time: 104 minutes.)

Feature Films with Librarians in Supporting or Minor Roles

As mentioned earlier in this chapter, over 100 movies have a librarian in them. In some cases their appearance in the film is of little consequence. But in others, the librarian leaves a lasting impression. So these films are worth mentioning in case you haven't seen them yet.

BECAUSE OF WINN-DIXIE

Based on the book of the same title, the movie focuses on a girl named Opal and her dog Winn-Dixie. Eva Marie Saint plays the town's spinster librarian, Ms. Franny. Despite the stereotypical librarian image, you can't help but fall in love with Ms. Franny's sweet character. When we first meet her, she tells Opal the story of how a bear wandered into the library and she chased him out by throwing a copy of *War and Peace* at him. The bear left but took the book with him!

Ms. Franny gives Opal a container of candy invented by Ms. Franny's grandfather whose first name was Litmus. The candy, named Litmus Lozenges, has a secret ingredient only some people can taste. Those who have experienced sadness can taste it. It's sorrow.

(Twentieth Century Fox, released 2005. Running time: 106 minutes.)

IT'S A WONDERFUL LIFE

It's no surprise that librarians appear as minor characters in movies more often than lead characters. Some of the most memorable librarians in motion pictures were minor characters. Who can forget Donna Reed's role as George Bailey's wife Mary in *It's a Wonderful Life*? When angel-in-training Clarence shows George what life would be like without him, we see Mary as an old-maid librarian (wearing glasses — which as George's wife she does not do). Hmmm ... funny how the alternative of getting married was to become an old maid librarian!

(Republic Pictures, released 1947. Running time: 130 minutes.)

UHF

The librarian character in this movie is not even a supporting character but worth mentioning nonetheless. If you've ever heard the phrase "Conan the Librarian," watching this movie will give you the origin of the phrase. The story centers on "Weird Al" Yankovic as a guy who has a hard time holding on to a job until he lands one at a bottom-rated television station. Things turn around though when Yankovic begins offering offbeat programming. One of the shows being "Conan the Librarian." But you need to watch closely because what appears in the film is a TV advertisement for the series "Conan the Librarian." It's about 51 minutes into the film and only lasts about one minute.

(Orion Pictures, released 1989. Running time: 1 hour, 37 minutes.)

Feature Films: Documentaries

At the time of this writing, *The Hollywood Librarian: Librarians in Cinema and Society* was still in production. But by the time you read this, it should be released. It will definitely be a "must-see" film for anyone curious about librarians.

Besides being the first full-length film to focus on librarians and their work in the movies and in real life, the film is also unique in that it was written and directed by a professionally educated librarian. Ann Seidl, the writer and director, holds a master's degree in library and information services from the University of Denver. She's also an example of the diverse background many new librarians bring to the profession. Before earning her MLIS degree, she worked in a variety of jobs ranging from hosting a television news magazine to working as a voice-over actor.

The Hollywood Librarian looks at librarian characters in dozens of films like *Desk Set, It's a Wonderful Life*, and *The Shawshank Redemption,* and at a variety of real life new, midcareer, and veteran librarians. The work of librarians in the movies is compared with the real work of today's librarians. The film covers the spectrum of librarians from those who work in public services, to those who work behind the scenes in technical services, and from libraries of all types and sizes.

Librarians in Books

Librarians have appeared in books and stories as long as there have been people called librarians. If you're dying to read as much fiction as possible with a librarian in it, then be sure to get your hands on a copy of Grant Burns' *Librarians in Fiction* (McFarland, 1998). This annotated bibliography contains descriptions of books, short stories and plays with librarians in them. Even if you don't have time to read all the items on the list, you'll enjoy just reading the story synopsis of each one in this book.

If you're a fan of bibliomysteries or romance novels with librarian characters in them, there are two websites you should be aware of. The first is Bibliomysteries.com. If you're wondering what a bibliomystery is, it's a mystery that has a plot, setting, or character related to libraries, books, archives, or writers. There are often librarians in bibliomysteries. The second website is www.jenw.org/home.htm. If you're a romance reader, be sure to check out this site of library career romances.

If you're not a really big fan of librarian characters, but occasionally just feel like reading a book with a librarian character, you may want to check out one of these recent books.

THE BOOK OF FLYING, BY KEITH MILLER. RIVERHEAD, 2004.

Set in a city by the sea where residents are either winged or nonwinged, the main character is Pico, a librarian, a nonwinged man unable to fly. He falls in loved with a winged girl who cannot fully love him because he is not one of the winged people. So he sets off for the fabled Morning Town, where legend says he will be able to get his wings, and begins an unforgettable adventure.

LA CUCINA: A NOVEL OF RAPTURE, BY LILY PRIOR.
HARPER PERENNIAL, 2001.

Set in Sicily, this story is about Rosa Fiori; who grows up in a family where the kitchen, "la cucina," is at the core of the family. When Rosa is 18, her lover is murdered. So she flees to Palermo where she becomes a librarian for the next 25 years, while perfecting her cooking skills. Then one day an Englishman researching regional cuisine comes into the library, reawakening Rosa's passion for love and cooking.

A DEATH IN DULCINEA, BY LARAMEE DOUGLAS.
ALLIGATOR FREE PRESS, 2005.

The suspect in a murder of a woman in Dulcinea, Texas, is a former student of retired school librarian Darby Matheson. This prompts her to try and solve the murder.

THE DEWEY DECIMAL SYSTEM OF LOVE, BY JOSEPHINE CARR.
NEW AMERICAN LIBRARY, 2003.

Ally Sheffield, a self-described spinster librarian, works at the Free Library of Philadelphia. But she is definitely not the stereotypical librarian. A fun loving librarian, Ally falls in love with Aleksi Jullio, the new conductor of the Philadelphia Philharmonic. The only problem is he's married. But this is a romance, and there is more than one man in this novel. Who does Ally end up with? You'll just have to take the time to pick up this fun novel to find out.

THE HISTORIAN, BY ELIZABETH KOSTOVA. LITTLE, BROWN, 2005.

This book involves a search for Dracula—Vlad the Impaler. Although librarians only appear as minor characters in this book, they are noteworthy. Also of note is that the author's mother is a retired librarian. That's a good enough reason to pick up this book!

HOW I FELL IN LOVE WITH A LIBRARIAN AND LIVED TO TELL ABOUT IT, BY RHETT ELLIS. SPARKLING BAY BOOKS, 2003.

An amusing easy read, this book has a librarian as a major character. The beautiful Myra Findley is the new librarian at the Clegmore Public Library. Ms. Findley is literally crazy when she's not on her meds. Add in the town preacher who's smitten with the new librarian and the fun begins.

ICE QUEEN, BY ALICE HOFFMAN. BACK BAY BOOKS, 2006.

The book centers around a New Jersey librarian who, as a child, wished her mother would disappear. Unfortunately, her mother subsequently dies, and the librarian grows up to be an ice queen, emotionally frozen. Her brother convinces her to move to Florida where he lives. She does, and one day is struck by lightning. She survives the lightning strike, but the strike changes her entire perspective on life.

THE LIBRARIAN, BY LARRY BEINHART. NATION BOOKS, 2004.

Due to budget problems, university librarian David Goldberg must end Elaina Whisthoven's employment in the library. Months later she reappears and asks for his help. She needs to take a leave of absence from her present job in the private library of the wealthy and powerful Alan Stowe. Fearful of losing her job, she asks David Goldberg if he will cover for her while she's gone. He agrees and begins moonlighting in the Stowe library. Soon he's involved in political intrigue, mystery, and danger.

THE LIBRARIAN'S PASSIONATE KNIGHT DYNASTIES: THE BARONES, BY CINDY GERARD. SILHOUETTE, 2003.

Shy librarian Phoebe lacks self-confidence. To her rescue is rich Bostonian Daniel Barone. This book is part of a series of books focusing on the Barone family.

OPEN SEASON, BY LINDA HOWARD. POCKET BOOKS. 2001.

Librarian Daisy Minor is the epitome of the stereotypical librarian. She lives with her mother and aunt, dresses conservatively, and the last date she had was over ten years ago with a guy who her aunt fixed her up with. So on her 34th birthday, she decides she needs to make a lifestyle change to get what she wants out of life — sex and a husband. She moves into her own house, undergoes an exterior makeover, and hits the local bars in search of love. But she inadvertently witnesses something she shouldn't. But no romance novel would be complete without a hunky hero. And in Daisy's case, it's chief of police Jack Russo.

POPPY DONE TO DEATH: AURORA TEAGARDEN MYSTERY, BY CHARLAINE HARRIS. ST. MARTIN'S, 2003.

Aurora "Roe" Teagarden works as a part-time librarian in a small Southern town. A widow and a member of the Uppity Women literary club, she gets concerned when her step sister-in-law, Poppy, fails to show up for a meeting. When Roe goes to her house, she finds Poppy murdered. While attempting to solve Poppy's murder, Roe must also deal with her half brother who moves in with her, a romantic involvement, and town gossip regarding Poppy and her husband's extramarital affairs.

UNTAMED, BY KATHLEEN LAWLESS. POCKET BOOKS, 2005.

Librarian Paris Sommer travels to Forked Creek, Nevada, a restored ghost town and the site of a bordello once owned by her great great grandmother. Since this is a hot romance novel, our librarian finds passion in a masculine sexy cowboy and a treasure map. What does the map lead to? You'll have to read the book to find the answer.

WHAT THE LIBRARIAN HEARD, BY LINDA BINGHAM. EAKIN PRESS, 2001.

In this mystery set in Oklahoma, the library shares a building with the police. And we know librarians are well suited to help the police solve a string of murders. In this case, the sleuthing librarian is Elinor Woodward. See if you can solve the crime before Elinor does!

THE WRITING ON THE WALL, BY LYNNE SHARON SCHWARTZ. COUNTERPOINT PRESS, 2004.

New York librarian Renata's life is full of tragedy. At 16 her twin sister has a baby, then mysteriously dies. Not long after that, her father dies and her mother goes crazy. So Renata ends up raising her sister's child, who disappears one day in the park, never to been seen again. Years later Renata finds herself in a relationship with a man named Jack. Then, on the morning of September 11th, the World Trade Center towers are attacked. This sets the backdrop for the rest of this emotional story.

6

The Comical Librarian

Those of us who work in libraries often experience humorous events during the workday, while some individuals outside the profession find librarians to be the focus of good humor. Whichever the case, librarians, and some of the situations they encounter, have been immortalized in comics and cartoons. If you need a good laugh, make some time to read some of the comics or cartoons in this chapter. You're sure to find some amusement in them.

Comic Strips Featuring Librarians

ALEX... THE LIBRARIAN

If you've been waiting for a comic strip about a librarian, your wait is over! You need only to look for *Alex... The Librarian*. Created and drawn by a real librarian, the strip is loosely based upon his library experiences. Here's a sample of one of his strips that can be viewed on his website (www.geocities.com/cartoonmeister).

Alex, a dark-haired male librarian with glasses, is complaining to a female coworker about equal rights issues going too far. He tells the female coworker about getting a memo from his library board claiming that his display is discriminatory toward women. The caption in the last box reads "Yep .... they say I can't have a display of toy Mailboxes. I can only have a display of toy Personboxes!"

You can obtain the comic strip for your library newsletter, flyer, or other publications by contacting creator Alex Krentzin at cartoonmeister@yahoo.com.

Who is the real Alex upon whom the character is based? The real Alex is a youth services librarian at the Madison Heights Public Library in Michigan who also holds a degree in fine arts from the University of Michigan. He told me by phone he has had a desire to draw things his entire life. One day at the library, the mother of a child told her son to ask Alex the librarian for assistance. Hence, the comic strip was born.

"Hey Professor!" Copyright Kevin Guhl, used by permission.

Mr. Krentzin has also invented children's board games. In the late eighties and early nineties he developed a library board game called *Check-It Out, The Library Game* for children ages 5 and up.

HEY, PROFESSOR

Although this strip focuses on the antics of a mad professor, it features a librarian in a recurring role. *Hey, Professor* by Kevin Guhl appeared weekly in *The Signal* (the newspaper of the College of New Jersey) from 1999 to 2001. But thanks to the Internet, you can view all of the strips on the web at www.geocities.com/heyprofessor/200616.

The strip centers around an unconventional college science professor. One of the frequently recurring characters is Edna, the college librarian. Edna wears glasses, her hair up in a bun, and a dress buttoned up to her neck — a common stereotypical image upon first glance. But Edna also wears spiked combat boots and is "the only one who sees through the Professor's nonsense." Edna and the Professor frequently battle over a five-cent book fine the Professor wants deleted.

According to its creator, *Hey, Professor* is somewhat based upon themes in an unreleased song by Arizona rock band "The Refreshments." The strip is of course drawn in good fun and should be enjoyed as such.

Kevin Guhl describes himself as a mild-mannered journalist working beats for a New Jersey newspaper. But by night, his pen flies across bristol boards as he depicts the adventures of his comic strip creations. Although *Hey, Professor* only had a limited run, Mr. Guhl notes he might bring it back to life in the future. At present, he continues to work on his current strip, *Detective Fork*. *Detective Fork* is a classic detective noir serial set in the world of talking silverware.

Although he doesn't make money off his comics, Mr. Guhl is committed to posting his comics for the readers he's found online. Readers appreciate this commitment. *Detective Fork* can be read at www.detectivefork.com. The site also offers a link to *Hey, Professor*.

"Unshelved." Copyright 2006 Overdue Media LLC, used by permission.

UNSHELVED

Are you ready for a comic strip set in a library? If so, check out *Unshelved*. Created by Bill Barnes and Gene Ambaum, the strip takes place at the Mallville Public Library. The cast of characters includes librarians and library workers that, if you work in a library, may resemble some of your coworkers!

The characters include Dewey, a young adult librarian who prefers reading comic books over working; Colleen, a reference librarian; Tamara, a children's librarian; and Mel, the branch manager. Other characters include Buddy the Book Beaver, who's a library page and former library mascot who still wears his mascot uniform, and Merv, a 12 year old who prefers activities other than reading but hangs out at the library frequently nonetheless.

Let's take a look at a strip that appeared on *Unshelved*'s website (www.overduemedia.com) on May 15, 2006. The first cell of the strip shows the branch manager behind a closed door telling staff that the library is implementing a new staff-sharing program that combines disciplines, brings together the branches, and finds hidden strengths. In the second cell a staff member asks why. The manager struggles with a reply saying it will increase flexibility. And in the last cell, Dewey says, "They didn't tell you why, did they?" The branch manager replies, "I'm sure I can find a way to justify this."

You can view the current strip and random past strips on the website. If you need a daily or weekly pick-me-up, you can have the strip delivered to your e-mail box free of charge. Just go to their website to sign up for a free subscription. You can join the over 30,000 readers of the series, 75 percent of whom happen to work in libraries.

And if you like the strips, it's highly recommended that you purchase their books, which are compilations of their strips from the very first one. This will allow you to see the evolution of the characters and events at the Mallville Library. It's like being able to read a good book starting at the first page.

The strip began in 2002 when Bill Barnes and Gene Ambaum decided to work on a strip about a library. Mr. Barnes was developing a different comic strip, but his wife's friend, Mr. Ambaum, had such wickedly funny stories about working in the library they decided to create *Unshelved*.

Gene Ambaum holds a MLIS degree and works as a librarian in the Pacific Northwest. His name isn't really Gene Ambaum. He uses the Ambaum name to separate his *Unshelved* career from his librarian career, and he is fairly secretive about his library life.

Bill Barnes is a cartoonist and a computer programmer. He chose a technical path in college, but didn't let the lack of formal art training deter him from his desire to be a cartoonist. And although he may not be a librarian, he's a regular library user who told me he checks out 90 percent of his reading material and 75 percent of his movies from the library. Better yet, his children have also become regular library users.

When I questioned Barnes about the impact he thought the strip was having on the way people view libraries and librarians, he responded that he hoped people gained some understanding of the challenges inherent in the profession. He replied that many nonlibrarian readers say they've gained a lot of respect for librarians. As a librarian, just the thought of the positive impact *Unshelved* is having on the public's view of librarians and libraries, and having the strips freely accessible on the web brightens my day.

Librarians in Comics and Cartoons

If you're interested in librarians that have appeared in either a cartoon or comic book, two bibliographies accessible on the web provide a good place to start. Steven Bergson's annotated bibliography "Librarians in Comics: Sources" contains over two dozen entries, the bibliography can be found at www.ibiblio.org/librariesfaq/combks/combks.htm.

A good webliography of library cartoons can be found on the web at http://pw1.netcom.com/~dplourde/cartoons/index.html. Compiled by Denise Plourde, this annotated bibliography lists close to 100 library cartoons that have appeared in places ranging from *Dilbert* and *Garfield* to *Blondie* and *Hagar the Horrible*.

Library Cartoons from the Cartoonist Group

You can find librarians who have appeared in comic strips like *Frank and Earnest* and in editorial cartoons by searching the website of the Cartoonist Group at www.cartoonistgroup.com. The group originated from the artists' "belief that digital technology offers new ways for people to access and utilize this art." Twenty-two artists belong to the group, including Nick Anderson (editorial cartoons), Mike Peters (*Mother Goose and Grimm*), Bob Thaves (*Frank and Earnest*), Mike Twohy (*That's Life*), and Signe Wilkinson (editorial cartoons).

You can search the website using the words "librarian" or "library" and retrieve and view all the cartoons and comic strips in the database. You can also search by cartoonist. It's great fun looking at the various cartoons and strips that have featured librarians, even though, sadly, a number of the strips feature a stereotypical librarian.

If you find a cartoon you like, you can purchase the right to reuse the cartoon or strip in your newsletter, magazine, book, presentation, or on your webpage, with the cost starting as low as $50 per cartoon. You can also have a cartoon customized and find out how to have artwork commissioned. The Cartoonist Group is a great source for a cartoon for your next newsletter.

Library Cartoons from the Cartoon Bank

If you like the cartoons that have appeared in the *New Yorker* magazine, be sure to bookmark www.cartoonbank.com on your computer. This website contains *New Yorker* cartoons, cover prints, original art, gifts and merchandise. You can search the site by keywords, or browse it by topic or artist. You can then select and view the cartoon or item online.

Artists including Ed Arno, Harry Bliss, Ed Fisher, Warren Miller, Bernard Schoenbaum, Peter Steiner, Robert Weber and others have drawn *New Yorker* cartoons dealing with librarians or libraries. The library topics have addressed everything from late fines to cataloging.

One of my favorite library cartoons on the site is by Bernard Schoenbaum. It shows a young girl at the reference desk speaking to the librarian. The cartoon caption reads, "Anything on romance at the entry level?"

Once you find your favorite library cartoon, you can order a matted or framed print of it directly from the website. Or, you can purchase the ability to use the cartoon in your presentation or newsletter. Customized books of cartoons are also available. You can even have custom cartoons created by Cartoon Bank artists. Check out their website for more information on these products and services.

Librarians in Comic Books and Graphic Novels

Rex Libris

Whether you're ready for it or not, Slave Labor Graphics publishes a series of comic books featuring Rex Libris, a librarian who travels through time and space to retrieve those long overdue library books. He's what some readers would consider a library cop, but in the series he's the head librarian at the Middleton Library. Rex Libris is far from your stereotypical librarian. He's able to travel through time using a teleportation crystal.

In a ComicReaders interview with creator James Turner about the *Rex Libris* series (which appears on their website, www.comicreaders.com), Turner states "librarians have been subtly guiding human civilization for almost two thousand years. By emphasizing, or de-emphasizing, strains of knowledge, they are able to influence the development of our societies."

Rex is a member of the Ordo Bibliotheca. Through the ages the Ordo's combat-trained librarians have protected information and knowledge. Of course, every story needs conflict, so there are bad guys as well. Each title in the series is provided below with a brief synopsis.

"I, LIBRARIAN"

In this first comic book, we're introduced to Rex Libris, head librarian at the Middleton Library. He travels the galaxy battling foes in his quest to retrieve overdue book and late fines.

"LABYRINTH OF LITERATURE"

This second book finds Rex preparing for a trip to the planet Benzine V in search of overdue books. But first he must rescue a patron from the library's labyrinth of literature and adjust to roommate Simonides and a new librarian named Hypatia.

"LEAP OF FAITH"

Rex leaps from orbit straight into danger on Benzine V as he encounters hostile aliens. While he's away from the library, unknown hostile forces take over the reading room and send patrons running.

"BATTLE ON BENZINE"

Rex's problems on Benzine V continue in this fourth book. Meanwhile, back on Earth, vandals are set on burning down the Middleton Library.

"TEA WITH VAGLOX"

The story that began in "Battle on Benzine" continues in this fifth book.

"Tea with Vaglox" and a sixth comic book titled "Book of Monsters" were not yet released at the time of this writing, but they will be in print by the time you read this.

The comic books are available for $2.95 each from Slave Labor Graphics, 577 South Market St., San Jose, CA 95113, (800) 866–8929, www.slavelabor.com.

James Turner broke into the graphic novel scene in 1995 with *Nil: A Land Beyond Belief.* He followed *Nil* with *Rex Libris.* A Toronto-based illustrator, he attended Ontario College of Art and worked in multimedia for years before changing to a career in illustration. If you want to read more about Mr. Turner, check out "In Nothing We Trust: An Interview with James Turner by Matt Rawson" which can be found on the web at www.comiccritique.com/interview_james_turner.html or Creative Behavior's "Interview with James Turner" at www.creativebehavior.com/index.php?PID=74. If you're interested in finding out more about him and his earlier work, *NIL*, you may want to read the interview that appears on www.popthought.com/display_column.asp?DAID=899. You can also view samples of his illustration work on his website, www.jtillustration.com.

THE TIME TEAM

This online comic strip, which is likely to eventually become a graphic novel, follows the adventures of a team of time travelers led by H.G. Wells. The time team includes Chip, a teenager and the story's hero; Clio, the Muse of History; Jade, a librarian at the Cerritos Library who is also a shape-shifter. Psychon is the story's villain, one of those ruthless leaders whose goal is to rule the world. Psychon is seeking the Time Unity Amulet, most likely to destroy it. The amulet brings harmony to the world, a world that Psychon wants to control through chaos. So the Time Team (Chip, Clio, Jade and H.G. Wells) seeks to beat Psychon to the amulet.

Created and produced by the Cerritos Public Library in California, the strip is edited by Michael Cart and illustrated by Topper Helmers. Why would a public library produce a time-travel comic strip? The answer is on their website. It states that "time travel is a metaphor for reading, for learning, and even for itself.... Just image the things we could see and the people we could meet on our trips through time.... It is our desire to replicate this experience for children through the various facets of the Time Team program, which will be rooted in the comic strip quest of the Time Team members...."

This innovative comic strip approach to reach children is just one part of the library's larger effort to involve children. The comic strip is "only part of the Time Team experience. We intend to use it as a portal to the whole world of imagination and learning that the Cerritos Library offers. The library itself is a virtual time machine in which every member of the community can equally share the adventures of discover and learning in a welcoming environment where the past and the future come together." Talk about a wonderful means of promoting the library!

This award-winning library offers many fabulous features including a full-size replica of a *Tyrannosaurus rex* in the children's area and a 15,000 gallon saltwater aquarium at the entrance of the building. The building's exterior is titanium clad and has a golden skin that changes color as atmospheric conditions change. This is definitely a library to see the next time you're in Southern California. And the facility definitely ties directly into the theme of their *Time Team* comic strip.

The strip can be viewed on the Cerritos Public Library's website at www.ci.cerritos.ca.us. Just select "Time Team" from the main menu. On the site you'll also be able to read more about the characters, the editor, and the illustrator.

Librarian Cartoon Books

BIBLIA'S GUIDE FOR WARRIOR LIBRARIANS: HUMOR FOR LIBRARIANS WHO REFUSE TO BE CLASSIFIED

Although the primary audience of this book (Libraries Unlimited, 2003) written by Amanda Credaro, with illustrations by Peter Lewis, seems to be librarians, anyone with a sense of humor will enjoy it. In the book you'll find laugh-out-loud advice on everything from becoming a librarian and working in a library, to those daily challenges librarian encounter.

Amanda Credaro is a teacher librarian in Australia. She holds a master's in education, and in applied science. At present she is the project officer at the NSW Department of Education.

DEWEY DECIMAL SYSTEM DEFEATS TRUMAN!

For a good laugh, pick up a copy of *Dewey Decimal System Defeats Truman!* by Scott McCullar (McFarland, 1998). The cartoonist, who works in a public library, provides over 80 pages of laugh-out-loud cartoons every library employee or user is bound to appreciate. From cartoons about library workers, such as zombie book shelvers, to cartoons about library work, like the toughest reference question, the cartoons in this book cover all aspects of libraries and library work.

To get an idea of McCullar's sense of humor, you need only look at a few cartoons in his book. For example, one of the cartoons depicts a male patron standing at a reference desk. The reference librarian is touching a crystal ball sitting on the desk and says, "Wait! Despite what you say, I can see the information you are truly seeking...." The caption below the cartoon reads, "The Library Psychic-Friends Network finds the hidden truth again."

Another cartoon shows a female patron standing in front of a computer. As a male library worker walks by, the woman says, "excuse me, I'm looking for a particular book I used once, but the keyword search 'blue cover' doesn't call it up." Almost anyone who has worked at an information desk in a library will recognize this often real situation.

Scott McCullar has an inside working knowledge of libraries. At the time he created this book, he was the materials selection assistant for the children's specialist at the Harris County Public Library in Houston.

The *Unshelved* Library

UNSHELVED, VOLUME 1 (2003)

This book of comic strips contains the first year of the *Unshelved* strips by Bill Barnes and Gene Ambaum. The strip takes place at the Mallville Public Library where you'll meet Dewey, a young adult librarian, his fellow library workers, and some regular library patrons. What goes on in the Mallville Library may seem like madness to some, but it's just a typical day at the library! Start your humorous journey into library land with this first book.

WHAT WOULD DEWEY DO? (2004)

Continue to follow the adventures of Dewey the librarian in this second compilation of *Unshelved* comic strips. Laugh as you follow Dewey's ongoing conflicts with fellow staff, patrons, and even the FBI.

LIBRARY MASCOT CAGE MATCH (2005)

Life at the Mallville Library continues in this third book of strips from year three of *Unshelved*. Loyal fans also get a special treat in this book. It includes the new graphic novelette, *Empire County Strikes Back*.

BOOK CLUB (2006)

It's hard to believe over four years have passed since the first *Unshelved* strip. But it has, and the fourth year of strips appears in *Book Club*. The book includes some bonus material, such as a never-before-printed story time as sung by Dewey. The book sells for $17.95.

The books can be ordered from Overdue Media at www.overduemedia.com and other sources such as Amazon.com. The first three books sell for $14.95 each, with the fourth book selling for $17.95. (Hint: You get a great deal when you order all four books as a bundle from Overdue Media.)

YOU CAN TELL YOUR KID WILL GROW UP TO BE A LIBRARIAN WHEN... CARTOONS ABOUT THE PROFESSION

Written and drawn by librarian Richard Lee, the cartoons in this book (McFarland, 1992) say a lot about the men and women who make up the profession. Despite the title, the book also looks at parents who are librarians, people who love the profession, the ins and outs of library school, the reference desk, patrons, and other topics. To give you some idea of Mr. Lee's humor, in the first chapter of the book there's a cartoon showing two girls, one holding a toy, the other a writing instrument and piece of paper. The caption "she is generous with her toys but requires their prompt return in two weeks." And in the chapter on parents who are librarians, there's a cartoon of a man wearing a T-shirt that says "I Love the Clark County Library," and he is looking at a tote bag filled with posters, books, and balloons bearing vendor logos. The caption reads "they bring you dumb presents from goofy conferences."

At the time he penned this book, the author ran the jail library for the Las Vegas–Clark County Library District. He's taken art classes at Utah State, and holds a master's degree in library science from Brigham Young University.

Humor Books

Everyone interested in library humor should be familiar with Will Manley. Former *Wilson Library Bulletin* columnist and current columnist for *American Libraries*, Will Manley has authored numerous humor books about the library profession, often teaming up with illustrator Richard Lee or illustrator Gary Handman. To get a sense of Manley's humor, you need only look for his column, "Manley's World" in a current issue of *American Libraries*.

For a dose of amusement, check out one of his many books listed here.

The Truth About Reference Librarians (McFarland, 1996)
The Truth About Catalogers (McFarland, 1995)
Uncensored Thoughts (McFarland, 1994)
For Library Directors Only: Talking About Trustees (McFarland, 1993)
The Manley Art of Librarianship (McFarland, 1993)
Unsolicited Advice (McFarland, 1992)
Unprofessional Behavior (McFarland, 1992)
Unintellectual Freedoms (McFarland, 1991)
Snowballs in the Bookdrop (Shoe String Press, 1982)

A FUNNY THING HAPPENED ON THE WAY TO THE SCHOOL LIBRARY: A TREASURY OF ANECDOTES, QUOTES, AND OTHER HAPPENINGS

Anyone who has worked in a library has funny stories to tell. School librarian Larry Parsons shares funny library stories, excuses, policies and other library humor with readers in his book (Libraries Unlimited, 1990). And as a library media specialist, he has some wonderful ones dealing with students and other library staff.

Divided into seven parts, the book offers topics including librarians as seen by others, library technology, those blessed and blasted machines, kid stuff, things I didn't know were going on, and book selection and deselection. The book contains numerous quotes and other content from real life librarians across the country. If you are a library user, you'll enjoy this humorous journey into the many issues faced by librarians on a daily basis. If you're a library worker, this book will bring a smile to your face as you identify and sympathize with the situations and experiences in the book.

7

Songs and Poems About and for Librarians

Songs About Librarians

To be immortalized in song is a great honor. Despite that frumpy, cold, spinster stereotypical image of librarians, many a songwriter has composed a song about a librarian. In fact, most of the songs written about librarians surprisingly have been love songs. Maybe it's that secret desire for that which is forbidden, or maybe it's just the idle daydreaming of a librarian letting her hair down and shedding her frumpy clothes that have prompted the creation of librarian songs. We'll never know. Strangely, librarians haven't penned any love songs about libraries.

And yes, there are librarians who are also songwriters and singers. Take for example multitalented Rob Lopresti. In addition to being a librarian, he's also a prolific mystery writer and singer/songwriter. His album *Can I Blame You?* has a song titled "Reference Librarian" that anyone who's ever worked a reference desk can identify with.

The songs listed in this chapter are but a sample of the many songs about librarians. Information on the albums on which the songs appear is provided in case you want to add the item to your music collection. In most cases you can hear a sample of the song on a variety of websites to help you in your decision as to whether or not to purchase the CD.

Love Songs (Including Unrequited Love)

"HEAVEN SENT"

Artist: INXS. Album: *Welcome to Wherever You Are* (Remastered). Type: Pop/Rock. Label: Rhino Records. Release Date: 1992. List Price: $11.98.

The sparse lyrics in this song are about a librarian and a library. A sample of the song can be heard on the CD Universe website (www.cduniverse.com).

Other songs on the album: "Questions," "Heaven Sent," "Communication," "Taste It," "Not Enough Time," "All Around," "Baby Don't Cry," "Beautiful Girl," "Wishing Love," "Back on Love," "Strange Desire," "Men and Women," "The Answer," "Wishing Well" (version 2), "All Around" (version 2), "The Indian Song," "Heaven Sent" (original demo waltz version).

"IN THE ARMY KID"

Artist: Of Montreal. Type: Pop/Rock. Album: *Bedside Drama: A Petite Tragedy.* Label: Kinde. Release Date: 1999. List Price: $49.98. Album: *Horse & Elephant Eatery.* Label: Columbia (Japan). Release Date: 2000. Price: $37.85

These song lyrics are bound to make most librarians smile. The song, about "Jen she's a librarian" contains lyrics like "sorry but you're just not my type" and "did you know I had a funny dream and in it I was in the army." The *Bedside Drama* album contains 17 additional songs, and the *Horse & Elephant* album contains 14 additional songs.

"KAREN"

Artist: The Go Betweens. Album: *That Striped Sunlight Sound.* Type: Pop/Rock. Label: Yep Roc Records. Release Date: 2006. List Price: $24.97.

The lyrics are about "this very special girl she works in a library...." A sample of it can be heard on the CD Universe website (www.cduniverse.com). Other songs on the album: "Black Mule," "Clouds," "Boundary Rider," "Born to a Family," "Streets of Your Town," "Here Comes a City," "Draining the Pool for You" "Finding You," "Spring Rain," "Was There Anything I Could Do," "Surfing Magazines," "Devils Eye," "Too Much of One Thing," "People Say," "The Clock."

"THE LIBRARIAN"

Artist: Hefner. Album: *Breaking God's Heart.* Type: Pop/Rock. Label: Beggars Banquet. Release Date: 1998. List Price: $13.98.

The lyrics pertain to a man's love and dreams of a certain librarian. Unfortunately the love is not returned. A sample of the song can be heard on the CD Universe website at www.cduniverse.com. Other songs on the album: "The Sweetness Lies Within," "The Sad Witch," "A Hymn for the Postal Service," "Love Will Destroy Us in the End," "God Is on My Side," "Another Better Friend," "Love Inside the Stud Farm," "Tactile," "Eloping."

"LISA LIBRARIAN"

Artist: Velocity Girl. Album: *Copacetic.* Type: Pop. Label: Sub Pop. Release Date: 1993. List Price: $11.98.

This is another love song involving a librarian named Lisa. A sample of the song can be heard on the Amazon website (www.amazon.com). The Velocity Girl ringtone is also available for download to your cell phone at www.lyricsdownload.com.

Other songs on the album: "Pretty Sister," "Crazy Town," "Copacetic," "Here Comes," "Pop Loser," "Living Well," "A Chang," "Audrey's Eyes," "57 Waltz," "Candy Apples," "Catching Squirrels."

"Love in the Library"

Artist: Jimmy Buffet. Album: *Fruitcakes*. Type: Country. Label: MCA Nashville. Release Date: 1984. List Price: $9.98.

The delightful lyrics in this song tell a story of a man who falls in love with a woman he sees in the library. It's unclear whether the woman is a librarian or a patron but my guess is the object of his affection is a librarian, who is trying to get a hard-to-reach book, and not a patron.

"Marian the Librarian"

Album: *The Music Man*. Type: Pop. Label: Warner Bros. Release Date: 1962. List Price: $11.98.

This is the famous love song from *The Music Man* movie that made Marian the Librarian a household name. Other songs on the album: "Main Title/Rock Island/Iowa Station/The Traveling Salesman Medley," "Ya Got Trouble," "Piano Lesson/If You Don't Mind My Saying So," "Goodnight My Someone," "Seventy-Six Trombones," "Sincere," "Sadder but Wiser Girl," "Pick-a-Little Talk-a-Little," "Being in Love," "Gary Indiana," "Wells Fargo Wagon," "Will I Ever Tell You," "Shipoopi," "Till There Was You," "Goodnight My Someone."

"Miss Clara"

Artist: Bobbie Gentry. Album: *Patchwork*. Label: Capitol LP. Release Date: 1971. List Price: no longer available for purchase.

Through the lyrics, the listener finds out that Miss Clara, a librarian, receives a letter from a library patron who is a student who professes his love for her. The only problem is she doesn't know his name.

"Sweet Librarian"

Artist: Railroad Jerk. Album: *Third Rail*. Type: Rock/Alternative. Label: Matador Records. Release Date: 1996. List Price: $15.98.

The song lyrics are from the perspective of a patron who is definitely sweet on a librarian. From asking her to be friends, what her days off are, to whether or not she'd like to go rollerblading, this patron has a bad crush on the librarian. A sample of the song can be heard on the CD Universe website (www.cduniverse.com). Other songs on the album: "Clean Shirt," "Objectify Me," "You Forget," "Natalie," "You Bet," "Well," "Dusty Knuckle," "Middle Child," "This Is Not to Say I Still Miss You," "Another Night at the Bar," "No Sleep."

Songs About Being a Librarian

"I Am the Sub-Librarian"

Artist: Piano Magic. Album: *Seasonally Affective: A Piano Magic Retrospective.* Type: Pop/Rock. Label: Rocket Girl (UK). Release Date: 2001. Price: $26.05. (The song also appeared on the album *Low Birth Rate*, released in 1999, by the same label, price $31.55.)

In the lyrics a sub-librarian describes herself. A sample of the song can be heard on the CD Universe website (www.cduniverse.com). Other songs on the album: "Wrong French," "Non-fiction," "General Electric with Fairy Lights," "Wintersport/Cross Country," "Angel Pie/Magic Tree," "Magnetic North," "For Engineers A," "For Engineers Aa," "Fun of the Century," "Sharpest Knife in the Drawer," "Industrial Cutie," "Music for Rolex," "Music for Annahbird," "Music for Wasps," "Me at 19," "How Does It Feel," "French Mittens," "Biggest Lie," "Amongst the Books an Angel," "C'est Un Mauvais Presage Lorsque Ton Aureole A Tombe," "There's No Need for Us to Be Alone," "Canadian Brought Us Snow," "Sketch for Joanne," "My Password Is a Dead Aunt's Name."

"Librarian"

Artist: Jonathan Rundman. Album: *Public Library.* Type: Pop/Rock. Label: Salt Lady Records. Release Date: 2004. List Price: $15.00.

In the lyrics a librarian tells us why he loves being a librarian. You can hear the acoustic demo of "Librarian" on the artist's website at www.jonathanrundman.com/audio.html. Other songs on the album: "Smart Girls," "Falling Down," "Second Language," "Narthex," "747s," "Almost Never See," "The Serious Kind," "Park River Bridge," "Cuban Missile Crisis," "Every Town's the Same."

"Reference Librarian"

Artist: Rob Lopresti. Album: *Can I Blame You?* Type: Folk Music. Label: Live Music Recordings. Release Date: 2003. List Price: $15.00.

Anyone who has ever worked at a reference desk will identify with and appreciate the lyrics of this song. The album contains 18 songs, including "White Wolf," "Fifteen Iguanas," "Robert Carter III," "Take a Box," "Nachshon," and "Can I Blame You?" This CD with the "Reference Librarian" song is a perfect gift for anyone who is currently working, or has ever worked at an information desk. The artist knows what he's singing about because he's a librarian at Western Washington University. In addition, he's a singer/songwriter and the author of over 30 mystery novels. To find out more about the artist and his creative works, check out his website at www.nas.com/~lopresti.

Other Songs With and About Librarians

"The Librarian"

Artist: Nine Horses (David Sylvian, Steve Jansen, Burnt Friedman). Album: *Snow Borne Sorrow*. Type: Pop/Rock. Label: Samadhi Sound. Release Date: 2006. List Price: $15.98.

This song is rather dark, with lyrics like "keep your head down while they're firing low."

An MP3 sample of the song can be obtained from www.djouls.com. Other songs on the album: "Wonderful World," "Darkest Birds," "Banality of Evil," "Atom and Cell," "A History of Holes," "Snow Borne Sorrow," "The Day the Earth Stole Heaven," "Serotonin."

"Library Rap"

Artist: MC Poindexter and The Study Crew. This song was never released on an album. It was in an episode of the TV series *Sliders* which aired from 1995 to 1997 on the Fox Network and from 1998 to 2000 on the SciFi Channel. "Library Rap" was in the episode entitled "Eggheads" which premiered during the first season. You can hear "Library Rap" on the web at www.slidersweb.net/blinker/tracks/vocal.htm#.

"Library Song"

Artist: Tom Chapin. Album: *Just for Kids*. Type: Children's. Label: Sony Special Product. Release Date: 1996. List Price: $5.98.

The lyrics focus on a visit to the library by a youngster, but there is mention of the librarian behind the check-out desk. A sample of the song can be heard on the Amazon website (www.amazon.com). Other songs on the album: "A Song of One," "You'll Be Sorry," "Johnny Glockenspiel," "Good Garbage," "Great Big Worlds," "Someone's Gonna Use It," "Alphabet Soup," "Don't Make Me," "R-E-C-Y-C-L-E."

"When Spring Comes to the Library"

Artist: Robert Lopresti. Type: Folk Music. Album: This song is not yet available on an album. But you can hear it and read the lyrics online at www.nas.cm/~lopresti/spring.htm.

Anyone who works in a library or spends time in libraries will truly enjoy the lyrics of this song. They depict so much of what really happens during springtime in any public library from the perspective of someone who works in a library. The singer/songwriter knows what he's writing and singing about because he is a longtime librarian.

Poems About Librarians

Librarians are also immortalized in poetry. Some poems are serious and some are humorous. But unlike songs about librarians, most of the poems are not expressions of love.

The Cataloguer
by Sam Walter Foss
(From Foss, *Song of the Library Staff*
[New York: John A. Anderson, 1906.])

Oh, joy! to see the Library staff perpetually jogging,
And to see the Cataloger in the act of cataloging.
("Catalogs — Log-books for cattle," was the school-boy's definition,
A statement not to be despised for insight and precision)
Every language spoke at Babel in the books that pile her table,
Every theme discussed since Adam — song or story, fact or fable!
And she sweetly takes all knowledge for her province, as did Bacon,
All the fruit that's drooped and mellowed since the Knowledge tree was shaken,
All the ologies of the colleges, all the isms of the schools,
All the unassorted knowledges she assorts by Cutter's rules;
Or tags upon each author in large labels that are gluey
Their place in Thought's great Pantheon in decimals of Dewey;
Oh, joy! to see the Library staff perpetually jogging,
And to see the Cataloger in the act of cataloging.

The Children's Librarian
by Sam Walter Foss
(From Foss, *The Song of the Library Staff*
[New York: John A. Anderson, 1906.])

See the Children's gay Librarian! Oh, what boisterous joys are hers
As she sits upon her whirl-stool, throned amid her worshippers,
Guiding youngsters seeking wisdom through thought's misty morning light;
Separating Tom and Billy as they clinch in deadly fight;
Giving lavatory treatment to the little hand that smears
With the soil of crusted strata laid by immemorial years;
Teaching critical acumen to the youngsters munching candy,
To whom books are all two classes–they are either "bum" or "dandy";
Dealing out to Ruths and Susies, or to Toms and Dicks and Harries,
Books on Indians or Elsie, great big bears, or little fairies.
For the Children's gay Librarian passes out with equal pains
Books on Indians or Elsie, satisfying hungering brains;
Dealing Indians or Elsie, each according to his need,
Satisfying long, long longings for an intellectual feed.

The Head Librarian
by Sam Walter Foss
(From Foss, *The Song of the Library Staff*
[New York; John A. Anderson, 1906.])

Now my Muse prepare for business. Plume your wings for loftier flight
Through the circumambient ether to a super lunar height,
Then adown the empyrean from the heights where thou hast risen
Sing, O Muse! The Head Librarian and the joy that's her'n or his'n.
See him, see her, his o her head weighted with the lore of time,
Trying to expend a dollar when he only has a dime;
Tailoring appropriations–and how deftly he succeeds,

Fitting his poor thousand dollars to his million dollar needs.
How the glad book agents cheer him—and he cannot wish them fewer
With "heir greatest work yet published since the dawn of literature."
And he knows another agent, champing restive to begin
With another work still greater will immediately come in.
So perfection on perfection follows more and more sublime
And the line keeps on forever down the avenues of time—
So they travel on forever, stretching far beyond our ken,
Lifting demijohns of wisdom to the thirsty lips of men.
See him 'mid his myriad volumes listening to the gladsome din
Of the loud vociferant public that no book is ever "in";
And he hears the fierce taxpayer evermore lift up the shout
That the book he needs forever is the book forever "out."
How they rage, the numerous sinners, when he tries to please the saints,
When he tries to please the sinners hear the numerous saints' complaints;
And some want a Bowdlered Hemans and an expurgated Watts;
Some are shocked beyond expression at the sight of naked thoughts,
And he smooths their fur the right way, and he placates him or her,
And those who come to snarl and scratch remain behind to purr.
Oh, the gamesome glad Librarian gushing with his gurgling glee!—
Here I hand my resignation,—' tis a theme too big for me.

The Librarians' Omar
With apologies to the original and to recent eminent revisions
Author unknown
(From *The Library Journal*, v. 28, no. 3, March 1903, p. 113.)

Look at the Public all about us, "Lo,
Give us our Books," they cry, "and do not blow
About Self-Culture. Ain't Corelli Grand?
And Hall Caine's most as Fine as E.P. Roe."
Some for the Tale that Is Not plead in vain,
Some of the Tale that Is in Wrath complain.
One says, "I'd like that Elsie book by Holmes,"
Then weeps to find it isn't Mary Jane.
Each week its grist of Volumes brings, they say
Yes, but where shelve the Books of Yesterday?
And though we choose the living from the dead,
Time little heeds our wisest "yes" or "nay."
The Women's Clubs we set our Hearts upon,
Armed with our Larned, Poole, and Lexicon,
Set Homer in his place, and calmly turn
From Modern Painters to The Mastodon.
And she who serious Research Work essays,
And she who cribs from Chambers' Book of Days
Alike with calm self-satisfaction hears
Her fellow members' dulcet words of praise
Whether in Pittsburgh or in Kankakee
Whether our selves are Homemade or L.B.,
We need More Books, More Room, and ever strive

To make One Dollar do the work of Three.
Think, at each Conference of the A.L.A.
How Earnest Workers all the livelong day
Inspire, Instruct and Argue! Ev'n at night
The Moon gives Inspiration too, they say.
To Incunabula one gives his Zeal,
To one the Children's Room alone is Real
What matter Diverse Paths, so that they lead
Each one a little nearer The Ideal?

The Reference Librarian
by Sam Walter Foss
(From Foss, *Song of the Library Staff*
[New York: John A. Anderson, 1906.])

See the Reference Librarian and the joys that appertain to her;
Who shall estimate the contents and the area of the brain to her?
See the people seeking wisdom from the four winds ever blown to her,
For they know there is no knowledge known to mortals but is known to her;
See this flower of perfect knowledge, blooming like a lush geranium,
All converging rays of wisdom focused just beneath her cranium;
She is stuffed with erudition as you'd stuff a leather cushion,
And her wisdom is her specialty–it's marketing her mission.
How they throng to her, all empty, grovelling in their insufficience;
How they come from her, o'erflooded by the sea of her omniscience!
And they know she knows she knows things,–while she drips
   her learned theses
The percentage of illiteracy perceptibly decreases.
And, they know she knows she knows things, and her look is education;
And to look at her is culture, and to know her is salvation.

A Parallel
by Henry T. Coutts
(From Coutts, *Library Jokes and Jottings*
[New York: H.W. Wilson, 1914.])

Life is a volume, so they say,
And each page in it is a day.
"Tween covers all our days we crowd;
The blanket first, and last the shroud.
Glued to the "round" we crease and fray,
Some leaves and sections break away.
In paper, cloth, or leather dressed,
The shoddiest binding looks the best.
Some but as pamphlets they go home,
And some a thick and heavy tome.
But few, or thick, or thin, I ween,
Show binding sound and pages clean.
Dog-eared and torn, and rubbed and wan,
We meet the Great Librarian.
Ranged on his sleeves, a battered crew,
Fit for the dust-heap, I and you.

Casanova Was a Librarian

The Passionate Librarian to His Love
by Edmund Lester Pearson
(From Pearson, *The Secret Book*
[New York: Macmillan, 1914, pp. 111–112.])

Come live with me and be my love,
And we will dwell–oh, far above
The silly multitude who feed
On novels, and who fiction read.
For all day long we'll sit and pore
Upon the very dryest lore;
Some ancient gray-beard shall dispense us
The latest volumes of the Census.
And I, ah I! will hold our hand
And sing you songs of Samarcand–
Then you shall softly read to me
From Dr. Ploetz' "Epitome."
When through the fields of daisies wide
We stroll together, side by side,
I'll bind your brows with pink carnations
And read you from the "Wealth of Nations."
Each month I'll bring, my love to you,
The North American Review,
Nor, sweetheart, shall you ever lack
For Whitaker's great Almanack!
Why, Spencer, Kant, John Stuart Mill–
They all await your word and will;
Let me obey your fads and whims
And get you Cushing's "Anonyms."
In winter when the nights are cool
The "Index" made by Dr. Poole
Shall give you job, my dearest dove–
So live with me and be my love!

The Reference Librarian
by Edmund Lester Pearson
(From Pearson, *The Secret Book*
[New York:Macmillan, 1914, pp. 187–188.])

At times behind a desk he sits,
At times about the room he flits,—
Folks interrupt his perfect ease
By asking questions such as these;
"How tall was prehistoric man?"
"How old, I pray, was Sister Ann?"
"What should one do if cats have fits?"
"What woman first invented mitts?"
"Who said 'To labor is to pray'?"
"How much did Daniel Lambert weigh?"
"Don't you admire E.P. Roe?"
"What is the fare to Kokomo?"

"Have you a life of Sairy Gamp?"
"Can you lend me a postage stamp?"
"Have you the rhymes of Edward Lear?"
"What wages do they give you here?"
"What dictionary is the best?"
"Did Brummel wear a satin vest?"
"How do you spell 'anaemic,' please?"
"What is a Gorgonzola cheese?"
"Who ferried souls across the Styx?"
"What is the square of 96?"
"Are oysters good to eat in March?"
"Are green bananas full of starch?"
"Where is that book I used to see?"
"I guess you don't remember me?"
"Haf you Der Hohenzollernspiel?"
"Where shall I put this apple peel?"
"Ou est, m'sieu, la grande Larousse?"
"Do you say 'wo-spot,' or 'the deuce'?"
"Come, find my book,–why make a row?"
"A *red* one,–can't you find it *now*?"
"Please, which is right: to 'lend' or 'loan'?"
"Say, mister, where's the telephone?"
"How *do* you use this catalogue?"
"Oh, hear that noise! Is that my dog?"
"Have you a book called 'Shapes of Fear'?"
"You mind if I leave Baby here?"

Ko-Ko's Song in "The Mikado Up to Date"
by Paul Herring
(From Herring, *The Librarian*, v. 3, no. 3, October 1912.)

There are some people living who, I entertain a hope,
Will eventually dangle from a bit of hempen rope.
There's the fiend who fills our magazines with "puffs" of someone's soap–
I've got *him* on my list — I've got *him* on my list.
There's the waggish young librarian who knows too much by half,
Classes Smiles and Theirs together, and in hopes to get a laugh,
Puts Bacon, bound in pigskin, on a shelf with Lamb, in calf–
He never will be missed — he really won't be missed.
There's the discontented reader who sends letters to the press,
And invariably doesn't put his name and his address,
Though at his personality we can generally guess–
I've got *him* on my list — he's down upon my list.
And the cataloguing faddist, who declaring everything
Is quite an easy matter if to rule of thumb you cling,
Puts "Sesame and Lillies" under "market-gardening,"
I'm sure he wouldn't be missed — he never would be missed.
There's the fellow who'd be "favoured" with a "sit" upon our staff;
The man who sends you "poems" and inscribes his autograph:
And that terrible affliction that the comic paper chaff–

The lady novelist — I've got her on my list.
There's the amateur collector who will drop a quiet hint
That he picked a lucky "find" up when you passed it; which he didn't–
And the binder who will guillotine deep down into the print–
They'll presently be missed — they'll all of 'em be missed.
He will have them by and by.

The Discovery
by Ron Barnes. 2006.

A boy sat quiet, small and still,
His mom watched through a window still,
She saw his face and knew the look;
Her child was traveling through a book
Time after time, his mom would say,
"It's nice outside! Go out and play!
There's life and laughter in the sun–
A boy your age should play and run!"
How oft he'd heard his mother's pitch,
Yet in his mind remained an itch
A hunger deep, the need to know,
Despite his youth the need did grow
The questions — how his thoughts did run!
How far the moon? How hot the sun?
How does the bumblebee take flight?
How soft the clouds? How dark the night?
Who wrote the themes of his favorite stories
And filled his mind with allegories?
Gulliver's Travels? The Brothers Grimm?
A Christmas Carol with Tiny Tim?
Who wrote the Bible, filled its pages?
Who put zoo animals in their cages?
Who wrote the dreams that filled his head,
put monsters underneath his bed?
His mom sighed deep, yet she was wise,
she saw desire in his eyes
and knew the hunger of his mind;
there was a treasure he must find
Next morning mom had formed her plan,
A trip designed for her young man
To gain what caused his mind to grow
And he, though young, desired to know
The building, quaint and somewhat small,
had wood and brick along the wall,
Its wooden doors were opened wide
inviting him to look inside
He stepped within to spy the land
while holding tight his mother's hand,
He gave his mom inquiring looks–
And then his eyes fell on the books

His heart is stilled by what he sees;
This land had books like fruit on trees!
The rows were long, the shelving tall,
With endless books along the wall
The smell of pages filled the air,
attesting to the writings there
and literary treasures deep–
all that he found was his to keep
"What is this place?" He asked with awe,
still wondering at the books he saw,
His mom then whispered in his ear,
"The library — you're welcomed here.
"There's knowledge here for you to gather,
Books to read, or if you'd rather
use computers, they will let
You research on the Internet."
Now every week, for hours on end,
He took his hunger and would spend
Some time inside the library
Enjoying this great discovery
The trips he took! The stories read!
With many tales he filled his head,
He learned of knowledge deep and fair,
And never left his reading chair
There was time to run and time to play,
But twice a week he'd spend a day
In book-filled corners where he'd find
A quiet place to feed his mind.

Books of Library Poems

For more poems about librarians, be sure to check out *Overdue Notice: Poems from the Library* by David Drake (McFarland, 1995). Containing almost 200 poems, the book offers poems about librarians, patrons, libraries, books and more. Whether you need a poem for a retirement, for the Friends of the Library, for story hour, or the bookmobile, this book is the place to find what you're looking for.

And if you just can't get enough library poetry to feed your soul, you should also look for *Each of Us Is a Book: Poems for the Library Minded* (McFarland, 2003), also written by David Drake.

8

Just for Librarians

Every profession is full of diversity. How the media portrays a profession as a whole, and how a profession prefers to portray itself, is often as different as day and night. Unless you're a member of that profession, you'll have a hard time determining which portrayal is more accurate. But looking at the merchandise and gifts designed for and purchased by individuals in the profession can give you a lot of insight into the profession.

For librarians, these gifts and products range from naughty librarian thongs and calendars featuring disrobed librarians, to "Harried Librarian" duster pens and fine art prints featuring librarians. After you peruse the following gift items for your favorite librarian, you be the judge. Are librarians meek, mousy individuals, radical militants, intellectuals, or something very different?

Sexy Items

When you think about librarians, underwear is probably the last thing that comes to mind. But believe it or not, a wide selection of sexy underwear designed just for librarians is available for purchase. Librarian underwear makes a unique gift for your spouse or intimate librarian friend. Or, if you're a librarian who wants to make a statement in the bedroom, or if you want to secretly make a statement at work wearing special underwear, you have the opportunity to do so through the purchase of a librarian thong, camisole, or boxer shorts.

For Her

CAMISOLES

For librarians who want to feel sexy during the day, a thin, tight-fitting camisole is the perfect undergarment. Once the day ends, it's a perfect top for late evening club hopping. And when it's time for bed, it can serve as sleepwear.

Made of 100 percent ultra-fine baby-rib cotton, these white camisoles can be purchased with lettering across the front of the garment. For librarians needing a hug, they may get one that reads "Have You Hugged a Librarian Today?" (product #43069782, $21.99). For librarians who can and want to flaunt themselves, there's a camisole with an image of two books and the words "Stacked Librarian" on the front (product #23780587, $16.99). And for those who aim to please, there's even a camisole with the silhouette of a shapely female librarian on the front and the words "Ensuring User Satisfaction at the Library" (product #10159149, $18.39). Several dozen different graphics and messages are available. To explore the options, go to www.cafepress.com and search for "librarians" then select "Women's and Junior's Apparel" on the toolbar on the left side of the screen.

The camisoles are available in small (for dress sizes 0 to 2), medium (dress sizes 4 to 6), and large (dress sizes 8 to 10), and certain camisoles are also available in extra-large (dress sizes 12 to 14). Order these camisoles online at www.cafepress.com, or by calling (877) 809–1659.

THONGS

Useful if you like wearing low-rise pants, 100 percent ultra fine-combed ring-spun baby-rib cotton thongs can be purchased with a variety of different designs and messages on the front of them. They are made in the United States, and three sizes are available: small (for dress sizes 2 to 6), medium (dress sizes 8 to 10), and large (dress size 12). The thongs fit snugly and bear an elastic trim.

Over 50 different designs or slogans are available. Although you can purchase a thong with a playful saying such as "Ha-Ha! Made Ya Read" (product #31364715, $12.99), most of the designs are geared toward naughty librarians. They range from "Desperate Librarian, the Book Stops Here" (product #34789690, $10.99) and "Librarians Do It By the Book" (product #31242071, $13.99) to a red heart with the words "Kiss Me I'm a Librarian" in the center of the heart (product #3746160, $9.00). You can view the wide selection of thongs available online at www.cafepress.com. Once on the site, do a search for "librarians." All the thongs can be purchased online from www.cafepress.com or by calling (877) 809–1659.

WOMEN'S SPAGHETTI TANK TOP

Sometimes the message that appears on a piece of clothing says more about its wearer than the piece of clothing. So you may be surprised to know there's a spaghetti tank top and other clothing with a graphic of a book bound with leather straps. The caption reads "Librarians Do It Best With Things Bound in Leather." Made in the United States of 100 percent fine-combed ring-spun rib cotton, the tank sells for $22.09 (product # 53550017). It can be ordered from Tease, 8570 Commerce St. #113, Cape Canaveral, FL 32920, (800) 416–0548, www.teasecatalog.com.

For Him

BOXERS

Male librarians are not to be forgotten. Boxer shorts are available with designs ranging from one with a red and yellow "Super Librarian" logo (product #39209915, $15.99) to ones with a simple statement such as "Proud To Be a Librarian" (product #39871638, $16.99). And of course there are boxers with more risqué designs for naughty male librarians. These include one with "Save a Horse Ride a Librarian" and the image of a horse head (product #37754436, $15.99), and one with simply "Dewey and I are a Number" (product #31172307, $16.89).

The boxers are made of 100 percent cotton and have an open fly. They're available in small (waist size 28" to 30"), medium (waist size 32" to 34"), large (waist size 36" to 38"), and extra large (waist size 40" to 42"). These and other librarian boxers are available online at www.cafepress.com or by calling (877) 809–1659.

Other Adult Clothing

Fleece Jacket

When the temperature drops, your favorite librarian will enjoy having a comfortable warm fleece jacket, especially one designed just for librarians. A wonderful gift, this navy blue fleece jacket features side seam pockets, elastic cuffs, and a full zip front. Machine washable, it's accented with a blue and gold "librarian" logo. Available in small, medium, large and extra large, it's priced at $65, with American Library Association members receiving a discount. The jacket can be ordered from the American Library Association, 50 E. Huron St., Chicago, IL 60611, www.alastore.ala.org or by calling (866) 746–7252.

Sweatshirts

Whether they're worn in the library or at home, sweatshirts are always a practical and useful gift for your favorite librarian. If you're buying a sweatshirt for a children's or young adult librarian, you may want to consider an ash grey sweatshirt with "Librarians Rock" on the front (product #34802653, $26.99). For your other favorite librarians, consider a white sweatshirt with "Librarians possess novel information" on it (product #40796842, $26.99) or one with "Everyone Loves a Librarian" on it (product #23543607, $24.99). For a sweatshirt with a little more flair, try a grey sweatshirt with a color graphic of the inside of a library in a box on the front. Below the graphic it reads "Librarians Have the Best References" (product #31240886, $26.99). Or, for something simple, you can order a sweatshirt with "Librarian" embroidered in blue on the front (item #K63–44368, $39.95).

You also have the option of purchasing a hooded sweatshirt. Great for joggers, they are available with a wide variety of slogans and graphics. For your librarian friends who are always struggling to increase their library's budget, you might want to consider a budget-challenged librarian hooded sweatshirt. On the front of this sweatshirt is a drawing of a tired, middle-aged male librarian holding a cup with "Please give" on it, and in his other hand he's holding a sign reading "Library to Support" (product #9999799, $28.99).

The sweatshirts are made of a 90/10 cotton/polyester blend. They're available in several sizes: small (fits chest size 34" to 36"), medium (chest size 38" to 40"), large (chest size 42" to 44"), extra large (chest size 46" to 48"), 2X-large (chest size 50" to 52"), 3X-large (chest size 54" to 56"), 4X-large (chest size 58" to 60"). All the sweatshirts, except for the "Librarian" sweatshirt can be purchased online at www.cafepress.com or by calling (877) 809–1659. The "LIBRARIAN" sweatshirt can be ordered from Upstart, W5527 State Road 106, PO Box 800, Fort Atkinson, WI 53538–0800, (800) 448–4887, www.highsmith.com.

T-Shirts

T-shirts abound with phrases about librarians. They run the gamut from an ash grey T-shirt with "8th Commandment 'Thou Shalt not Steal' Remember to Return Your Library Books" (product #41481444, $16.99), available from www.cafe-press.com, 877–809–1659) to a T-shirt with the emblem of the "Ordo Bibliotheca — International Order of Librarians" designed by James Turner on the front of it ($19.95, available from http://store.slavelabor.com). Or, if you're looking for a T-shirt with a contemporary design, check out the T-shirt from Upstart that has a Google-like design on the front reading "Librarians" in big colorful letters and "The Ultimate Search Engine" in the search bar (product # K77–11109, $14.95, www.upstartpromotions.com).

Long-sleeved T-shirts are also available. For your favorite reference librarian, there's a great one with "Ask Me!" in big letters, with "I'm a Reference Librarian" in smaller letters below it (item #23595152, $20.99, available from www.cafepress.com, 877–809–1659). If you just want to support a good cause, you can always purchase a "Desperate Librarians — The Buck Stops Here" long-sleeved T-shirt (product #34789666, $22.99, available from www.cafepress.com, 877–809–1659). If you're not familiar with the slogan, it was developed by a group of rural Wisconsin libraries as a way to raise some money for their libraries.

Ties

BOOKS

This black 56"×3.75" polyester necktie by Steven Harris displays shelves upon shelves of books and is perfect for librarians and book lovers. The tie sells for $11.99

(SKU: NS217272) and is available from Neckties.com, 10372 Stanford Ave., Suite R, Garden Grove, CA 92840, (800) 289–2843, and can be ordered online at www.neckties.com.

DR. SEUSS LIBRARY CAT TIE

This 100 percent silk jacquard tie features shelves of books up and down the tie. In the lower portion is the Cat from the *Cat in the Hat*. This colorful tie can be purchased from the American Library Association, 50 E. Huron St., Chicago, IL 60611, (800) 746–7252, www.alastore.ala.org. The tie sells for $31.95 and association members receive a discount.

SCHOOL BOOKS

Perfect for a school librarian, this colorful tie features stacks of schoolbooks, each with an apple on top. The tie can be purchased for $16.95 from Homeroom, PO Box 388, Centerbrook, CT 06409–0388, (800) 222–8270, www.homeroomdirect.com.

Woman's Track Suits and Hoodies

There are even track suits with librarian logos available for purchase. Made of preshrunk 100 percent spun cotton, the sweat pants are straight legged with a drawstring waist. The zip-up hoodie has a white body and the sleeves are color coordinated to the pants. Most are available in black/white, baby blue/white, or pink/white color combinations. Again, the librarian logos or sayings available on these outfits run the gamut from "Boolean Operator" (product #17641345, $45.99), to the more common "I Love Librarians" (product #35659090, $54.99). The track suits are available in small (dress size 0 to 6), medium (dress size 8 to 10), large (dress size 12 to 14), and extra large (dress size 16 to 18). They can be purchased online at www.cafepress.com or by calling (877) 809–1659.

If you're not interested in the complete track suit, you have the option of purchasing a variety of hoodies alone. For that hard-to-buy-for cataloger, consider a hoodie with "Catalogers Work by the Book" on it (product #23595875, $28.99). If promoting library use is a big issue for the individual, you can purchase a hoodie with "Get Thee to a Library" on it (product #14698357, $31.99). They also can be purchased online at www.cafepress.com or by calling (877) 809–1659.

Children's Clothing

Kids' T-Shirts

For children who want to follow in a parent's footstep, there's a T-shirt just for them. It reads "I Want to Be a Librarian" in a variety of different colored letters on the front. Made of 100 percent preshrunk cotton, it's available in small (chest 27", length 18"), medium (chest 31", length 20.5"), and large (34", length 23") and sells for $15.99 (product #8183428). You can order this item online at www.cafepress.com or by calling (877) 809–1659.

Infant and Toddler Wear

For librarian moms-to-be and librarians with children or grandchildren, there's even a choice of infant and toddler wear promoting reading, books, and librarians. Forget the standard store-bought baby gifts for ones that will stand out from crowd. These make perfect gifts for expectant librarians and new moms.

"BORN TO READ"

You know a child will grow up to be a reader when at least one parent is a librarian. There's no better gift than a bib with "Born to Read" in the middle of a heart on the front. To complement the bib is a "Born to Read" knit cap and a T-shirt. Each of the items is sold separately, but the three make a nice set for a gift.

All items are white except for the logos. The bib measures 7½"×8½", is made of 100 percent washable cotton terry with a vinyl backing and sells for only $6.50 (item #5270–0200). The cap is designed for newborns and is made of orlon. It has a tiny pompon on the top of it. It sells for only $6.50 (item #5270–0700). The infant T-shirt is also made of 100 percent cotton. It fits infants (6 months) and sells for only $10 (item #5270–0100). The items are also available in Spanish.

"READ, PLEASE!/LEA POR FAVOR!"

This set of infant wear features drawing of the heads of two children. The caption above one of the children is "Read, Please!" and "Lea Por Favor!" appears in the caption above the other. This logo appears on a white vinyl-backed bib with a red trim and a snap at the back. It sells for $7.50 (item #5272–0201). It also appears on a newborn bodysuit made of 100 percent cotton with a nap crotch and lap shoulder that sells for $16 (item #5272–0202). Body suits are also available for infants (6 months — item # 5272–0203 and 12 months — item #5272–0204) for $16 each.

You also have the option of purchasing the logo on a red romper made of 100 percent jersey cotton with long sleeves and pants bearing ribbed cuffs and ankles and a snap crotch. A red romper (6 months — item #5272–0205, 18 months — item #5272–0207) sells for $22.

All of the "Born to Read" and "Read Please" items are available for purchase from the American Library Association, 50 E. Huron St., Chicago, IL 60611 (866) 746–7252, www.alastore.ala.org.

"LIBRARIAN IN TRAINING"

For librarians who are determined to have their offspring follow in their footsteps, an infant creeper with "Librarian in Training" is the perfect baby gift. Made of 100 percent cotton jersey knit, the creeper features a standard T-shirt neck and three snap bottom. The nicest feature is its $9.99 price (product #8183532). It's available in six sizes: 6 months (19" to 21" chest, length 12¼"), 12 months (21" to 23" chest, length 13"), 18 months/2T (25" chest, length 14½"), 3T (26" chest, length 15"), 4T (28" chest, length 16"). The creeper can be ordered online at www.cafepress.com or by calling (877) 809–1659.

Warm Fuzzies

Medium Plush Animal: Bear

This cute 11" soft plush white bear will bring a smile to anyone's face. The bear comes wearing a red ribbon tied around its neck and a white T-shirt with "Librarians work in a Booking Joint" on the front of it. This is a great gift for children or adults. Selling for $16.89 (product # 31173173), this bear can be ordered online from www.cafepress.com or by calling (877) 809–1659.

Small Plush Bear

The next time you want to treat yourself or your favorite librarian to a warm and fuzzy gift, think about a cuddly teddy bear. You can find a white, 11" plush teddy bear with cute black eyes and nose, a red bow, and choice of T-shirts perfect for librarians on the Cafepress.com Website. The prices range from $13 to $16.99, depending upon which T-shirt the bear wears.

For example, you can purchase a bear wearing a white T-shirt with the numbers "688.724" printed in black on the front of the shirt. This is definitely a bear for a librarian since most people don't know that 688.724 is the Dewey Decimal number for — you guessed it — teddy bears! This bear (product # 45930645) sells for $13.99.

Or for that special librarian who is wild about bears, or just a child who likes to read, you can select a bear wearing a white T-shirt with a picture of a happy brown bear sitting up. The caption above him reads, "Beary Wild About Books." This bear sells for $16.99 (product # 14953258), and you can opt to purchase the bear with a slightly different caption over the graphic. That caption is "Beary Happy Reader" (product # 14693832).

Or for a perfect baby shower gift for a librarian mother-to-be, consider giving a bear with a T-shirt bearing "Read to Me" on the front, with the drawing of a mother, father and baby bear in brown above the wording, a blue drawing of a buccaneer on the bottom right of the wording, and a green drawing of a fairy to the left. This unique baby gift sells for $16.99 (product # 14695092).

All the bears can be viewed and ordered online at www.cafepress.com.

Toys and Collectibles

Librarian Action Figures

When you think of action figure toys, librarians generally don't pop into your mind. But the image of librarians is constantly changing. Over five librarian action figures can be purchased for the children of your favorite librarian, or other fans of librarians.

LIBRARIAN ACTION FIGURE (NANCY PEARL)

Modeled after former Seattle Public Library librarian Nancy Pearl, this original librarian action figures features a bespectacled Nancy attired in a plain dark blue jacket and ankle length skirt. Completing her outfit are black frumpy (oops, excuse me, "sensible") flat shoes. Push a button on her back and this 5" librarian raisers her finger to her mouth to silently shush anyone making too much noise.

Packaged with Nancy are a tiny stack of books, a replica of her book *Book Lust*, two bookmarks, and a Librarian Action Figure Trading Card. A great deal for only $8.95. To see a picture of the action figure, go online to www.mcphee.com. This item can be purchased from Archie McPhee, PO Box 30852, Seattle, WA 98113, (425) 349–3009, www.mcphee.com.

DELUXE LIBRARIAN ACTION FIGURE (NANCY PEARL)

If you just can't get enough of Nancy, or want her attired in a different color, there's the Deluxe Action Figure. In the deluxe model Nancy sports the same clothes and sensible shoes but they are burgundy. She's also accompanied with a tiny book cart, a computer, a pair of book stacks, and a tiny replica of her second book, *More Book Lust*. And yes, she can still "shush" you with the push of a button. This deluxe version is also available from Archie McPhee for only $12.95.

BATGIRL

Every fan of the Batman comics will remember Barbara Gordon, the daughter of police commissioner James Gordon and head librarian of Gotham City Library. Regarded by fans as the one true Batgirl, she wasn't the first batgirl to appear in DC Comics, but she is definitely the most memorable. (The first Batgirl in DC Comics was Betty Kane, a teen sidekick to Kathy Kane's Batwoman who appeared in the late 1950s and early sixties.)

A number of Batgirl action figures are available. Fans of Barbara Gordon's Librarian Batgirl should consider the Secret Files: Unmasked!: Series 2: Barbara Gordon/Batgirl Action Figure. Dressed in her famous blue Batgirl outfit with yellow gloves, belt and boots, this 6" figure "transforms from librarian to crime-fighter with the flip of her cowl! This figure features multiple points of articulation, a display base, an alternate head and character-dedicated accessories." Retailing for $14.99, this action figure is available for sale from a variety of online sources and comic stores. A picture of the action figure can be found at www.dccomics.com/dcdirect.

RUPERT GILES

Fans of the television show *Buffy, the Vampire Slayer* know Rupert Giles as Buffy's Watcher, the person who trains her and looks after her. Giles also happens to be the school librarian at Sunnydale High School. Fans of this Watcher/Librarian have a choice of action figures.

The first ever Giles action figure, the Rupert Giles Series 2 Buffy Figure has Giles dressed in a grey vest with matching pants, a tie and long-sleeved shirt. He comes with a tombstone base, crucifix, slayer battle-axe, two stakes, and a watcher book, and sells for $29.99.

A Palz block figurine of Giles is also available. The figurine comes with two quarterstaffs, a Vampyr book, a tombstone, additional body and clothing parts, and a collector's card. This figure currently sells for under $15.

Both action figures can be purchased from a variety of online sources, including Fadtoys.com and emerchandise.com.

CASANOVA

Best known for his notorious love affairs, Casanova was also a soldier, author, gambler, and yes, a librarian. A Casanova action figure makes the perfect gift for any male librarian who wants to shatter the image of male librarians as mousy geeks and replace it with the image of a suave, adventurous individual.

The 5½" Casanova figure features the legend in a dashing blue topcoat with a black masquerade mask in hand. The packaging notes he was a soldier, author, spy, gambler and librarian. At only $8.95, he's the perfect counter companion for the Nancy Pearl action figure! This item can be purchased from Archie McPhee, PO Box 30852, Seattle, WA 98113, (425) 349–3009 and can also be viewed on their website at www.mcphee.com.

LAURA BUSH

Collectors will want to check out the limited edition action figure of school librarian and First Lady Laura Bush dressed in a pale blue suit and flat white pumps. This talking action figures features the First Lady speaking five different statements. Statement #1: "Education is not a Republican issue or a Democratic issue. It's an American issue." Statement #2: "I think teaching is really one of the most important professions. A teacher impacts children. And they certainly impact our whole country and our future." Statement #3: "All of us want what's best for our country. We may see different ways to get there, but in the end we all really want what's best for our country." Statement #4: "We've benefited always, because of the expertise, or the interests, or the passions of our first ladies." Statement #5: "Americans are willing to fight and die for our freedoms. But more importantly, we're willing to live for them." Limited to a production of only 10,000 figures, each one comes with its own individually numbered certificate of authenticity and sells for only $29.95. It's available online at www.toypresidents.com or by calling 1–877-TOY-PREZ.

BENJAMIN FRANKLIN

Remembered by most people as an inventor and statesman, this one-time librarian is immortalized in a hard vinyl action figure with moveable arms and legs. Outfitted with black-rimmed glasses and appropriate brown attire from his time period, he comes complete with a kite and key so you can re-enact his famous experiment. To bad books are not part of the accessories. But who can complain with the price of $8.95. Available at selected retailers and from Archie McPhee, PO Box 30852, Seattle, WA 98113, (425) 349–3009, www.mcphee.com.

Collectible Art Prints

THE BOOKWORM

This fine art print by German artist C. Spitzweg is available in 12.5"×22", 16"×20", 24"×36", and as a framed art print in 18"×22", and 23"×27". Prices start as low as $15.99. A wonderful gift for any librarian or book lover, *The Bookworm* features an elderly gentleman, his nose in a book, standing on a ladder in a library with floor to ceiling wood bookcases filled with books. This full color print is available from Art.com, 2100 Powell St., 13th Floor, Emeryville, CA 94608, (919) 831–0015, and can be viewed on their website.

THE LIBRARIAN

By artist Roy Carruthers, this 18"×24" Giclee print contains a cartoon-style male librarian dressed in a suit and tie standing next to a tabletop card catalog. On top of the card catalog is a book with a hole in it. In one hand the librarian is holding a hammer, and in the other hand he's holding a nail on top of the book. He's poised to add another hole to the book. The print is perfect for anyone who's ever questioned the normality or sanity of librarians. It's available for viewing and purchase at www.art.com, which sells the print by itself for $64.99. For a higher fee you can purchase the print mounted with a rounded metal moulding and acrylic glazing. You can contact Art.com at 2100 Powell St., 13th Floor, Emeryville, CA 94608, (919) 831–0015.

LIBRARY 1969

Library 1969 was created by famed African American Harlem Renaissance painter Jacob Lawrence (1917–2000), who refined his painting skills while attending a Harlem art workshop held at the New York Public Library. He later spent months doing research in the Schomberg Collection at the New York Public Library. It can definitely be said the library had an impact on this artist's life. *Library 1969* is a colorful depiction of a library scene that conveys a vibrant place due to the frequent use of red, orange and purple. This fine art print measures 28"×26" and is available for only $24. But you'll want to invest a little more to have this wonderful print mounted and framed. Available for purchase from Art.com, 2100 Powell St., 13th Floor, Emeryville, CA 94608, (919) 831–0015.

QUIET PLEASE LIBRARIAN PINUP GIRL POSTER

No art aficionado's collection would be complete without this librarian pinup girl art print. Created by artist Richie Fahey, famous for creating the covers of 14 James Bond novels, the print measures 9"×12" and features a voluptuous sexy librarian in a low-cut V-necked white sweater and tight black skirt standing behind a library desk with a "quiet please" sign on it against a blue background of book shelves. Despite her glasses and dark hair swept up on top of her head, this sexy librarian will never be labeled frumpy! The print itself sells for only $14.99, but once you see this print, you'll want it mounted. It's also available with a SoHo onxy moulding and acrylic glazing and a variety of frames for a higher cost. The print can be viewed online at www.art.com. Available for purchase from Art.com, 2100 Powell St., 13th Floor, Emeryville, CA 94608, (919) 831–0015.

Renaissance Library Collection

Any librarian or book lover will appreciate this beautiful collection of 16"×12" color prints. The libraries shown in the collection each reflect their architect's love and worship of books. Although each print is sold individually, you'll want the entire collection since it will be difficult to choose a favorite among the prints. The six libraries featured in the prints are as follows:

ABBEY LIBRARY, ST. GALLEN, SWITZERLAND, 1758

This print shows the interior of this fabulous baroque library. From the walnut and cherry book and display cases to the ornate ceiling, this library is stunning. It would probably even outshine any library found in a royal palace.

ABBEY LIBRARY, WALDASSEN, GERMANY, 1585

This abbey library in Waldassen will take your breath away. Also designed in baroque style, the library features detailed woodcarvings and a lovely vaulted ceiling, showcasing murals. You feel inspired just by looking at this print.

CATHEDRAL LIBRARY IN FREISING, GERMANY, 1734

If libraries with natural light and art appeal to you, this is the print for you. The tall windows in this library provide natural lighting for the statue of Apollo that stands in the center of the room featured. The white wood display cases, floor and detailing in the library really create a light, welcoming environment.

LIBRARY OF ST. WALBURGA, ZUTPHEN, HOLLAND, 1564

This library has architectural features often found in cathedrals. In the print, you'll notice books are displayed on pulpits.

NATIONAL LIBRARY OF RUSSIA, ST. PETERSBURG, 1795

The print of this library shows the grandeur of the Russian National Library. From the elegant wood furniture to the patterned ceiling design, the comfortable environment of this great library just begs visitors to sit and read a good book.

THE NEW LIBRARY OF THE ROYAL COLLEGE OF PHYSICIANS, EDINBURGH, 1682

Physicians undoubtedly find comfort in this grand wood paneled library. With comfortable chairs, study tables, and carpeting, the library is visually pleasing as well as comfortable.

Each print is sold individually for $8.99 each. (Note: These items are shipped from Sweden so the shipping cost will be higher than what you're accustomed to paying for materials shipped from within the United States). The prints are products of Information Strategy & Information Management, Torsvagen 7b, 192 67 Sollentuna, Sweden, +46 8754 15 55. The prints can be ordered online at www.renaissancelibrary.com.

Posters and Prints to Collect Just for Fun

BATGIRL POSTER

Batgirl fans and librarians will enjoy this poster with the bottom banner reading "Librarians Are Heroes Everyday!" When she's not saving the world, Batgirl, whose real identity is librarian Barbara Gordon, spends her days working at the Gotham City Library. This 22"×28" poster contains original artwork that depicts Ms. Gordon working in the library, with a reflection of her as Batgirl in the window. Available for $13 from the American Library Association, 50 E. Huron St., Chicago, IL 60611, (800) 545–2433. You can view the poster at www.alastore.ala.org.

LIBRARIAN

This 8"×10" matted print contains the word "Librarian" near the center, with a computer in the lower right hand corner. On the left side of the print is an artistic rendition of several shelves of books on top of a reading table. This print can be viewed online at www.applesangelsandmore.com/library.html. It's available for purchase from Apples, Angels & More, 2148 16th Avenue SW, Largo, FL 33770 (800) 441–8600.

REX LIBRIS POSTER

Comic book fans know Rex Libris as the head librarian at Middleton Public Library who will travel to the edge of the galaxy in pursuit of overdue books. Illustrated by James Turner, the writer of the Rex Libris comics, this 12"×17" color poster features Rex pointing his finger at you. The caption reads, "Have you returned your library books? Don't force me to hunt you down like a wild animal with my semi-automatic Beretta M92F pistol." The poster can be purchased for $6.95 from SLG Publishing, 377 Market Street, San Jose, CA 95113, (408) 971–8929, and can be viewed and purchased online at http://store.slavelabor.com.

For the Movie Buff

Librarian/Library Movie Posters

No true librarian movie buff's collection would be complete without a set of vintage-inspired movie posters with library themes. Demco Inc. offers four different full color 23"×17" posters designed with librarians in mind. The posters promote use of the library in a fun manner.

These inexpensive posters can be purchased individually or as a set for under $20. To see the posters online, visit the Demco website at www.demco.com and do a product search for "movie posters." Bookmarks featuring the poster images are also available for purchase. These materials can be ordered from Demco, Inc., PO Box 7488, Madison, WI 53707–7488, (800) 356–1200.

ATTACK OF THE ZOMBIE LIBRARIANS

With a poster banner of "Attack of the Zombie Librarians," this is a great gift for librarians with a sense of humor. The poster depicts two female zombie librarians with bulging glazed eyes posed in a Frankenstein-like walk, terrifying a female patron in the library. The caption at the bottom of the poster reads "Starring Horror Novels Now Showing in Libraries Nationwide!" Subtext within the poster includes: "They are Smarter! They are Stronger! They are Hungry!"

THE CARD CATALOG CRUSH

The stereotypical image of the librarian is far from the image of the librarian depicted in this poster. Reminiscent of a scene from *Casablanca*, a man in a trench coat stands by a lamppost. A seductive blonde librarian, carrying a flame red book that matches her lipstick, appears in the background above him. Text within the poster reads, "She checked out books and his heart! No man could escape her charm!" The banner at the bottom reads "Starring Romance Novels Now Showing at Libraries Everywhere!"

INTERGALACTIC BOOK MUTANTS

Librarians haven't made it into outer space in this poster. But if you like two-legged green space monsters giving a pair of astronauts a scare on a distant planet, this is the poster for you. "They Traveled the Galaxy in Search of Books, What They Found Were!" reads the text within the poster. The bottom banner reads "Starring Science Fiction Novels Now Showing at Your Local Library."

OVERDUE!

Reminiscent of a James Dean film, a young male library patron tries to outrun three cops in pursuit with their billy clubs drawn. "He Didn't Return His Books On Time! Now He Must Pay!" reads the poster text. With the bottom banner reading "Starring Adventure Novels Now Showing at a Library Near You!" This poster is bound to please librarians who are sticklers for the rules.

Movies

All too few movies have librarians in lead roles. Those that do make great gifts for librarians. From musicals to fantasy, here are some movies with librarians playing prominent roles. (If you're interested in a more movies featuring librarians as characters, see chapter 5.)

DESK SET (1957). TWENTIETH CENTURY FOX. DVD RELEASE DATE 2004. 104 MINUTES. LIST PRICE: $14.98.

A perfect gift, especially for young librarians who probably haven't seen it, the film features Spencer Tracy as an efficiency expert and Katharine Hepburn as the head of a research department. She's the equivalent of a head librarian in a corporate library. The sparks and the fun fly when Hepburn learns Tracy is installing a super computer known as an "electronic brain" in the research department. Hepburn and her staff are fearful the "electronic brain" will replace them. But you've probably guessed how the movie ends. There's comedy, romance, and a happy ending. What more can you ask for?

FOUL PLAY (1978). PARAMOUNT. DVD RELEASE DATE 2004. 116 MINUTES. LIST PRICE: $9.98.

Gloria Mundy, played by Goldie Hawn, is a single librarian in San Francisco who witnesses a murder. Add in Chevy Chase as a police detective, Dudley Moore as a musical conductor, a menacing dwarf, a dangerous albino, and a plot to kill the pope and you've got a somewhat dated, but still hilarious madcap comedy. Although the movies takes place in San Francisco, Southern California librarians may have a déjà vu feeling while watching the film because some of the library scenes were filmed inside the Pasadena Public Library. This comedy makes a perfect gift for any librarian who likes a good laugh.

THE GUN IN BETTY LOU'S HANDBAG (1992). TOUCHSTONE PICTURES.
DVD RELEASE DATE 2003. 89 MINUTES. LIST PRICE: $9.99.

Starring Penelope Ann Miller (*The Relic, Kindergarten Cop*) as Betty Lou, a meek librarian in a small town who's married to a police detective, this movie will make you laugh out loud. After a gangster is murdered, Betty Lou stumbles upon the murder weapon, a handgun, and puts it in her purse. After several unsuccessful attempts to alert others to her find, her frustration forces her to fire off the gun in a ladies room. She's promptly arrested, confesses to being the murderer, and is thrown in jail. From this point the fun really kicks into high gear as she transforms into a sexy, fearless, outspoken librarian. There are some priceless scenes, including one of a library fundraising event, that make me believe the screenwriter must have either been a librarian at one time, or is married to a librarian. Alfre Woodard, Eric Thal, and Julianne Moore are also in the cast.

IT'S A WONDERFUL LIFE (1947). REPUBLIC PICTURES. DVD RELEASE
DATE 1995. 130 MINUTES. LIST PRICE: $19.95.

Just the fact that this is a classic Christmas movie should be enough of a reason to give it to your favorite librarian. But if you need a little more convincing, don't forget that Donna Reed, who plays George Bailey's wife, is a librarian in George's alternate reality.

THE LIBRARIAN: QUEST FOR THE SPEAR (2004). A TNT ORIGINAL
MOVIE DISTRIBUTED BY WARNER BROTHERS. DVD RELEASE
DATE 2005. 106 MINUTES. LIST PRICE: $19.95.

What do you get if you make a librarian the hero in a *Raiders of the Lost Ark* type movie? You've got it! In this case Noah Wyle (from the television show *ER*) plays "The Librarian" at the Metropolitan Library, whose secret collection include legendary artifacts such as Pandora's Box and Excalibur. When the bad guys steal the Spear of Destiny, Wyle uses his knowledge to track down the bad guys and retrieve the spear. He's aided by a female action-type hero in the form of Sonya Walger. Bob Newhart and Jane Curtin also appear as fellow librarians.

Many librarians panned the movie after its initial airing on TNT. It was criticized as moronic, silly, and an inaccurate portrayal of librarians. But let's face it — the film was not intended to be a serious, accurate portrayal of librarians. It was meant to be entertainment, and it certainly is fun entertainment. Just the idea of a librarian being the action hero using his brain instead of his brawn is reason enough for this film to be a welcome gift. It's a fun action-packed film. Plus, don't we wish a lot of male librarians were as cute as Noah Wyle?

THE MUMMY (1999). MCA HOME VIDEO. DVD RELEASE
DATE 1999. 125 MINUTES. LIST PRICE: $14.95.

THE MUMMY RETURNS (2001). MCA HOME VIDEO. DVD RELEASE
DATE 2001. 130 MINUTES. LIST PRICE: @12.98.

What librarian can dislike a movie where a librarian helps save the world? In *The Mummy*, Brendan Fraser (*George of the Jungle, Bedazzled*), a hunky treasure hunter, rogue, and ex-soldier teams up with Rachel Weisz (*Runaway Jury, Constant Gardener*), an Egyptologist and librarian, to find the lost city of Hamunaptra. They find the city, but unknowingly bring a mummy, Imhotep, back to life. Imhotep begins to unleash evil upon the world and only Fraser and Weisz can stop him.

In *The Mummy Returns*, the mummy is once again brought back to life. Fraser and Weisz are now married with a son. The mummy kidnaps their son, which sets them on a quest to retrieve their son and once again try to defeat the mummy.

THE MUSIC MAN (1962). WARNER HOME VIDEO. DVD RELEASE
DATE 1999. 151 MINUTES. LIST PRICE: $19.95.

Aficionados of musicals will enjoy receiving a copy of this film. Starring Robert Preston *(Victor/Victoria)* as the music man/con man, this movie features all those memorable songs such as "Seventy-six Trombones" and "Gary, Indiana." And Shirley Jones as the old maid librarian Marian made "Marian the Librarian" a household term. This is a great gift, especially for those librarians who were born after the movie was released.

PARTY GIRL (1995). SONY PICTURES. DVD RELEASE DATE 2003.
94 MINUTES. LIST PRICE: $19.95.

This fluffy comedy features Parker Posey (*Waiting for Guffman*), as Mary, a young girl whose party lifestyle eventually lands her in jail and broke. So whom does she call for bail money, but a librarian, who happens to be her godmother. To pay back the bail money, Mary is forced to work as a library clerk at the public library. As you can image, at first this is a fate no party girl ever wants to endure. But eventually Mary tackles the Dewey Decimal System and transforms into a super library clerk. And of course there's some romance for her in the film as well.

For the Practical Side

Maybe it's an occupational hazard, but I know many librarians who are pack rats, myself included. For all those librarians whose home and offices are cluttered with too much stuff (excuse me — I mean potentially useful or valuable items), it's wise to think about purchasing a practical gift for them. Forget about the paperweight, trinket, cardholder and other stuff that will add to the clutter on a desk or shelf. Give them a useful gift that is less likely to end up in the recycle bin the next time they do a massive cleaning. Here are a few ideas.

APRONS

For librarians who prefer a sensible gift while displaying their pride in the profession, you can purchase an apron for them. Great for everyday use in the kitchen or for those occasional outdoor barbecues, these midlength aprons provide wonderful protection from all those cooking splashes and splatters. They even feature a handy bottom pouch for those cooking utensils, recipes and other things you want to keep at hand while cooking. The aprons are machine washable and made of 35 percent cotton and 65 percent polyester twill. If you're uncertain about your librarian's cooking abilities, you may want to purchase an apron with "Trust Me! I'm a Librarian" (product #40558909) printed on the front of it for $18.99. At least everyone will know that the person cooking can definitely read a cookbook!

Or, you may want to purchase an apron with a reproduction of the color cover of a 1960 book by Carla Green titled *I Want to Be a Librarian* (product #10715173) selling for $14.99. Aprons with an attitude are also available such as one featuring a rubber "Smite" stamp in the middle of a flame. Below the graphic it reads "Librarian Avengers" (product #26034401). This apron sells for $17.99. Both aprons can be ordered online at www.cafepress.com or by calling (877) 809–1659.

LIGHT SWITCH COVERS

For those librarians who seem to have everything, chances are they don't have light switch covers displaying their love of books or the profession. A practical gift for those "hard to buy for" librarians or a perfect white elephant gift or a secret Santa gift, light switch covers are available in a variety of different designs. Each single switch cover measures 3.5"×5" with a center switch slot measuring $^{15}\!/_{16}$"×$^{7}\!/_{16}$". The covers mount flush against the wall.

Cover designs include simple statements, such as "There's no such thing as too many books" with each of the words appearing in a different color (product #34151952, $10.99) and statements with simple graphics. For example, you can select a cover with a horizontal blue box in the middle of the frame with "Reading Is Sexy" across the top of the box and an open grey book lying below the words (product #38424738, $11.19), or a cover with "Book Addict and Proud of It!" running down the side and bottom of the frame, with a color graphic of a stack of books in the center (product #35035394, $7.99).

Or, you can select a cover with simply a graphic image on it, such as a Victorian era woman sitting in a chair reading a book (product #40482177, $9.99) or a 1940s era pinup girl sitting reading a book with her legs extended showing the garters holding up her nylons (product #29692978, $9.99). These and other light switch covers can be ordered online at www.cafepress.com or by calling (877) 809–1659.

PET COLLARS WITH DEWEY CLASSIFICATION NUMBER

I'm not sure what it says about the profession when you can purchase a pet collar displaying the appropriate Dewey decimal number on it! But for those catalogers you know who catalog and classify their home collection of books and own pets, these pet collars are bound to be appreciated and put to good use. These blue collars, with embroidered color designs and the Dewey classification number on them, feature a side release and a metal D-ring for the leash. The dog collar is ¾" wide and is available in three sizes, small (adjusting from 9" to 14" long), medium (adjusting from 12" to 20" long), and large (adjusting from 18" to 32" long). The cat collar is ½" wide and adjusts from 7" to 11" long. The cat collar sells for $14 and the dog collar for $16. And if you don't remember your Dewey Decimal Classification System, the Dewey number on the cat collar is 636.8 and 636.7 on the dog collar. Both are available for purchase from the American Library Association, 50 E. Huron St., Chicago, IL 60611, (800) 545–2433, www.alastore.ala.org. American Library Association members receive a discounted price.

DOG T-SHIRTS

For librarian dog owners, there's even a white dog T-shirt available with the Dewey number "636.7" in black on the back of the shirt (product #45930637, $14.99). Or for a more playful shirt, you can purchase a dog shirt with a color image of a dog sitting and reading a book (product #29271353, $18.99). These and other styles can be purchased online at www.cafepress.com or by calling (877) 809–1659.

For Paper Lovers

Technology is wonderful. But most of us still cannot live without paper in our lives. In certain cases, paper may be preferred over technology. When computers and other handheld items weigh no more than a 3"×5" notepad, don't require a manual, have self-generated power, and are indestructible, I'll give up my pen and paper. Below are some items designed for all those librarians who still love pen and paper.

Calendars

Calendars are usually a lovely, useful, and "not too personal" gift for your favorite librarian. At least, that's true for the last two calendars listed below. The same can't be said for the first one.

MEN OF TEXAS LIBRARIES

You've seen the calendars featuring hot firemen. But you probably haven't seen this calendar featuring the men of Texas libraries! The men featured in this eighteen month calendar are members of the Texas Library Association. The calendar is bound to bring a smile to every librarian who receives a copy. It's a humorous celebration of men who work in libraries. Printed in full color on glossy stock, the calendar is produced by the Association, and it benefits the association's Library Disaster Relief Fund. So if you need a good reason to explain your purchase of the calendar to co-workers who see it hanging in your office, you can tell them it was purchased in support of a good cause! For a sneak peak at the calendar and ordering information, go to www.txla.org/temp/TLAmen.html.

LIBRARIANS DESK CALENDAR

Designed for librarians, this month per sheet calendar features celebrations and other important dates of interest to librarians. From National Library Week and National Library Card Sign-Up Month to famous authors' birthdays and dates of major library conferences, librarians will find this calendar an indispensable reference tool. This 17"×22" calendar also provides ample space in each daily 2½"×3" square for notes and other jottings. It sells for only $11.95 and is available from Upstart, W5527 State Road 106, PO Box 800, Fort Atkinson, WI 53538–0800, (800) 448–4887, www.highsmith.com.

RENAISSANCE LIBRARY CALENDAR

For librarians and anyone who appreciates the interior beauty of some of the world's finest library buildings, the photographs in this calendar will leave you breathless. Each month features the interior of a famous historical library. The photos differ from year to year. In 2006, some of the libraries featured include the Library at the Abbey of Lilienfeld in Austria (1202), the Canterbury Cathedral Library in the United Kingdom (597 AD), the Trolleholm Castle Library in Sweden (late 18th century), the Palafoxiana Library in Puebla, Mexico (1646), and the Library Company of Philadelphia, in the United States (1731). The calendar sells for $12.95. But please note that the calendar is shipped from Sweden, so the shipping cost will be higher than what you're accustomed to paying for materials shipped from within the United States. The calendar is a product of Information Strategy & Information Management, Torsvagen 7b, 192 67 Sollentuna, Sweden, +46 8754 15 55. It can be ordered online at www.renaissancelibrary.com. Since words cannot describe the beauty of the libraries photographed, be sure to take the time to view the calendar photos online.

Duster Pens

Forget those old pens that hang from a cord around your neck. They may be practical, but they're far from fun. Duster pens are perfect gifts because they're useful and can bring a smile to any librarian's day. You'll have to take a peek at these on the Tease website (www.teasecatalog.com). Measuring approximately 6¼" from the footed base to the top of the duster, these shapely pens take on the caricature of a wide-eyed librarian with the duster brush serving as the hair. You can purchase a purple pen with the inscription "Harriet, the 'Harried' Librarian." A white pen with a black-footed base and black duster bearing the inscription "Hartley, The Reference Librarian" is available. And last, but not least, is a light blue pen with the inscription "Hannah, The Librarian Assistant." These pens are not only good for writing and dusting, but there's also a slot in the pen's mouth to hold messages. A true multitasking librarian pen! For only $6 each, you'll want the entire set. The pens can be purchased from Tease, 8570 Commerce St. #113, Cape Canaveral, FL 32920 (800) 416–0548, www.teasecatalog.com.

Journals

BAD LIBRARIANS

"Bad" librarians can record their thoughts in an unlined 5"×8" spiral bound journal whose cover features a sexy young woman in a short strapless evening dress and heels sprawled across a book. The caption reads: "For a well-rounded education, you could try curling up with good books and bad librarians"—Richard Needham. To see what the cover looks like, you can cruise on over to Molly Dolan's Girl-ish.com website. The journal (product #10965319) sells for $12.49 online at www.cafepress.com or by calling 1–877–809–1659.

Note Cards

"BOOK LOVERS NEVER GO TO BED ALONE!"

On the front of the card above this caption is a drawing of a person in bed reading a book. This black and white card is available in two versions, one with a woman in bed (product #20271026), and one with a man in bed (product #20271361). A packet of six cards of either version is available for $14.99 and can be ordered online at www.cafepress.com or by calling (877) 809–1659. You can view the cards at www.cafepress.com/readersshop.

"CHECK OUT YOUR LIBRARIAN"

Forget the frumpy shoes. From a red miniskirt a long pair of sexy legs extend diagonally across the front of this card. The librarian is sitting on top of a computer with books resting nearby. Her red high heels and red skirt are a stark contrast against the rest of this black and white card. "Check Out Your Librarian" appears in the right corner of the card. Brought to you by the Reader's Shop, a package of six cards (product #19912908) sells for $14.99 and can be ordered online at www.cafepress.com or by calling (877) 809–1659. You can view the card at www.cafepress.com/readersshop.

"I Love My Library"

A perfect gift for librarians who truly love their libraries, these top-fold white cards feature red and black hearts at the beginning and end of the message of "I Love My Library" on the front. A package of six cards sells for $14.99 (product #20133763) and can be ordered online at www.cafepress.com or by calling (877) 809–1659. You can see what the card looks like at www.cafepress.com/readersshop.

Lazy Lions

Lions in the library? Yes. Two lions lounging inside the library grace the front of these full-color note cards. They're framed by a green border and the back of the card is green. Measuring 6¼"×4½" and accompanied by matching green envelopes, a pack of 25 cards sells for $19. American Library Association members receive a discounted price. Available for purchase from the American Library Association, 50 E. Huron St., Chicago, IL 60611, (866) 746–7252, www.alastore.ala.org.

Librarians and Cocktails

Dispelling the old shoddy image of the librarian, these note cards feature a sexy librarian in a red cocktail dress with a low-cut back, holding a martini glass and smiling provocatively as she looks over her shoulder at the reader. The front of the card is black and white, except for the red dress, and it reads: "Perhaps the two most valuable and satisfactory products of American civilization are the librarian on the one hand and the cocktail in the other."—Louis Stanley Jast. Brought to you by the Reader's Shop, a package of six cards (product #201089840) sells for $14.99 and can be ordered online at www.cafepress.com or by calling (877) 809–1659. You can view the card at www.cafepress.com/readersshop.

"Libraries: An Investment for Life!"

To help your favorite librarian advocate for libraries, you may want to consider purchasing a package of these cards for her use. A brick-colored colonial-style library with a green roof graces the cover of the card. Above the library appears the word "Libraries" and below the library appears "An Investment for Life!" The words appear in green ink, curiously, the same color as money! A packet of six cards sells for $14.99 (product #19926579) and can be ordered online at www.cafepress.com or by calling (877) 809–1659. You can see what the card looks like at www.cafepress.com/readersshop.

Multilingual "Read" Notecards

If you ever wondered what the word for "read" was in other languages, these note cards are for you. The word "read" is displayed on the front in over 20 languages, including Hawaiian, Urdu, Swahili, Navajo, Wolof, Spanish and Chinese. A package of 25 of these 6¼"×4½" cards sells for $19. American Library Association members receive a discounted price. Available for purchase from the American Library Association, 50 E. Huron St., Chicago, IL 60611, (866) 746–7252, www.alastore.ala.org.

RENAISSANCE LIBRARY GREETING CARDS

Any librarian or library user will appreciate this collection of color note cards highlighting some of the world's loveliest libraries. The cards, measuring 8.27"×5.85" when folded (the fold is at the top of the card), feature a grand library on the front and information on the library's construction date, architect, and history is provided on the back. The set of 12 cards sells for only $24.95 and contains one card of each of the following libraries: 1) Abbey Library, St. Gallen, Switzerland, 1758; 2) Abbey Library, Waldassen, Germany, 1585; 3) Cathedral Library, Freising, Germany, 1734; 4) Chetham's Library, Mancheseter, UK, 1653; 5) Library of Parliament, Ottawa, Canada, 1876; 6) Library of the Sorbonne, Paris, France, 1897; 7) Marsh's Library, Dublin, Ireland, 1701; 8) National Library of Russia, St. Petersburg, Russia, 1795; 9) National Library of the Czech Republic, Prague, Czech Republic, 1727; 10) Parliamentary Library, Wellington, New Zealand, 1899; 11) Royal College of Physicians of Edinburg, New Library, UK, 1682; 12) Vilnius University Library, Vilnius, Lithuania, 1570.

These cards are shipped from Sweden so the shipping cost will be higher than what you're accustomed to paying for materials shipped from within the United States. The note cards are products of Information Strategy & Information Management, Torsvagen 7b, 192 67 Sollentuna, Sweden, +46 8754 15 55. The prints can be ordered online at www.renaissancelibrary.com.

"SUPER LIBRARIAN"

She travels the world to make sure the truth is never hidden. Dressed in her purple superhero outfit with a purple- and gold-lined cape, she's surfing on top of her computer mouse and she is "Super Librarian." Developed by the New Jersey State Library, she graces the cover of two different note cards. The first card, printed portrait style, bears a gold background and the words "Super Librarian" across the top above her picture (product #14589550). The other card, printed with a landscape, shows Super Librarian in the bottom right corner of the card. It reads "No Boundaries. No Limits. Know Your Library" (product # 14500498). Both cards are printed on coated glossy paper. A package of six cards sells for $11.99 and can be ordered online at www.cafepress.com or by calling (877) 809–1659. You can see what the cards look like by going to www.superlibrarian.com.

"TAKE ME TO YOUR LIBRARY!"

Perfect for anyone who enjoys science fiction, the front of the card features a green alien wearing a blue space suit with yellow detailing, who beckons you to take him to the library. Brought to you by the Reader's Shop, a package of six cards (product #20157118) sells for $14.99 and can be ordered online at www.cafepress.com or by calling (877) 809–1659. You can view the card at www.cafepress.com/readersshop.

Note Pads

For a useful gift, try a notepad with a logo designed for librarians. You can purchase white imprinted 100-sheet pads for $5 each. The pads measure 4.24"×5.5" and are available with the following imprints:

- "I Love Librarians" (a red heart is used for the word "Love")
- "Donde esta la biblioteca? Ou est la bibliotheque? Wo ist die Bibliothek? Huor er biblioteket? (Where's the library in an Asian language script) The most important question in any language."
- "Queen of Circulation" (a drawing of a queen appears to the right of the imprint)
- "Queen of Cataloging" (a drawing of a queen appears to the right of the imprint)
- "Queen of Processing" (a drawing of a queen appears to the right of the imprint)

(Sorry guys, there's no King of Circulation, Cataloging or Processing notepads.)

- "It's Library, not Liberry"
- "Librarians Do it Between the Covers" with a drawing of an open book, pages down above the words
- "Librarian" running vertical down the lower left side of the pad with each letter of the word starting the following list of words: "Libertarian, Independent, Bold, Revolutionary, Adventurous, Renegade, Individualist, Audacious, Nonconformist"
- "Librarian" running vertical down the lower left side of the pad with each letter of the word starting the following list of words: Loveable, Intelligent, Beautiful, Radiant, Amazing, Remarkable, Interesting, Astounding, Novel"
- A drawing of a tombstone reading "Marian the Librarian 1962–2003 R.I.P." and below the grave marker it reads "We Killed Marian."

The note pads can be ordered from Tease, 8570 Commerce St. #113, Cape Canaveral, FL 32920, (800) 416–0548, www.teasecatalog.com.

Postcards

BAD LIBRARIANS

Forget the old spinster librarian! These 4"×6" glossy postcards feature a sexy young woman in a short, strapless evening dress and heels sprawled across a book. The caption reads: "For a well-rounded education, you could try curling up with good books and bad librarians"—Richard Needham. The postcard can be viewed on Molly Dolan's Girl-ish.com website. A pack of eight postcards can be purchased for only $10.99 online at www.cafepress.com or by calling (877) 809–1659. A package of eight greeting cards is also available for $15.99 (product #10965327).

"Librarians Give It Away for Free"

We all know that information is free and accessible at your local public library. But if you like postcards with a little twist on that fact, check out these black and white postcards featuring the drawing of the head of a female librarian next to the words "Librarians Give It Away for Free!" on the front. A package of eight of these 6"×4" postcards (product #26676757) sells for $8.99 and can be purchased online at www.cafepress.com or by calling (877) 809–1659.

Gift Cards

Book Cards

Who can resist a set of gift cards with a book on them? Definitely not librarians. Sold in packs of four, these gift cards from the American Library Association are adorned with a gold open book on the front of the card, with a matching golden border. These die-cut, foil-embossed cards measure 3¼"×3¼" (too small to send through the U.S. mail) and are accompanied by white envelopes. Selling for $4.50 a pack, they're available for purchase from the American Library Association, 50 E. Huron St., Chicago, IL 60611, (866) 746–7252, www.alastore.ala.org.

Holiday Greeting Cards

"Seasons Readings"

The American Library Association sells the perfect holiday cards for use by librarians. These bright red three-fold cards proclaim "Season's Readings." The cards measure 4⅜"×6" with a pack of 25 cards selling for $19. American Library Association Members receive a discounted price. Available for purchase from the American Library Association, 50 E. Huron St., Chicago, IL 60611, (866) 746–7252, www.alastore.ala.org.

Glitz and Gold

Giving jewelry is just as pleasurable as receiving it. Even librarians love a little "bling." Whether it's 14-karat gold or gold plated, jewelry with a book or reading theme is sure to be a welcome gift by any librarian. Remember, it's the thought that counts!

Earrings

Blue Book Earrings

If you're looking for an artistic pair of earrings, check out this offering from Bas Bleu (www.basbleu.com). These sterling silver pierced earrings hold a pale blue rectangular shaped blue chalcedony stone. Are they shaped like books? Since art is in the eye of the beholder, go check out the picture of these earrings on the vendor's website and you be the judge. Whether or not you think they look like books, these earrings are definitely eye catching! They're available for $59.95 (item #4299) from Bas Bleu, PO Box 93326, Atlanta, GA 30377–0326, www.basbleu.com, (800) 433–1155.

14K Book Earrings

For an elegant gift for that special librarian, think 14-karat gold book earrings. These "open book" pierced earrings are available in two sizes. The small size (⅜"×⁷⁄₁₆") sells for $70, while the larger size (½"×¹¹⁄₁₆") sells for $90. A matching necklace is also available. The earrings and necklace can be purchased from Tease, 8570 Commerce St. #113, Cape Canaveral, FL 32920, (800) 416–0548, www.tease-catalog.com.

Sterling Silver Book Earrings

A sterling silver version of the 14K gold earrings listed above, a small pair sells for $45, and the larger pair sells for $55. A matching sterling silver necklace is also available. These items can be purchased from Tease, 8570 Commerce St. #113, Cape Canaveral, FL 32920, (800) 416–0548, www.teasecatalog.com.

Necklaces

14K Book Pendant Set

Fine jewelry is always a great gift. This 14K gold "open book" set includes an 18" Guicci link chain with a ½"×¹¹⁄₁₆" book charm and a pair of small (⅜"×⁷⁄₁₆") pierced book earrings. The set sells for $165. If you want, you can order the set with larger (½"×¹¹⁄₁₆") earrings that are identical to the size of the charm. The larger set sells for $190. These items can be ordered from Tease, 8570 Commerce St. #113, Cape Canaveral, FL 32920, (800) 416–0548, www.teasecatalog.com.

Sterling Silver Book Pendant Set

A sterling silver version of the small 14K pendant set listed above is available for $100. A set containing the larger earrings sells for $110. These items can be ordered from Tease, 8570 Commerce St. #113, Cape Canaveral, FL 32920, (800) 416–0548, www.teasecatalog.com.

"Read" Necklace

Four square silver-colored beads spelling "READ" adorn a 24" nickel-plated brass bead chain. A wonderful inexpensive gift for yourself, a librarian or a reader you know. The necklace can be purchased for $6.95 from Upstart, PO Box 800, Fort Atkinson, WI 53538–0800, (800) 448–4887, www.highsmith.com.

Bracelets

"READ" BRACELET

Profess your love of reading with a bracelet with squares featuring books and the word "READ" printed on plastic set in epoxy in a silver-tone frame. Featuring an elastic band, the bracelet sells for $9.95 and is available from Upstart, PO Box 800, Fort Atkinson, WI 53538–0800, (800) 448–4887, www.highsmith.com.

Pins

BOOKS PIN

A collage of little books and book stacks in silver, bronze, and brass-plated metal, this broach features a safety clasp and sells for $14.50. The pin is available from Homeroom, PO Box 388, Centerbrook, CT 06409–0388, (800) 222–8270, www.homeroomdirect.com.

"BORN TO READ" PIN

If reading is your passion, here's a pin for you. Against a heart-shaped background are the words "Born to Read." Plated in 24K gold, this ½" pin is available for $6 from the American Library Association, 50 E. Huron St., Chicago, IL 60611, (866) 746–7252, www.alastore.ala.org.

ENAMEL LIBRARIAN PIN

Show how you love being a librarian with this blue enameled pin. Across the top of the pin it reads "love (a red heart is used for the word "love") being your" and the word "Librarian" is along the bottom of the pin. In the center is a librarian reading to three children. For only $2.00 each, you'll want to order it for all your coworkers as well. It's available from Apples, Angels & More, 2148 16th Avenue SW, Largo, FL 33770 by calling (800) 441–8600 or by ordering online at www.applesangelsandmore.com.

FILIGREE BOOK PIN

This gold-plated pin displays an intricate filigree pattern. Seeing it immediately triggers thoughts of the elegance of yesteryear. "Adapted from a nineteenth century silver card case," this gorgeous pin will become a favorite piece in any librarian's jewelry box. Selling for $22.50 (item #6422), it can be ordered from Bas Bleu, PO Box 93326, Atlanta, GA 30377–0326, (800) 433–1155, www.bassbleu.com.

LIBRARY PIN

Featuring a one-story building with a "Library" sign on it, this handcrafted 1 ½" sterling silver pin features brass and copper accents. It's available for $29.95 from Homeroom, PO Box 388, Centerbrook, CT 06409–0388, (800) 222–8270, www.homeroomdirect.com.

"Read" Artistic Pin

This artistic, goldtone pin has a pair of eyes above the word "Read" with a dangling book charm. It measures 1½". If you take the time to look at this unique pin on the vendor's website, you'll fall in love with it. Selling for under $5, it can be viewed and purchased from Homeroom, PO Box 388, Centerbrook, CT 06409–0388, (800) 222–8270, www.homeroomdirect.com.

"Read" Oblong Lapel Pin

This 1½" long pin has the word "Read" in bold lettering in red. It's available with a black or blue background. It sells for $8 with members of the American Library Association receiving a discount. Purchase this item from the American Library Association, 50 E. Huron St., Chicago, IL 60611, (866) 746–7252, www.ala-store.ala.org.

"Read" (Books)

The word "Read" appears over a background of four books on this pin. It has a safety clasp and sells for $13.95. The pin is available from Homeroom, PO Box 388, Centerbrook, CT 06409–0388, (800) 222–8270, www.homeroomdirect.com.

For Car Lovers

Automobile aficionados are found in all professions. Librarians are no exception. So here are some gift ideas for that librarian/automobile aficionado.

License Plate Frames

Occupational

Librarians proud of their profession can display that pride as they cruise down the highway. Whether the car is a ten-year-old economy car, or a jazzy new sports car, these license plate frames will make a statement. Constructed of chromed steel and measuring 12"×6", the graphics are applied with permanent adhesive waterproof decals. Selling for under $15 each, they can be purchased online at www.cafe-press.com. Frames are available with the following statements:

- Proud to Be a Librarian (product #39871632)
- Librarians Possess Novel Information (product #40796808)
- Trust Me! I'm a Librarian (product #40558903)
- Radical Militant Librarian (product #41247347)
- Cyber Librarian (product #31065267)

For parents who are proud of their child's profession, there's a license plate frame with the statement "Proud Parent of a Librarian" (product #44224569). And for library school students, there's "Librarian in Training" (product #8242613) and "I Want to Be a Librarian" (product #8242368).

And for librarians who really take pride in their profession, there's a special plate frame just for them. Measuring 12"×6" and made from chromed steel, this frame has black lettering that reads "Nobody Knows I'm a Librarian" on the top and on the bottom "Celebrate Librarian Pride." The words on the bottom of the plate are blue, red, and then purple. Selling for $11.99, this frame (product #45066755) can also be ordered online at www.cafepress.com or by calling (877) 809–1659.

PROCLAIM YOUR LOVE OF BOOKS

A black plastic license plate frame measuring 12¼"×6¼" with the words "I'd Rather Be Reading" in white on the bottom of the frame sells for only $3.95. The frame can be ordered from Upstart, PO Box 800, Fort Atkinson, WI 53538–0800, (800) 448–4887, www.highsmith.com.

PROMOTING READING AND BOOKS

For librarians who like being a leader in promoting libraries and reading while driving down the roadways, the American Library Association offers a white license plate frame with red lettering reading "Follow Me to the Library" on the top of the frame, and "Read" on the lower portion of the frame. Selling for only $6, American Library Association members receive a discount off this low price. The frame can be ordered from the American Library Association, 50 E. Huron St., Chicago, IL 60611, (866) 746–7252, www.alastore.ala.org.

Magic Dash Mat

If you think your favorite librarian has everything, he or she probably doesn't have a nifty skid-proof dash mat for the car. The mat is designed so that it sticks to the dashboard without the use of adhesive or magnets, and you can place your cell phone, sunglasses and other item on it and they won't slip off while you're driving. Measuring 6¾"×4", the mat bears a drawing of a tombstone reading "Marian the Librarian 1962–2003 R.I.P." The logo below it reads "We Killed Marian." This makes a nifty gift for only $6. The mat is available for purchase from Tease, 8570 Commerce St. #113, Cape Canaveral, FL, 32920 (800) 416–0548, www.teasecatalog.com.

Special Gifts

The most memorable gifts are frequently those that don't come from a department store. These special gifts may or may not be material items. Here are some ideas for special gifts for that favorite librarian.

Weekend at the Library Hotel (New York)

A stay at this themed hotel will definitely be a memorable gift for that special librarian. The hotel is a 1900 landmark brownstone that features ten guest floors, with each floor dedicated to one of the ten major categories of the Dewey Decimal System. Each guest room is designed to resemble a gentleman's library with art and books that relate to the theme of the guest room. For instance, on the floor dedicated to literature, there's a themed room for poetry, another for the classics, etc.

The hotel offers complimentary refreshments throughout the day, a complimentary evening wine and cheese reception, complimentary access to the hotel's video library of the American Film Institute's top 100 films. And for guests who are tired of reading in their rooms, the hotel also features a greenhouse known as the Poetry Garden, and a paneled room with a fireplace known as the Writers Den. Both make excellent places to read a good book.

The icing on the cake is that the Library Hotel is close to both the New York Public Library and the Pierpont Morgan Library. The hotel is located on Madison Avenue and 41st Street. This is the perfect hotel for those librarians who just can't stand to be away from a library for very long. Room rates range from approximately $225 to $475 per night. (The Library Hotel, 299 Madison Ave., New York, NY 10017, (877) 793–7323, www.libraryhotel.com.)

Library Gifts

The next time you need to buy a gift for that librarian who has everything or receive a wedding invitation where both the bride and groom to be are librarians, consider a not-so-ordinary gift. Libraries never seem to have a sufficient budget for the purchase of books and other materials needed in the library. That's why there are so many Friends of the Library and Library Foundations out there to help support and provide additional funding to their local library.

So forget giving that toaster or other fancy paperweight as a gift. Instead, purchase and give multiple copies of that new bestseller the library needs to the librarian's library. Or purchase and give the library those new bean bag chairs or plastic book bags the children's section needs. Or better yet, just make a donation to the library's Foundation or Friends of the Library in honor of that special librarian. The gift is tax deductible and will be used and appreciated by potentially thousands of library users.

If you're a librarian who doesn't need another reading light or planner, the next time you're approaching another birthday, you can start dropping those hints about a donation to your Friends of the Library as the perfect thoughtful gift. Or, if you're about to get married again, or for the first time, think about creating a wedding gift registry with a list of all the books and other materials needed by your library.

9

The Ideal Librarian

Through the years much has been written on what a model librarian should be like. Surprisingly, literature from the late 1800s and early 1900s often identify librarian traits and abilities that are still relevant to today's librarians. However, you may disagree with some of the desired skills and traits. But read on and then make your own judgment.

The Librarian

The following appeared in chapter 4 of the *A.L.A. Library Primer,* which was printed in *Public Libraries,* v. 1, no. 1, May 1896, p. 7.

The librarian should have culture, scholarship, and executive ability. He should keep always in advance of his community, and constantly educate it to make greater demands upon him. He should be a leader and a teacher, earnest, enthusiastic, and intelligent. He should be able to win the confidence of children, and wise to lead them by easy steps from good books to the best. He has the greatest opportunity of any teacher in the community. He should be the teacher of teachers. He should make the library a school for the young, a college for adults, and the constant center of such educational activity as will make wholesome and inspiring themes the burden of the common thought. He should be enough of a bookworm to have a decided taste and fondness for books, and at the same time not enough to be a recluse and so lose sight of the point of view of those who know little of books.

As the responsible head of the institution, he should be consulted in all matters relating to its management. The most satisfactory results are obtained in those libraries where the chief librarian is permitted to appoint assistants, select books, buy supplies, make regulations, and decide methods of cataloging, classifying, and lending; all subject to the approval of the trustees. Trustees should impose responsibility, grant freedom, and exact results.

An Ideal Librarian appeared in Public Libraries, *v. 5, no. 9, November 1900, p. 399.*

The perfect librarian is a subjective being, and moves more within than without the world of books that surrounds him. He is subdued to the reverence of what he works in, and has the student's perceptions, discreet and catholic. He helps to create the ambient with which a library should be permeated, and even to those who have no feeling for the right spirit of the place his manners and personality are an instruction, unconsciously absorbed, and leading them to a humaner attitude. In short, the most precious qualifications that a librarian can have are precisely such as cannot be taught; exactly as is the case with teachers, and very notably with teachers of the primary grades of education, whose true efficiency is dependent upon some priceless personal gifts which are wholly incommunicable.—-Scribner's magazine, The point of view.

The Up-to-Date Librarian

The following was part of a report of a library meeting that appeared in *Public Libraries*, v. 6, no. 4, April 1901, p. 217.

Miss Marvin, of the Library commission, then gave a most interesting talk on The up-to-date librarian.

Miss Marvin said that the up-to-date librarian must have, besides her knowledge of books, and her technical training, a business training; she must be, first of all, a practical business woman. For the up-to-date librarian is a woman. She must have tact and must adjust herself to her community, accepting the conditions and making the best of them.

She must be a good housekeeper, keeping the books in order and mended, and the rooms clean and attractive. And up-to-date building has a study-room, a conversation room, and a children's room — open shelves. The up-to-date library has an annotated catalog.

But Is There Such a Being as a Model Librarian?

The following excerpt is from "Dual Control of Libraries and Museums," by A.H. Millar, LLD, chief librarian, Dundee. Read at the Dunfermline Meeting of the Scottish Library Association, June 1, 1910. *The Librarian: The Independent Professional Journal for the Professional Man*, v. 1, no. 2, September 1910

But is there such a being as a Model Librarian? Consider what are his requisite qualifications. He must know all the literature which thousands of years have accumulated, upon every conceivable subject. The lore of ancient Egypt must be as familiar to him as the most recent sex-problem novel. He should be able to direct the students to the best sources of information upon the infinite topics embraced within the range of Ancient and Modern History. He ought to know the latest pronouncements in Medical Science, Philosophy, Literature, Biography, Natural History, Psychology, local events, and the countless other themes that haunt the readers in a Public Library. The mere choice of books in different departments of Science and Art must have exercised his powers to an extreme degree; and thus he ought to be familiar with the last word on Science, Art, and Letters. Surely one so accomplished might easily take up the additional duties required from the Curators of a Museum or Picture Gallery! If there be doubtful points raised in either Science or Art, the Librarian ought to know the best sources for information and guidance. His knowledge of books must be encyclopedic, and he will turn with ease and alacrity to the works which are accepted as authoritative. Evidently it would be too much to expect the Scientist of the Art-Connoissseur to have such an intimate acquaintance with books on all subjects such as intimate acquaintance with books on all subjects as that which the Librarian, in the exercise of his profession, must have acquired. When there is need to make a choice between the three officials the Librarian's claims to superiority are overwhelming; and until the Rate is sufficient to provide three experts in Literature, Science, and Art, the Librarian must exercise full control. He alone can apportion the Rate at his disposal so that each of the three Institutions under his charge shall have its due and adequate share.

Librarianship as a Profession

"Librarianship as a Profession," by Katharine L. Sharp initially appeared in *Public Libraries: A Monthly Review of Library Matters and Methods*, v. 3, no. 1, May 1898, pp. 5–7.

A gentleman of experience was asked what was needed to fit the inquirer for a librarian's position, and whether the profession was remunerative. He replied as follows:

My dear young friend, if you want all the conceit, natural and acquired, taken out of you, by all means adopt the librarian's profession. As for requirements for librarianship, the following desiderata may be of use to you. You will find that in addition to whatever store of knowledge you possess, you must know not only all that you ought to know, but what everybody else ought to know besides. You will find it convenient to be able to tell anyone whatever he wants to know on any given subject, and where to find all important references to it. You will need to have the bibliography of every subject at your tongue's end; to know what books have been published in any country from the time of Caxton down to the present day; to know what books are to be published and when; to know what books are out of print and what not. You will have to be familiar with the name of every writer and every noted character in all ages. Furthermore, you will have to be such an acute mind reader that you can infallibly distinguish the right person under the wrong name; to know for example, that when one asks for Silliman's travels in South America, he means Schlieman's Ilios or Troja. Moreover, you must be able to tell the authorship of any extract, prose or poetry, in any language, and where to find it; to know the author of any poem, the correct rendering of any phrase and by whom first used, and, if in a foreign language, the meaning in addition; to know definitely all about history, genealogy, and heraldry.

In short, you must be a combined edition of the encyclopedia, the dictionary, the dictionary of phrase and fable, the universal history, the bibliographer's manual, and general biography.

Then, my dear young friend, when you know all this thoroughly, you stand a pretty good chance of being able to answer correctly one question a day out of several hundred!

This ought to appeal to the budding ambition of a college senior. Here is a new world to conquer, a new profession to enter. It appears to legal, medical, domestic, and above all to philanthropic instincts. It is a true profession and so recognized. It is a profession in which there is not only room at the top, but all along the ladder. It now leads to the degree of Bachelor of Library Science at the University of the state of New York, and this degree represents as much professional work as a doctor's or a lawyer's degree, covering two years of technical instruction beyond college work. It is raising instead of lowering the value of degrees, and we are far from the danger predicted by a New York senator that the University would next be turning out Bachelors of Hemstitching.

The New York state senator was only one of the great majority who wonder what there is to study in library work, who think it just so easy to hand the book out over the counter, and who envy the fortunate librarian who can read all the new books.

Alas! for the fortunate librarian. Tradition has already decreed that the librarian who reads I lost, and most library trustees have further guarded him, ruling that no new books shall be loaned to the library staff. Conditions in library work are rapidly changing, but sometimes begrudged them to others. The over-praised modern librarian knows his books, but sometimes begrudged them to others. The over-praised modern librarian knows his methods, but often misses the goal through his zeal in administering them. The day has passed when a fugitive from justice can take refuge in a library reading room without fear of detection. The library is a laboratory, a workshop, a school, a university of the people, from which the students are never graduated.

It is the library as a neglected factor in education which appeals to college graduates. Their peculiar fitness has been comprehensively stated by the faculty of the New York state library school, who say: We greatly prefer college-bred men and women in selecting new librarians.
1. Because they are a picked class, selected from the best material throughout the country.
2. Because the college training has given them a wider culture and broader view with a considerable fund of information; all of which will be valuable working material in a library as almost anywhere else.
3. Because a four years' course of successfully completed is the strongest voucher for persistent purpose and mental and physical capacity for protracted intellectual work.
4. Chiefly because we find that the training of the course enables the mind to work with a quick precision and steady application rarely found in one who has not had this thorough college drill. Therefore, we find it pays to give higher salaries for college graduates.

But much energy will be misdirected if college students enter the work without specific training. The college studies of most direct use to them are history, literature, and the languages, and it must be confessed that most college graduates are deficient in a familiarity with general literature.

Until 1887, candidates for library positions had to obtain training in one of three ways: 1) by writing to experienced librarians for answers to their questions; 2) by serving an apprenticeship in a large library; 3) by securing the services of some neighboring librarian for a limited period.

The first method is still used as a cheap substitute for training, as busy librarians know to their sorrow. It is not uncommon to receive a letter asking, Can I learn the decimal classification by correspondence? or, I have just been appointed librarian of this small town and find many difficulties. What methods would I better adopt? Any information will be thankfully received. Their innocent authors would not have presumed to ask similar advice from a doctor or lawyer without considering it a matter of business. But the librarian is a true missionary and the instances are few where he has not given his leisure time to answer such letters. These answers have formed the basis for some existing library manuals.

An apprenticeship in a large library is very difficult to secure and at best gives a training limited to the methods of one library.

The third method, of securing the temporary services of some neighboring librarian, is equally limited.

Neither of these ways would satisfy the college student.

In 1887, systematic library instruction was first given at Columbia college, New York, and later transferred to the state library at Albany. This school has been followed by others at Pratt institute, Brooklyn; Drexel institute, Philadelphia; Armour institute of technology, Chicago;

Los Angeles public library, California; Denver public library, Colorado, and Maine state college, Orono, Maine.

Limited bibliographic instruction is also now given in many colleges and should be extended and made compulsory in the freshmen year, that students might learn to use their college libraries.

But you ask, what is there to study? Consider the technical side first. There is the accession department, with its details of ordering, importing, and buying from regular bookstores, second-hand stores, and auctions, of duplicates, exchanges, gifts and acknowledgements.

There is cataloging, with bewildering rules from Panizzi to Cutter and Dewey, and a wealth of mechanical accessories with which to become familiar.

There is classification, more correctly speaking, there are classifications, and therein lies the trouble. Shall we learn Dewey Decimal or Cutter Expansive? One is enough for one mortal librarian to have with him night and day, but both are required, and of course, one must also be familiar with the systems of Schwartz, Edmands, and Lloyd Smith. At this stage the poor library student classifies everything which he eats, drinks, wears or otherwise possesses.

There are loan systems in great numbers to be studied comparatively, and illustrated by examples.

There is binding, with samples of practical work, and visits to binderies.

There is the shelf department with shelf lists of various kinds, book supports and dummies, the care and preservation of pamphlets, maps, clippings, etc., and stock taking.

Library architecture includes location, arrangement, plans, lighting, heating and furniture.

Government and service is studied with reference to relations between trustees and librarian, librarian and staff, hours, vacations and salaries.

Regulations for readers bring up questions of hours of opening, holiday and Sunday opening, and special privileges.

Still the greatest work has not been touched; that is, reference work. This cannot be taught. It is a growth, the development of an instinct, which can only be directed.

The library must be brought in touch with the schools, with factories, with clubs, with University extension, with the *people*, without respect to age, race, color, sex, or previous condition of servitude.

It is not a trained librarian who put up the notice Children prohibited, and gave as an excuse that the children used the books so much that they wore them out.

It is not the trained librarian who keeps her crochet work in the library because she has so much spare time.

Nor is it the trained librarian who tells the club women to look up their own reference because he is busy.

The trained librarian welcomes the child as cordially as the adult, and counts it his greatest joy when he has been the means of bringing the right book to the right person.

The library is what the librarian makes it and he can easily become a potent force in his community.

His profession possesses all the pleasures of teaching, without its attendant nervous strain. Instead of spending his days with young people dependent upon him and his ideas, he is constantly quickened by contact with vigorous minds and kept from a rut by the scope of his work.

A young teacher must specialize to win great success. This necessitates his reading in one line. A librarian must generalize and cover many subjects even at the risk of being superficial.

Educated trustees are needed as much as librarians. Here is a distinct field for college men and women. A director cannot direct until he knows how the work should be done.

Voicing these sentiments, Mr. W.E. Foster of Providence, R.I., says: In what other occupation or profession are the necessary and inherent disadvantages attended by so many and signal compensations? In what other line of work or study are there such opportunities for depth of culture, side by side with breadth of culture? In what other is the motive so strong to make one's self thoroughly master of some one line of research, while, side by side with it, is an imperative pleasure to carry one's attention in other directions? The librarian would not be an idle or unscholarly man if he could. He could not be the embodiment of intellectual narrowness and one-sided-ness if he would. The two tendencies — happiest of all ideal conditions — the two tendencies correct each other. Who would not be librarian?

There is no course more permanently valuable, if not put into practical use, than that of library science. There is no system of culture more broad. There is no work more absorbing, and its followers feel that it is second only to the church in its possibilities for good.

Librarians and Readers

"Librarians and Readers" by Edmund Lester Pearson appeared in *The Library and the Librarian: A Selection of Articles from the Boston Evening Transcript and other Sources.* Published by Elm Tree Press in 1910, it was also book number two of the Librarian's Series edited by John Cotton Dana and Henry W. Kent.

"Librarians," said someone, "librarians are the people who keep you from getting the books you wish."

It is curious that the notion persists of the librarian as a modern dragon. There is scarcely a public library which does not know one or two persons who are constantly in trouble with its rules. Like the politician who could not see why the Constitution should be allowed to come between friends, they are eternally annoyed to find that the usual regulations apply to them as well as to others. One man was forever sending the librarian (scorning to deal with the humble assistant) to ascertain if he must really obey this or that rule. He was disturbed to find that he must, and finally ventured the opinion that the librarian was a "bureaucrat." This sounding, as it did, of St. Petersburg and bombs, was a terrible thing to call a man, but the librarian was forced to put up with it.

"We are not fond of making rules," he explained; "every one we make is so much more trouble for us. It would be infinitely easier if we could put all the books in a heap on the floor and let whoever liked take what he pleased for as long as he desired." The explanation was probably wasted. If the vague complaints against librarians could be boiled down into the brief articles of an indictment, some of them would probably run like this: First, that no book is ever "in" when it is wanted; second, that the librarian sets himself up as one having authority to say what books people shall not read; third, that readers asking for bread in the shape of books are frequently offered a stone in the form of a card catalogue.

These accusations are more or less familiar to everyone. There is some ground for them, though it would be preposterous to blame the librarian for the first. His share of responsibility in the other two is limited, or, at most, a matter of difference of opinion. Instead of going over well-ploughed ground and attempting a defense, it will, perhaps, be more entertaining to consider the counter charges which librarians might bring against their readers. "Might bring" for as a matter of fact they seldom or never do bring them. It is a well-recognized convention for a librarian to represent his clientele as composed entirely of reasonable and serious minded folk. The motives for this may not be unmixed, but in general the thing does not show to the discredit of the profession. "We prefer," they seem to say, "to speak of the sensible people whom we have tried to satisfy, rather than the occasional crank or bore, whom no one could please."

A discussion of these latter gentlemen does not belong here. They are not peculiar to libraries: they occur everywhere. There are, however, these classes of people whose reform would rejoice the hearts of librarians. It is significant of the fact that the complaint is not a bitter or ill natured one when it appears that the reformation would simply permit libraries better to serve these persons. They are, then, the reader who will not ask for what he wants; the one who does not want what he asks for; and the one who desires imaginary books.

Speaking of the first of these classes, Mr. William Warner Bishop, the superintendent of the reading room of the Library of Congress, said recently: "We could devote an hour to telling the experiences which we all have had in arriving at that most elusive object of inquiry — the thing a reader really wants to know about. The chief art of a desk assistant or a reference librarian is, as we all know, the knack of divining by long experience what is actually wanted by inquirers. The fact that so few readers will ask directly for what they want, even when they have a clear idea of their needs — which is seldom the case — is perhaps a greater obstacle to successful reference work than poor equipment, poor catalogues, poor bibliographies."

To find what a reader really wants is sometimes a little like the game of "Twenty Questions," and the reference librarian might well begin, on occasions, with the inquiry: "Is it animal, vegetable, or mineral?" This hesitation of the reader to disclose his real needs comes from shyness, or a belief that he is saving the librarian trouble, or a feeling that he ought to be ashamed not to know where to look for the thing himself. Often he begins far off in his inquiries — thousands of miles away; and works toward his real object by almost imperceptible degrees. At other times he asks a number of wholly unrelated questions, casting a sort of fog over the situation, and then suddenly springs his real inquiry like an attorney during cross-examination.

An instance of the first of these methods occurred when a woman came into a reference library, leading a small boy by the hand. "Have you any books of travel" she asked. They had about twenty or thirty thousand, though the reference librarian did not say that. He merely replied in the affirmative and asked what she wished. "Oh, just some books of travel — haven't you got some handy? What are those over there?" "Those over there" were a miscellaneous assortment of new books, and there were some which described travels. She is a casual reader, thought the librarian, come in to while away an hour, and he brought her four volumes — the latest South Polar expedition, somebody's adventures in Tibet, a work recounting pleasures and perils in British Guiana, and a very much illustrated book about the missions of Southern California. With these the two readers retired to a table, and began turning over the leaves at great speed. The woman soon returned to the reference desk, but as it chanced to be a busy hour she had to wait a few minutes while the reference librarian listened to the complaints of an old gentleman who had found that some miscreant had cut out a picture from the Scientific American — an act of vandalism which sadly interfered with his enjoyment of the other side of the page. After him, in order of precedence, came a little girl who said that the teacher over in the children's room had told her to come over here and you would tell me how I can address a letter to Mr. Rudyard Kipling so he will get it all right. Then came a man who wanted last week's Saturday Evening Post as he had missed that installment of "The Firing Line," and then came Mrs. Homer Maclay.

Mrs. Maclay was in trouble as usual. She had been at the library early that afternoon to get a life of Watts — George Frederick Watts, you know, the painter. She had found out that he was Ellen Terry's first husband and so she wanted to read about him, and she had taken out a book that she had supposed was his life, and then gone all the way home and opened it and it wasn't about Watts the painter at all, but Isaac Watts the hymn-writer, and she had brought it back, and the young lady out at the desk said it was against the rule to return a book the same day it was taken out, and that they were told they must not break the rule, and so she came in here to see if the reference librarian couldn't do something about it. She didn't want Isaac and she did want George Frederick, and it had cost her two extra car fares and all this trouble, and she thought the library was to blame anyhow, or that boy who got here the book was — why didn't he find out which Watts she was after? And she certainly didn't intend to go all they way home again with this old Isaac. The reference librarian felt very sure that Mrs. Maclay had merely asked for "A Life of Watts," and he knew that Edgar, the fifteen year old page, did not profess mind-reading, nor have any particular interest in discriminating between a Watts who wrote hymns and one who painted pictures. Neither of them was on a league nine, and both of them were dead, anyhow. But he also knew that in the end Ms. Maclay would get what she wanted and it was best to give in gracefully at the start. So the rule was broke, as rules are always broken for persons who make themselves sufficiently obstreperous, and Mrs. Maclay went away with the book she desired.

All this time the travel lady was waiting impatiently. "Can't you let me see some more books on travel?" she asked. Certainly he could, and four or five more were fetched. Lady Cicely Waynflete's 'Captured by the Moors'; Dr. Von Hohensticker's "Land und Leute in Samoa"; a motor tour in Spain, and so and so forth. These entertained her and her son for about half an hour. Then she returned in apparent bad humor. "These are not what I want," she remarked shortly.

The librarian thought he saw his chance. "What do you want?" he inquired. "Some books on travel — haven't you got any others?" The librarian groaned in spirit. He saw now what he had to deal with — a person who would not make known her specific want, but would waste her time and his trying to achieve it herself. And so it proved. The afternoon wore on and books of travels were deposited by the ton, so to speak, on the table where the woman sat. Finally she consented to narrow the field by admitting that she was particularly interested in Africa. The resources of the library on the subject of that continent passed in review before her eyes. She grew more and more acid in her manner. Finally she gathered together her bag and her boy, put on her gloves, and sailed down the room, stopping a minute at the reference librarian's desk. "I cannot find what I want; I shall have to go now." The librarian made one last effort: "Just what did you want?" he asked. The woman looked at him in the manner of one imparting the most delicate family secret. "My little boy," she said solemnly, "wished to see a picture, a large picture, of an elephant. He wished to copy it. There was only one in all these books, and it was very small. I am very much surprised, and Leander is disappointed." The librarian moaned aloud as he took a large volume on zoology from a shelf nearby. He silently exhibited a very fine elephant, indeed. The lady said: "Well, it is too late now", and out she went.

"Now why," asked the librarian, addressing the ceiling of the reading-room, "why couldn't she have told me that in the first place? Why is it a base and shameful thing to desire a view of an elephant? Why was it only extorted from her at the eleventh hour?" And he called Edgar, the lightning page, and set him at work carrying off the one hundred and fifty volumes of the elephant lady's books, as a punishment for not having divined the unspoken thought of Mrs. Homer Maclay in regard to Watts.

The reader who does not ask for what he wants, and the one who does not want what he asks for are frequently combined in the same person. The traits overlap. A man came into a reading-room one evening and asked if there were any "essays" there. "I don't supposed you've got any essays here, have you?" was the form of his inquiry. Yes, they had, Macaulay's and Emerson's — would he like to see them? No, not those, exactly. Some others, then? Yes, some others. Whose, please? Oh, just some essays. So essays were brought. But they failed to please, and finally the man brought them back. He drew near the librarian. "To tell the truth," he remarked, as though there were a strong temptation to lie about it, "what I want is 'Quo Vadis',—have you got that?"

The reader wants imaginary books appears in various forms. Sometimes he is of that familiar type, dear to the heart of all librarians, who wants "a red book." Or it may be "a brown book", but that is the limit of his information about it. He had it a year ago and he wants to read it again. What was the title? That, he doesn't remember. Who wrote it? Oh, he never knew that. What was it about? Oh, about a lot of things, it was full of information. He does wish he could get it. You must have it around here, somewhere — it was about so high. And he indicates with his hands the not very unusual height, known (in old times) as "duodecimo."

Some time or other there will be a librarian with a testy disposition and a strong right arm. And he will deal with this man. The accumulated and righteous wrath of years will be visited upon him. The librarian will grab him by the throat and run him back to the nearest wall, and bang his head against it hard. "You wearisome ass!" he will say: "suppose you went to a city of half a million inhabitants, and went up to a policeman at the station and told him that you wanted to see a man who lived there. And that you didn't know the man's name, nor his house, nor his business. And that all you knew about him was that he wore a blue suit, or may-be a black one, and that he was five or six feet all. Wouldn't that policeman ring for the patrol and have you before an expert in lunacy pretty quick? Well, here goes for you! The door? No, the window, by the shade of Sir Thomas Bodley! Heads, below, there!" And out the man would go.

That librarian would lose his job, and he would be held up to reprobation as woefully lacking in library ideals, and he would be openly denounced everywhere. But five thousand of his colleagues would gather in secret and they would send him an illuminated address, and vote each one to give a month's salary, and thereby they would collect $900, and they would send him that, and they would pray for him every night, too.

A Librarian and His Constituency

The following excerpt is from a report of a spring meeting held at the Young Men's Institute of New Haven (Connecticut) on Wednesday, May 14, 1902, which appeared in *Public Libraries*, v. 7, no. 6, June 1902, p. 256.

Prof. [Albert] Cook [of Yale] compared the relations between a feudal lord and his dependents with those between a librarian and his constituents. The lord's benefits consisted largely in the defense of the subject people against enemies, while those of the modern baron of books consisted of aid to advancement in life. The castle was not the prime defense, neither was the security and prosperity of the feudal community to be found wholly in its willingness to provide needful supplies. The chief dependence was ever upon the wisdom, the skill, the leadership of the castellan. Every librarian is a castellan or a chatelaine, in possession of a building devised for its uses, with a community to serve and stores to distribute. He has not done his duty when he has bought the books that someone has suggested, or that a committee has prescribed, has labeled, shelved, and cataloged them, has handed out what happens to be asked for, and duly recorded the issue. All this is necessary, may be irksome or even arduous, but it is the lowest, if not the smallest, part of a librarian's function. The librarian is the castellan, and to issue stores on demand is the least part of his business. He must see that the proper stores are brought in; must make suggestions if the wrong stores are called for; must indicate the best use to make of each article. He should know his books and his constituency, that he may be a power and not a servant. Librarianship may be a profession, not in the sense of an occupation which requires a certain apprenticeship in order to acquaint one with the details of external management, but in the sense that it gives one a commanding position in society. Advice is asked of a lawyer or a physician because they know more of certain vital matters than the inquirer; when a librarian is consulted in the same way the same deference and esteem are his due. If the librarian be a mere clerk, charging a book when an inquirer has made his own choice, he is merely entitled to courtesy; but in proportion as he knows more than the reader, and thus becomes a guide, he is entitled to respect. To gain an intimate knowledge of the books committed to his custody is the foundation of the librarian's ability. This may involve self-denial. He cannot read all the new novels if he is to be a man of light and leading in his community. He may perhaps be forced to let his constituents read them, if they will not hearken to his sager counsels; but at least he can refuse active complicity. Nor need he fear that he will thus forfeit the regard of anyone whose regard is worth having. He can only be a leader on condition that he does not follow a multitude.

The Librarian as Censor

"The Librarian as Censor" by John Cotton Dana appeared in *Suggestions*, F.W. Faxon, 1921.

The librarian of a public library is a censor of books and reading. Of the millions of books already in the world, and of the thousands of new ones published each year, he can buy only a few. Those he buys he approves of as the better ones for his community to own and read. All the others he disapproves of, for the time being; that is, he exercises his power of censorship against them.

I do not say that the librarian rejects books of which he does not personally approve, or selects books which uphold his personal doctrines. The censorship which is the outcome of the usurped power to use a community's money to promote his own personal views is entirely reprehensible, no matter how "moral," "loyal," "religious," "constitutionally sound," "patriotic," or "acceptable to the majority" may be the opinions or theories the librarian may hold and try, by skillful selection of books, to promote.

The Librarian as a Unifier

"The Librarian as a Unifier" by Andrew Keogh was an address delivered at the commencement exercises at the Library School, the New York Public Library, June 11, 1915.

To maintain mental health and to attain professional success a librarian must have abiding consciousness of unity in his work. The need of such a consciousness varies with different kinds of libraries, but it exists in all. The lack of such a conscious aim and ideal is shown in the small library in a sense of isolation, and a consequent tendency to judge results by purely local standards; it is evidenced in larger libraries by a want of harmony between departments:

it accounts for the absence of a community consciousness between libraries of the same locality or character, and the failure to secure the greatest results for the community by co-operation. Wanting such an ideal the individual librarian confuses unity with uniformity, and energy with efficiency; becomes immersed in details; makes of work a routine without enthusiasm; and loses, if he ever attains, that balance and harmony which is characteristic of the normal mind.

The evil is unfortunately inherent in the librarian's occupation. Dissimilarity is the keynote of the stuff with which he works, and distraction is the penalty of working with it. The daily round of the ordinary librarian is a dissipation, a frittering away, a scattering, of his mental energy. He handles books on a hundred different subjects, and answers questions relating to as many different topics, in the course of a day. If he is not careful, his mind becomes a thing of shreds and patches, lacing in a sense of perspective and relative importance. Accustomed to jump from one thing to another, all things become of equal importance or unimportance, and it is only by keeping constant watch that he can preserve himself whole. His very office requires the twofold function of scholar, and administrator, and he must meet each of these requirements in a superlative degree if his library is to be thoroughly successful at all points. Yet the librarian's function is not an impossibility; and no other profession gives greater opportunity for unifying one's work, and unifying one's mind while doing that work.

A librarian has to do with buildings, with books, and with men. A suitable building must house his intellectual properties and activities, with due regard to the arrangements of rooms, heating, lighting, ventilation, cleanliness, and absence of noise; with care for the provision of shelving, tables, and other conveniences for ease, order, and dispatch. It is obvious that the planning and operation of such a literary workshop gives opportunity for unifying talents of the highest order; but as building committees often make contracts before the librarian is appointed, and allow the architect to work from the outside in, instead of from the inside out, the librarian cannot always be blamed if his building is monumental rather than serviceable. A noble collection of books should have an appropriate setting; but many libraries are still in the stone age, spending on maintenance the income which should be available for their real function.

In the acquisition of books a librarian usually has a much freer hand. Book committees often determine the general policy as to purchases, and leave specific recommendations to the librarian as the responsible officer; but in any case the wise librarian will ensure harmony and unity by seeking the advice and respecting the wishes of those for whom he acts. Selection, the, and not mere gathering, is the librarian's method of procedure. But selection implies judgment in the selector, for choice without purpose is mere chance, and the result is meaningless. Book purchase, then, must be unified, both in the apportionment of funds to each class of literature, and I the method of choosing individual books. Exchanges, again, are too often haphazard, and should be systematized. Even gifts should be questioned unless we are to be content with such an absurdity as a collection of local histories in a small college, while a nearby historical society is burdened with many hundreds of volumes on the drama.

Yet a mere accumulation of books, however carefully chosen, is no more a library than a selection of carefully chosen bricks is a building. The man in the streets thinks of a museum as a place where curiosities are kept, but the expert knows that it is an exhibition of objects illustrating some subject or idea with reference to a definite region or period; that it is, in fact, a systematic arrangement of careful descriptions illustrated by specimens. Books, in the same way, must be organized for use, and the library authorities of this state have wisely decided that they will not recognize a library an unorganized collection of books. The solution here, again, is unification. To a unifying mind it is a welcome task to take a miscellaneous lot of books, and shelve them in such a scholarly and lucid manner that all on the same subject shall be together, and all on a related subject near at hand. Moses should surely be counted as one of the great classifiers, from the evident delight he took in describing the process of bringing order out of chaos, and in his ascription to the Creator of satisfaction at the successive steps in this progress. He describes the earth as without form and void, and then details the division of light from darkness, day from night, dry land from sea, and so on stopping six times to remark that "God saw that it was good." At the end of the sixth day, when the work was all done, the narrator adds that "God saw everything that He had made, and behold it was very good." The classifier who is not thrilled by the first chapter of Genesis should immediately resign his position.

The catalogue, too, should be a unit in the choice of subject headings and in the network of references that bind the headings together. The work should be ideally the plan of a single mind, but one remembers that the great epics have not lost their unity because the original framework was expanded and interpolated.

With a suitable building, and with a sufficient provision of books carefully selected, classified, and catalogued, the librarian's task would seem to be ended. Yet the most important duty of his office still remains. To be successful the librarian must master the psychological aspects of his problem, and this is more difficult because, being personal, they cannot be reduced to rules. The librarian may have but slight interest in a certain field of knowledge, and yet save his professional soul; with individual books he may live on terms of friendship, or indifference, or even detestation, and none need be the wiser; but he must have acceptable human relations with all who come in contact with him. The people he meets are just as varied as the books. There are directors and colleagues, the users of his library, and his fellows in general: an infinite variety of temperament, and education, and training, and experience, and requirement. Since the trustees have appointed the librarian as their unifier, it becomes his business to gather up the human threads, and weave them into the desired pattern. The librarian organizes the library for the public; he also organizes the public for the library. He calls upon individuals for help in book selection, and in classification and cataloguing, if they can serve in this way; he provides reference assistants as personal guides to save from desultory or wasteful reading those users of the institution who look for guidance, and to interpret and supplement, and on occasion to supersede, written and printed helps; he calls upon experts for lectures and book annotations, and upon collectors for exhibits. He deals, too, with the corporate public, with the schools, the reading clubs, the churches, the trade-unions, with every kind of organization that can help him or be helped by him. He has relations, directly or indirectly, with other library boards, or with individual members of such boards, striving to cooperate in book purchases, in the joint preparation of bibliographies, and I every other way by which the library resources of the country may be unified, and freed from unnecessary duplication. He feels that he is a debtor to his profession, and so has relations with other libraries, taking his share in their associations and enterprises, and seeking to leave his calling better than he found it.

He looks upon his staff as a particularly important field for his unifying endeavors, and he begins by determining his own place in the personnel. He remembers that he has to be a custodian for property and an efficient superintendent of buildings; a scholar, selecting the best books and using them and teaching others to use them in the way most economical of time and energy; and an efficient administrator and organizer, working harmoniously with others for a common end. By self-analysis, or by noting or even inviting the criticism of others, he tries to estimate aright his strong points and his weak ones. Such an analysis he makes early in his professional career, for a man's estimate of himself ought to determine to some extent his choice of a field of service. After making this inventory, he can, by taking thought, add to his mental stature, or perchance supply what is lacking. There is, however, a diversity of

144

gifts, and the normal man in unequally developed, because he has the defects of his qualities. If a man is *this*, he is not likely to be *that*, so he must complete himself by association with those who have the qualities that he himself lacks. If he be a scholar by taste or training, he sees that there is on his board or on his staff someone capable of looking after the business side of his institution. If he be primarily an administrator, he is careful to have as aids those who are expert in various fields of knowledge. If he cannot find among his trustees or his assistants those with the special ability required, he does not hesitate to call upon his professional brethren or upon outsiders for competent and necessary help.

He sees to it, also, that every member of his staff has opportunities for self-development. Assistants of peculiar skill or attainments are necessary for special posts, but they should be developed to their greatest efficiency and prosperity. If we need monotony for our mental health, we also need variety, and the moving of an assistant from one post to another, even for a little while, gives him a greater interest in the library's doings and a better understanding of them. Staff meetings, a library club, a bulletin board, will keep assistants in touch with other departments of the library, and give them a chance to see the proper relation of their own departments to the institution as a whole. Without knowledge of the end, the assistant is the servant of detail; it is the idea that liberates. But if the assistant has rights, he also has duties. There is no position in a library that is unrelated to the centre, that is not unifiable, of the occupant choose. A sentry on outpost duty is lonely, but his eyes and ears are keener because he is conscious of the bond between him and another sentry a thousand miles away, and between them both and the life of their common country.

To ask that the librarian shall unify his work, is equivalent to asking him to do what all skilled and artistic workers do, whatever the stuff the mound into form. The dramatist builds upon the unities of time and place and action. The painter reproduces nature, not with photographic fullness, but by selecting that which is vital and significant. The baseball coach sifts out nine men, and by training and organizing turns out a victorious team. The university president gathers students from every quarter, and selects specialists having little in common save the love of knowledge, and makes an institution that is everywhere recognized as a thing distinct. The statesman takes people and colonies with conflicting interests and standards and ideals, and makes a nation whose motto is E Pluribus Unum. Nature itself is not an aggregate of independent parts, but an organic whole.

By unifying his work the librarian not only attains professional success, but unifies his own mind. The frayed edges of his mental fabric disappear. The details of his daily task acquire their proper perspective in his even larger view. Balance and harmony become characteristics, and, like Sophocles, the librarian sees life steadily, and sees it whole.

Librarianship a Profitable Profession

Any librarian can tell you librarianship is not a wealth-building career. But John Drury thought otherwise during the seventeenth century. A passage from an article by Richard Garnett (*The Library Chronicle: A Journal of Librarianship and Bibliography*, v. 1, 1884 issued by the Library Association of the UK) quotes Drury as saying, "The library-keeper's place and office in most countries are looked upon as places of profit and gain." However, that article's author goes on to state:

Rather a startling statement to us, who have been accustomed to look upon librarianship as under the special influence of the planet Saturn, which is said to preside over all occupations in which money is obtained with very great difficulty. It would seem, however, that mean as the prizes of librarianship might be, they were yet scrambled for.

Women as Librarians

"Women as Librarians," by Dr. C. Norrenberg, Kiel, appeared in *Public Libraries*, v. 6, no. 3, March 1901, pp. 156–158.

A great deal of foolish matter concerning the women's movement in America is written in German newspapers. Women as mayors, lawyers, preachers, they delight in noting, and with sarcastic comments. Of other callings the great public hears little, and especially of such as offer large numbers of women an independent existence, and a satisfactory, successful activity well adapted in womanly qualifications. To this class of callings belongs that of librarian. As in teaching, so in the library profession over there women predominate, and on library conference form the majority of participants and speakers, and stand on a footing of perfect equality and good understanding with their masculine coworkers.

The library calling demands no publicity, and nothing which is opposed to our inherited German conception of womanliness. It demands a sense of order, faithfulness in small things, and in some of its branches a certain pedagogical inclination or impulse to instruct and help others. The calling is, therefore, one well adapted for women, and if in Germany there have been hitherto only a bare dozen women librarians, while in American they have many hundreds, if not thousands, it is because America has long since possessed, and in large number, a type of libraries which we in Germany are only now creating.

There are two main types of libraries, and, accordingly, two different callings. The scholarly libraries, such as the university and great state libraries, and many of our city ones, serve the purposes of science. Their higher officers must be specialists; familiarity with such fields as higher literature, art, and art industries, matters which lie within the comprehension and interests of women, is less essential, and knowledge of this kind will for the most part lie fallow. Furthermore, in these libraries it is a question of a small and diminishing number of positions for which numerous applicants are already waiting. For instance, there are at the present time, according to the Centralblatt Fur Bibliothekswesen, in the Prussian scientific libraries, 48 applicants for positions (23 for assistant librarians, 9 for assistants and 16 for volunteers), while (according to the average of the last eight years), there are only 42 library positions to fill, and this number is likely to diminish rather than increase on account of the comparative youth of the present librarians.

The hopelessness of the learned library career for woman need not trouble her, however, for the field of woman is not that of learning, but rather of culture, and that of the librarian not in the scholarly, but in the public library. This public library is to most Germans, even cultivated ones, an unfamiliar conception. That there are scholarly libraries for science, and peoples' libraries for the people (the great mass of those with little means and culture), is familiar to everyone, because we have always known such. But that there should be, along with the scholarly ones, libraries in which everybody, the most cultivated as well as the simplest workman, may find reading for culture of every kind and every degree, and also, for good literary entertainment; that such public libraries are something wholesome and reasonable, because they give the cultivated man his due, and open to the intelligent man of the people the way to higher culture; that the people's libraries (Volks Bibliotheken) should be developed in these real libraries of culture — at least in the cities — that is a conception that only in these latter years, and very slowly, makes its way. The administrative bodies of many German cities still wear blinders, see only the so-called common people, and arrange libraries only for the needs of the lower grades of intelligence, while the need of inspiring reading for those standing somewhat higher intellectually is more pressing. Here, and there beginnings are being made toward improving the conditions. A number of real public libraries have already been created, and more will follow.

Here, then, as in America, in the public library, the woman as librarian is in place. But let no one think that the cultivated woman can make a claim to the head positions of the larger institutions. In the large cities the tendency is to bring all library institutions: a scholarly city library, perhaps, with the people's libraries and reading rooms, into one organization under a city librarian, who naturally must be a professional, and possess the most comprehensive scientific and literary culture. Generally, also the medium and large public libraries, which have not a scientific aim, but merely that of general culture, demand as head a man academically trained and thoroughly conversant with library economy, and it is well that women should cherish no false hopes in regard to such leading positions. Even in America the leading library positions occupied by women are few, although there, for a much longer time than with us, opportunities for study have been open to women. But even as head of one of the smaller public libraries in the medium and smaller towns, or as cultivated assistant libraries in the large public libraries, woman will find a rich field of labor. She must, however, make clear to herself what the calling demands of her and what it offers. It offers outwardly no high honors, and not much money or means. It will be reasonable to make the salaries equal those of teachers of a corresponding grade of culture, and it is to be desired that these public libraries should be municipal institutions, assuring their officials at least a certain livelihood. The calling demands an almost complete renunciation of visible success. The teacher survives in what his scholars become; the librarian works and knows not for whom, for even when he has been to his readers a zealous counselor, how many thank him, or from how many does he learn how the good books are valued? Above everything, however, the library calling demands thorough preparation. First, in belles-letrres. Experience shows that three-fourths of all the books loaned fall into this class, and it is the opinion of a barbarian that this is an evil. Belles-lettres, including novels, although read most for entertainment only, not for purposes or artistic enjoyment, form, nevertheless, one of the foremost factors in education. The choice of the books must be made accordingly. It is not enough for the librarian to know at second-hand which novel writer is a poet and a respectable man, and which a shallow or lying one, pandering to bad instincts of the public; she must also be able to judge every new book by an unknown author which comes under her eye. She needs not only a comprehensive knowledge of home and foreign literature, but also literary judgment, taste, if she is to be the instructor of her public. She must have the same taste in the plastic arts. Her own judgment must tell her with audible voice whether she shall put the Illustrirte Zeitung, or the Woche, Kunst fur Alle, or Moderne Kunst in the reading room. She must also be informed, not exactly in all sciences, but as to the output of books in all fields; not only the nearest ones, like history and biography, geography and travel, natural science and physics, but also the political, industrial, etc. And all this knowledge of books must be no mere mass of material, but the whole field of literature must be surveyed, and so intellectually comprehended that the librarian has the system of all departments clearly laid out before her eyes, and according to that, can plan and carry through a subject catalog of her collection of books, and give each book its proper place. To make even an author catalog requires a great amount of knowledge and skill of a literary, historical, and practical kind, and logical thinking. Anybody can make a poor catalog, but for the making of a good one the requirements are many; among others a good, plain handwriting, an indispensable requisite for the librarian. A sense of order and painful exactness, even to pedantry, must permeate the whole activity. These things do not come to one of themselves, but can only be acquired, even by the gifted, through earnest work, and that requires time. Let no one undertake the conduct of ever so small a library who has not thoroughly prepared and trained herself, by preference in some well conducted public library, for one learns the practical, administrative calling only by experience. For this reason I consider Hottinger's plan for a library school for women unconnected with active library work as an impractical.... What cannot be learned, however, but must be inherent, is the impulse to teach and help others. Many users of the public library will come to the loan desk without knowing what they want to read, or the book they want is out, then it is the business of the librarian to estimate the reader with tact and judgment, and to advise, and to do this gladly and heartily. The book counter is a place from which the most manifold and richest influence may go out to the whole intellectual life of a city, and the public library should be, as much as possible, the intellectual center of the town.

But even the people's libraries of the lower sort, which are planned wholly for the common people and only used by them, offer a field for the cultivated woman not without its reward. But these town institutions are not in a position to pay their own officials, and where it is possible in the cities, it is to be hoped that these libraries will soon give place everywhere to the public library for all classes. The tendency of the time is favorable to this, and it will come with economic advancement; the prospects in this branch of the library profession are, therefore, not bad. If women who are really cultivated, and take pleasure in spreading culture, devote themselves to this work, may they be perfectly clear as to what is required in the way of natural gifts, character, knowledge, professional training and skill; for if unsuitable elements enter the field and make a failure, it will put back the whole woman's movement. For such a calling as this only the best powers are good enough.

10

Everything Librarian

The fascinating facets of librarians are too many to be listed in any single book. But this chapter will give you a taste of the many other interesting aspects and data about librarians. So sit back and enjoy a glimpse at image-busting librarians, multitalented librarians, librarian exam questions, and more.

Librarian Barbie

Unfortunately, there's not a librarian Barbie yet. But several years ago a poll was posted on the Barbie.com website asking parents and children which Barbie they would most like to see: an architect, policewoman, or a librarian.

In response to the poll, *Library Journal* created a picture of what a librarian Barbie might look like. If you're curious, you can see the picture of page 13 of the September 1, 2005, issue of *Library Journal.*

Librarian Trading Cards

Baseball players have their trading cards, so why not librarians? There's no reason, which is why, yes, there are librarian trading cards. All you need to do is look online (http://librariantradingcards.blogspot.com) or http://flickr.com/groups/80982632@N00/pool).

Created by Amy Pelman while a student at the graduate school of library and information studies at the University of California at Los Angeles, the cards are designed to help viewers learn fascinating facts about librarians across the globe. Besides containing a photo, the cards also contain information about each librarian, like what's on their MP3 player, what's their favorite book, and what they wished more people knew about libraries.

If you're a librarian, go to the site to find out how you can create and add your own trading card to the pool.

Librarians of Congress

Only 13 individuals have held the title of Librarian of Congress to date, all of them men. By law, the position requires no special education or qualifications and no specific term of office is specified. Nominated to the position by the president of the United States, the individual must be confirmed by the Senate.

Chronologically, the men who have held the office follow.

John J. Beckley (1757–1807)
Term of office: 1802–1807

Despite having been born in England and spending his early childhood there, Mr. Beckley had the distinction of serving concurrently as both the first clerk of the House of Representatives, and as the first Librarian of Congress. Appointed to the position by President Thomas Jefferson, Beckley's salary as Librarian of Congress was no more than two dollars a day. Although the library had been established in the Capitol building in 1800, it was two years later that the office of the librarian of Congress was established.

Patrick Magruder (1768–1819)
Term of office: 1807–1815

Also nominated by Thomas Jefferson, Mr. Magruder, a former newspaperman, also served concurrently as the Librarian of Congress and clerk of the House of Representatives. But during his term of office, the Library of Congress was destroyed in 1814 when the British invaded Washington and burned the area of the Capitol building housing the library. The following year Magruder resigned from both his posts.

George Watterston (1783–1854)
Term of office: 1815–1829

A journalist and novelist, Mr. Watterston was appointed to the office by President James Madison. But unlike his predecessor, Mr. Watterston did not voluntarily leave the post. He was removed from his post when Andrew Jackson was elected president.

John Silva Meehan (1790–1863)
Term of office: 1829–1861

Printer and publisher John Meehan served as the fourth Librarian of Congress. President Andrew Jackson appointed fellow Democrat Meehan to the position, replacing the partisan Whig who had held the office. The political nature of appointment to the office of Librarian of Congress continued when Meehan was replaced when Abraham Lincoln was elected president.

John Stephenson (1828–1882)
Term of office: 1861–1864

Physician John Stephenson was appointed Librarian of Congress by President Lincoln as a reward for having been one of his political supporters. But he resigned from the office after serving in the post for just four years.

Ainsworth Rand Spofford (1825–1908)
Term of office: 1864–1897

President Lincoln appointed Mr. Spofford the sixth Librarian of Congress. Spofford's work at the library actually began three years earlier when John Stephenson appointed him assistant librarian. During Spofford's term as Librarian of Congress, the library was moved out of the Capitol and into a separate building. Holding the post for over 30 years, he was in his seventies when he was replaced. But recognizing his value, the new Librarian of Congress appointed him to serve once again as the assistant librarian, a position he held until his death.

John Russell Young (1840–1899)
Term of office: 1897–1899

Journalist John Young was appointed by his friend and fellow Republican, President McKinley, to serve as the seventh Librarian of Congress. Like the first librarian, Young was also born abroad, in Ireland. He held the position until his death.

Herbert Putnam (1861–1955)
Term of office: 1899–1939

Appointed by President McKinley after the death of former librarian John Young, Herbert Putnam held the distinction of being the first person to hold the office who had previous experience as a librarian. He had been a librarian at the Boston Public Library. After officially retiring as Librarian of Congress, he briefly served as librarian emeritus until a new librarian was appointed.

Archibald MacLeish (1892–1982)
Term of office: 1939–1944

Poet and writer Archibald MacLeish was nominated by President Franklin D. Roosevelt to succeed Herbert Putnam. Controversy surrounded his appointment.

The American Library Association opposed his nomination due to his lack of prior library experience. But despite their opposition, MacLeish was confirmed by the Senate and held the position for almost five years before resigning to serve as assistant secretary of state.

Luther Evans (1902–1981)
Term of office: 1945–1953

President Truman nominated Luther Evans, the Chief Assistant Librarian of Congress to succeed MacLeish. Because he was an experienced library administrator, there was no opposition to this appointment by the American Library Association. He held the office for eight years before resigning to become the third director-general of UNESCO.

L. Quincy Mumford (1903–1982)
Term of office: 1954–1974

President Eisenhower nominated a popular individual among librarians to the office of the librarian of Congress. L. Quincy Mumford, who was president-elect of the American Library Association and director of the Cleveland Public Library, was confirmed to the post without any objection. He successfully served in the position until his retirement at age 71.

Daniel Boorstin (1914-)
Term of office: 1975–1987

Historian, author, and former director of the National Museum of History and Technology, Boorstin was nominated to be the Librarian of Congress by President Gerald Ford. He had no library experience or training, so his nomination was opposed by the American Library Association. But despite their opposition, the Senate confirmed Boorstin's nomination without debate. He held the office for over ten years until his retirement.

James Billington (1929-)
Term of office: 1987-

President Ronald Reagan nominated the current Librarian of Congress, James H. Billington, to the office. Billington, a historian and former director of the Woodrow Wilson International Center for Scholars at the Smithsonian Institution, had no prior library experience or training. However, the American Library Association did not oppose his nomination.

Multitalented and Image-Busting Librarians

Despite what some people think, librarians are talented, creative people. If you don't believe me, keep reading. And hopefully you'll change your thinking about librarians.

Barbarian Librarian

If the picture of the Barbarian Librarian on her website doesn't dispel your image of librarians as frumpy old maids, nothing will. Wearing a barbarian outfit that reveals a lot of skin, this attractive blonde librarian answers the question, what is a barbarian librarian? The answer: "A person who collects and helps you access information resources about Barbarians, all while wearing leather and a big knife." The Barbarian Librarian's Lair can be found at www.angelfire.com/scifi/barbarian-librarian.

Belly Dancing Librarian

Without a doubt, librarians are talented individuals. By day, Eris Weaver, who holds a master's degree in library science, manages the Redwood Health Library in Petaluma, California. But Ms. Weaver's talent extends beyond the library into Raks Sharki, otherwise known as belly dancing. But she's just one of many belly dancing librarians. In the gallery of belly dancers on her website, you'll find belly dancing librarians across the globe. Who says librarians can't shake it? Check out the belly dancing librarian and her gallery at www.bellydancinglibrarian.com.

Biker Librarian

Many librarians are motorcyclists. But Shirl Kennedy stands out in the crowd. This Florida mother of two sons literally wrote the guide for beginning motorcyclists. *The Savvy Guide to Motorcycles* (Indy-Tech Publishing, 2005) offers wisdom and knowledge gathered from the author's own motorcycle experiences and those of others. By the way, if you're curious about her motorcycle, an editorial review on Amazon.com lists it as a 2005 Yamaha V-Star 1100 Midnight Custom motorcycle.

A former newspaper reporter, Ms. Kennedy holds an MLIS degree from the University of South Florida. She works as the base librarian at MacDill Air Force Base in Tampa. To find out more about this biker librarian and to see a photo of her and her bike, check out her homepage at http://home.tampabay.rr.cm/shirlk.

The Bodybuilding Librarian

Librarians have strong minds. But this lady librarian also has strong muscles. You can find out more detail about her bodybuilding training on the sumptuous.com website. On the site she chronicles her bodybuilding from 1987 to date. Although the site focuses on her journey through bodybuilding and not on her library career, it does reveal she attended library school at Syracuse. More importantly, this librarian can deep-squat 275 pounds! Hmmm ... I wonder how many library books it takes to total 275 pounds.

Butt Kicking Librarians!

In the movie *The Black Mask*, martial arts expert Jet Li plays a librarian. In real life, the folks featured on the following website are librarians who are also martial arts experts. Armed with black belts, it's wise not to pick on these librarians! Check out these butt-kicking librarians at http://hokken.uuft.org/librarian.html.

Kinky Librarians

Yes, librarians do like sex. And some librarians like kinky sex. For obvious reasons, most like to keep their real identities secret. But not all like to keep quiet. Take for example the Kinky Librarian, who has a blog and whose real identity is secret. The heading on her blog reads "KINKY LIBRARIAN — being an intelligent, academic woman can go hand in hand with being a horny, kinky slut!" Her blog can be found at http://kinkylibrarian.blogspot.com).

Librarian Authors

Many a librarian has authored a book. To get a taste of the many books written by librarians, you may want to check out http://ravenstonepress.com/libwritr. html, which lists "Librarians Who are Authors of Children's and Young Adult Literature."

Librarian Avengers

This website is actually run by a single individual, librarian Erica Olsen. If you are a librarian, you're bound to like her, even without knowing her. The reason is because on her website there's a footnote that reads "Saying 'I am a librarian' is like saying 'Please, remove $80,000 from my paycheck' so let's try and keep the librarian thing between you and me."

She is known for writing an essay titled "Why you should fall to your knees and worship a librarian," and her website has categories ranging from life, librarianship, and comics to library tourism and film. You can check out her website at http://librarianavengers.org.

Librarian Poet: David Drake

Although a number of librarians write poetry, few write considerably about libraries or librarians. But David Drake does just that. Having served as the director of several academic libraries, he's the author of not one, but two books of poetry dealing with libraries and librarians. His first book *Overdue Notice: Poems from the Library* (McFarland, 1995) contains a wealth of poems that have been used in new library buildings, as well as retirement parties. His second book, *Each of Us Is a Book: Poems for the Library Minded* (McFarland), was published in 2003.

Modified Librarian

Forget the librarians with their hair up in a bun or that blouse buttoned up to the neck and fastened with a cameo. These "modified" librarians accessorize with tattoos and body piercing. Yes, you read this right.

The Modified Librarian website (www.bmeworld.com/gailcat), which bears the subhead, "Librarianship and the Art of Body Modification" on the main page, provides a forum for the discussion of body modification in relationship to librarianship. You can click on a link to read "Rants of Modified Librarians," or you can click on links to the personal pages of modified librarians. The personal pages contain the stories behind the librarians' tattoo or piercing, plus a picture of his/her tattoo or body piercing.

If you're a library worker with a body modification who'd like to tell your story, you can do so on this website. Or if you're just someone who's having a hard time shedding your old mental image of the spinster librarian, be sure to check out this website. With tattoos ranging from tigers to outer-space themes, these are not your stereotypical librarians!

Singer/Songwriter/Writer Librarians

Multitalented Robert Lopresti works as a librarian at Western Washington University in Bellingham, Washington. He's also the author of over 30 mystery stories that have appeared in prestigious magazines such as *Alfred Hitchcock's Mystery Magazine,* and he's also won a Derringer Award from the Short Mystery Fiction Society. (Note: His short story "Uncle Victor on Watch" which appeared in the fall 1997 issue of *Murderous Intent* has a librarian as a minor character.) Kearney Street Books published his novel, *Such a Killing Crime* in 2005. But his talent doesn't stop here.

Lopresti is also a singer and songwriter. His folk music CD *Can I Blame You?* features 18 of his songs, including "The Reference Librarian." He's also written another library song since the CD was issued. His newest library song is titled "When Spring Comes to the Library" will absolutely delight anyone who works in a library. You can read the lyrics and hear the song at www.nas.com/~lopresti/spring.htm. If you want to find out more about this multitalented librarian, check out his website at www.roblopresti.com.

Spooky Librarians

The spookylibrarians.com homepage for this website is rather spooky with a drawing of two skulls on each side of the page. A picture of two "spooky" librarians also appears on the website. But you'll find yourself doing a double take because one of them, a male librarian, is nicknamed Bunny.

The website states it's "the virtual home of two slightly demented Capricorn librarians. Within this site, you'll find Bunny and Jeanne's individual and combined rantings, recommendations, remembrances, and other things that begin with the Letter R."

According to the website, Jeanne says "during the day, I struggle with the intricacies of copyright and distribution lists." Bunny is the director of libraries at the Cincinnati College of Mortuary Science, and hopes to one day own a souped-up hearse. (Hmmm ... I wonder if a hearse has ever been converted into a bookmobile.) These two librarians definitely defy the popular image of librarians.

The New Librarian's Alphabet

A is for Acquisitions
B is for Books
C is for Children's Services
D is for Dewey Decimal System
E is for Electronic Databases
F is for Fund Raising
G is for Government Publications
H is for Holds
I is for Internet Access
J is for Journals
K is for Kids
L is for Libraries
M is for Metadata
N is for New Library User
O is for Online Catalog
P is for Patrons
Q is for Query
R is for Reference
S is for Serials
T is for Technical Services
U is for Urban Libraries
V is for Virtual Library
W is for Web Page
X is for Gen X patrons
Y is Young Adult Services
Z is for Zero Censorship

Space Marine Librarians

Space marine librarians are metal figures used in the game Warhammer 40,000. Space marines are genetically modified warriors with close combat skills and superior firepower, who win almost every battle. They serve the emperor and are divided into several legions and chapters. The chapter of space marine librarians keep the records of the chapter. On the battlefield, they use their psychic abilities and precognition to fight their enemies. A valuable chapter within the space marines, "the path to becoming a Librarian is a difficult one, as they must not only be strong enough to survive their training, but possess enough mental discipline to fend off the demons and entities of the Warp, as these creatures see the enhanced form and mind of a Librarian as a strong prize."

You'll have to love this game as it holds librarians in high esteem. And what can be more fun than librarians as space marines! To read more about Warhammer 40,000 and space marine librarians, go to http://us.games-workshop.com/games/40k/spacemarines.

Library Superstitions

Are librarians superstitious? That's a hard question to answer. An easier question to answer is whether or not library superstitions exist. And according to W.I. Fletcher, they do. The following excerpts are from "Some Library Superstitions," by W.I. Fletcher, librarian of Amherst College. This article initially appeared in *Library Journal*, v. 14, no. 5–6, May/June 1889.

Our President has reminded us that any discussion of a subject should begin with definition. What, then, do I mean by "superstitions?" I find the dictionaries too strict in their definitions, the word being confined by them almost wholly to religious applications. I must, therefore, make a definition for myself; and I will ask you to let me call a superstition any idea of notion which is held as a matter of belief, and which is based on authority and accepted without reason, or the application to it of that ground principal in all good work — common sense...

If such be the age of the library as an institution, what wonder if, like other ancient establishments, it has become well encrusted with superstitions, or that some of these have become so firmly fixed in the very warp and woof of the fabric that they seem a part of it, and cling with the utmost tenacity even in the broad light of to-day?

To begin with the enumeration of them, we will ask what notions with regard to library *buildings* may justly be considered as superstitions. In the first place, there's the sacred style of architecture, with its lofty and capacious interior, into which a chastened light feebly struggles from narrow windows piercing thick walls or from a few skylights in the roof. In the presence of American librarians of to-day, this superstition need not be dwelt upon. It is for us a thing of the past. But who can tell how many of us may yet be called upon (as was one of our number within the year) to try to administer a modern Library in a magnificent new building erected on this old conventional plan? Just so often and so far as we can, it devolves upon us to denounce this superstition, and endeavor to create a sentiment with regard to it which reach and affect the building committees and architects who will yet be erecting libraries with one thought of the present and future and ten thoughts of the past.

But while speaking of library buildings, I wish to indicate two other notions quite prevalent about them which, while not old, seem to me to be properly but superstitions. First, that of excessive regard for fire-proofness.

Books, pamphlets, and papers are inflammable to a high degree; and while they are not rapidly consumed by fire, their backs, as exposed in a library, shelf above shelf, offer a ready food to the devouring element. This being so, there is but little security against a library's destruction by fire in metal shelves or uprights. Should fire once take in a iron stack of several stories in height, with perforated floors, I fear it would spread as quickly, and do as much damage, to say the least, as in a lower room with wooden shelving. It is conceded that the iron uprights are much more expensive than wooden ones of equal or at least sufficient strength. But the iron ones give an *appearance* of security against fire, and are often lauded on this account. This I call a modern superstition in library architecture. A library building ought to be fire-proof in so far as the structure of the building itself is concerned. But the book-shelving, being a mere shell filled with combustible materials, can gain little, if anything, from being itself combustible, especially, as in case of a hot fire, as much damage may result from its warping as from the burning of wooden shelving, or even more.

The second modern superstition to which I wish to refer as connected with library architecture is the idea of making available for book-storage every perpendicular foot in the building. Certain librarians and architects have fallen a prey to this superstition, and seem to have become infatuated with it. It is the great central idea of the stack system.

But it is not well grounded in reason. Why are not other kinds of buildings amenable to this principle? For instance, why does not a factory building fifty feet high to the eaves have seven floors? Or a dwelling-house have only seven and a half feet between joists?...

Not to dwell longer on superstitions connected with library buildings, I will mention some of a different class. First, there's the idea that a library must not part with anything which has once formed a part of its collections unless it be a duplicate. I dare say I shall here run counter to the feelings of many of my brethren, but I must maintain that there is an apparent lack of reasonableness about this notion of the sacredness of everything once in the library, so that it would be a sort of sacrilege to part with it.

Looking into the near future, are we not led to the conclusion that our libraries must come to the point of a healthy sloughing off of the outgrown and obsolete accretions of the past, to make room for the constant addition of that which is vital for the present and the future? One other thing is pressing upon us in the East, where considerable libraries are growing up in almost every town, and that is the necessity and advantage of a differentiation of libraries, one following out one line of development and another a different one, and all helping one another instead of being engaged in a short-sighted rivalry.

With the acceptance of these two ideas, — that of keeping down the size of a library by, getting rid of that which is useless and obsolete, and that of harmonious and mutually helpful differentiation of libraries, — comes in necessarily the abandonment of the old rigid rule of "Get all you can, and keep all you get," which seems to have prevailed hitherto, and which I do not hesitate to stigmatize as a superstition. I confess I have not yet seen indications of any decided escape from this superstition on the part of those having libraries in charge, but I expect to see them in the future. Reason will prevail here as elsewhere.

Right in this connection we come naturally to another superstition; namely, that of exchanging duplicates. We have had a great deal of talk about this matter of exchanging duplicates, and one proposition after another for a "clearing-house for duplicates." I have become satisfied that the best clearing-house for duplicates possible already exists in the form of the auction-room. And the only reason we have not all taken advantage of it is this mere superstition that a library ought not to sell for money what it may have to dispose of, but must exchange it for an equivalent. Now one of the greatest difficulties about an exchange is the fixing of prices. Whoever has tried it must have felt that he was put in a difficult and trying position. It is conducting a matter of trade. Prices on goods are supposed to have a definite relation to market value, as fixed by manufacturer or established by competition. But a great many library duplicates are not current in the market, so as to have any established price; and for all such there is but one fair way to set a price, and that is to submit them to competition. This the auction-room does effectively, economically, and equitably, and at the saving to the librarian of the immense labor involved in negotiating exchanges for any considerable number of volumes.

Another superstition is the worship of decimals. I had the pleasure formerly of the acquaintance of an army engineer, General T.G. Ellis, who was a decided and earnest opponent of the metric system. I recollect a conversation in which he said that one of the great difficulties in the way of the progress of his thumbs. Had he only stuck to a truly digital system, we should have had a perfect method of reckoning. But as he was so unwise as to bring in the thumbs, we are saddled with a system of tens, in which a larger unit can be divided by two only once without a fraction. By the octal system *three* such divisions give us the lower unit and no fraction. The issue of the conflict between the artificial system of tenths and the natural one of halfs, quarters, and eighths, who can tell? At any rate, Mr. Dewey will tell you this is a very hackneyed and puerile argument against the metric system. It is not presented here with the view of running amuck against that system, but simply as illustrative. Perhaps we may be allowed to remark that no interest of modern civilization would have been more the gainer, had our early ancestors not counted their thumbs, than the one we represent.

Since the days of Dr. N.B. Shurtleff, and his book on the decimal system as applied to libraries, we have been afflicted with a succession of efforts to run libraries on that system. Ten has been the sacred number with many librarians, as seven was with some ancient nations. There is something fascinating about the decimal system, it must be admitted; but it is when one is scheming on paper that this fascination is most strongly felt. In actual work a revolt against its artificiality almost inevitably sets in. By Dr. Shurtleff's method each range of bookshelves was regarded as having ten shelves, each alcove ten ranges, and a room was naturally to be so arranged as to have ten alcoves. The day of alcoves has pretty well gone by, and with it the high ranges of shelves, as well as the whole idea of numbering shelves as furnishing a notation for the books.

Driven out of this stronghold, the decimal system has entrenched itself in classification; and, just as one generation was captivated by the beauty of the former decimal system, the next has been largely carried away with the charms of this, its later applications. But it is hardly rash not to predict that the system will not stand the test of practical use longer in the classification field than it has in the shelf arrangement. Perhaps I have sufficiently paid my respects to the matter of classification, of late, in the columns of the *Library Journal,* and I will not dwell upon it at this time.

One more superstition I have noted, and that is the catalogue cult. I find that I have put myself on record on both sides in regard to cataloguing. I have sometimes placed emphasis on cataloguing as the one means of making a library available, as opposed to classification. Again, I have made light of the value of catalogues, as set over against bibliographical helps. I should like now to harmonize these two expressions, if I may. And I would do so by saying that I heartily believe in catalogues as the one means of guidance to books; but at the same time I am coming to place less and less stress upon the cataloguing of the individual library, and more on catalogues in the wider sense, including and referring mainly to printed catalogues and bibliographies, which may be made available, in lieu of elaborate cataloguing of the individual library. What I would point out, as the current superstition on this subject, is the idea that each individual library should have its very complete catalogue, and that a catalogue can be made which will be a sufficient guide to readers. I think that many of you must have had some of the same experience that has often come to me of late years, when I have found the great inferiority of the references in our own subject catalogue on some topic to the list published somewhere as a bibliography of the subject.

Such experiences must lead to a certain loss of interest in the effort to make a subject catalogue full and complete, and also to a desire to make the fullest use possible of such reference lists and bibliographies as we have or can get. And further than this, the idea is impressed upon us that any and all catalogues or bibliographies whatever fall far short of furnishing the guidance readers want. I quote a striking passage from the late annual report of Mr. Foster, of Providence, on this point.

He introduces it in connection with an interesting showing of the great number and variety of questions asked by persons who have consulted his library. Referring to these questions, he says:—

"If we analyze them, we find that an extraordinarily large percentage of them will not be answered by consulting even the most elaborate of the ordinary type of library catalogues."

There is nothing new to us in all this. It is the same ground gone over pretty completely by Dr. Green several years ago in his paper on "Personal Relations between Librarians and Readers." I only refer to it as cumulative testimony to the truth that implicit dependence cannot be placed on catalogues as guides, and to support my warning against that superstitious regard for the catalogue idea, which will lead to the devotion to elaborate features of this work of time and expense better put to other uses.

I have gone hastily over this ground, which is somewhat hackneyed, simply for the purpose of indicating that in *all* departments of our work we need to be on our guard against the growth of such sentiments or ideas as may be classed as superstitious and unreasoning, based on a mistaken apprehension of the value of things, either venerable for age and general repute, or coming to us as novelties in such a captivating garb that we accept them without brining them to the bar of good sense and rationality. "Prove all things, hold fast to that which is good," is a good motto for the modern librarian, as for the worker in any department.

I have referred thus far only to superstitions liable to be held inside libraries, by librarians and library officers. I had thought of devoting a few moments to the matter of superstitions about libraries held by outsiders. But time is short, and I will only name two of them and have done.

1. Librarians have nothing to do but to read the books.
2. Anybody can make a catalogue.

Think You Could Be a Librarian?

If you think you've got what it takes to be a librarian, you may want to take a couple minutes to try and answer the following questions. They initially appeared in the British periodical the *Librarian*, in various issues published from 1910 to 1911. They were intended to assist students in "progressing through the whole subject of the foundation, erection, furnishing, and equipment of a public library." Following are some questions and answers taken from various issues of the journal and rearranged for your pleasure.

If you find yourself at a loss for an answer, don't fret. This is the type of information taught to students studying to become librarians in the early 1900s. But a lot of the questions and answers are still valid today. If these questions intrigue you, then be sure to peruse the next section on books about library careers.

Questions:

1. What relationship does the size of a public library site bear to the district it is to serve?
2. What are the conditions essential in a public library site?
3. What are the desirable but not essential conditions of a public library site?
4. What are some of the considerations governing the use of the various materials that may be used in the building of a library?
5. What relationship does one department of a public library bear to another, and what arrangement of the rooms will best meet the needs of that relationship?
6. Should all the rooms or departments of a Public Library be maintained at the same temperature? What temperature should be maintained?
7. What are the two classes of methods of ventilation for public and other Libraries where many readers are together in a room?
8. What are the advantages of "natural" ventilation?
9. Name some of the floor materials in use in public and other libraries and describe the features of each.
10. Describe Point Lighting, General Lighting, Diffused Lighting.
11. Which system of lighting is best adapted for (a) Reading Rooms, (b) Reference Rooms, (c) Lending Libraries (open access)?

Answers:

1. It is impossible to lay down invariable rules for determining the size of the site of a public library in respect to the size of the district to be served owing to the differences that exist in the conditions of the locality and its population. The factors to be employed in any such computation however, are the relative density of the population: the class of the inhabitants; the methods of transit: and, not the size of the library district, but the size of the area to be served. It must be known before these factors are used, whether the district (not the immediate locality) is to be served by one library: by one central library and a certain, or uncertain, number of branches or delivery stations; or by several libraries of a similar size....
2. The essential features of a public library site are, 1) a sufficient superficial surface, 2) light on at least two sides, or on one side and top lighting on a single floor building.
3. It is difficult to draw a line between essential points, and those regarded only as desirable in a public library site, because necessity and advisability are relative terms having sufficient values in the minds of different people. It may be safely said that it is desirable that a public library should occupy a central position on a symmetrical site in the district it has to serve — not necessarily the library area. The site might be advantageously situated in a "good" side street in proximity to a main road. The library might stand in its own grounds, on a corner site, to secure easy possibility of two entrances and air and light on all four sides. It would be an additional recommendation if the site were flat, and not on a steep incline.
4. Although to a large extent the choice of materials for the building of a library lies with the architect chosen, some consideration must be given to the subject by the Librarian, to prepare him for formal or informal discussions with members of his Committee. This consideration should be in the direction, first, of the atmospheric conditions of the locality and their known effect on the varieties of stone, and the different qualities of brick, and terra-cotta; the next direction in which to turn attention, is the suitability of the appearance of the suggested material from the points of view of the use

161

to which the building is to be put and the aspect of the immediate surroundings. Another consideration is that of the relative cost of the various materials.

5. All the departments of a public library as it is at present organized are inter-dependent. The newsroom is generally regarded as the first step in the making of a reader, heading next to the magazine room, and thence to the lending library, after which the reader may become a student of the reference room. The logical arrangement of the various rooms under this scheme would be to place the newsroom at the nearest point to the entrance, followed by the general reading room. As the reader begins to realize his hunger for books, he will, of his own accord, proceed to the lending library and on to the reference library. This is, of course, the rough outline of the generally accepted theory, and is subject to innumerable considerations of various kinds in individual cases. The arrangement, however, has many points in favour of it: the most important being probably the situation of those rooms most needing quietness at the farthest point from the noise of the streets.

6. It does not appear desirable that all the rooms of a Public Library should be maintained at the same temperature. The Reference Room, being used by readers remaining some time, and frequently removing their hats and coats, might be reasonably kept at a temperature slightly higher than the other departments, say, 60 degrees. The Newsroom and Magazine Room might be kept at 58 degrees, or even less, while probably 55 degrees or 56 degrees would be found sufficient for the Lending Department of an open access Library where the borrowers are moving from shelf to shelf, if local heat is given in the staff enclosure. It was very generally held at one time that every room should be 60 degrees, but that is now admitted to be too high for some of the Library rooms.

7. Ventilation is usually divided into two classes, the natural and the mechanical. This is largely the result no doubt of the opposition and advocacy of two schools of ventilating experts.

8. The advantages or otherwise of natural ventilation can be best described by pointing out the various forms of natural ventilation. The first of these is undoubtedly open windows with flat sashes. This form has been developed in various ways: Small shutters and circles let into the glass of the windows; small windows in boxes or opening in certain prescribed ways to avoid draught; tubes in the walls at various heights from the ground with or without opening in the roof in the shape of wire ventilators, glass flaps, cowls on the roof, & c. The chief advantage of most of these is that there is no cost when once they have been fitted. The wind supplies whatever natural current of air there may be. Unfortunately there is seldom any protection from draught. There are several patents in natural ventilation, some of which are more successful than others as applied to public Library ventilation.

9. Apart from carpets of various qualities and other textile materials usually found in private and semi-private libraries, the floor materials referred to are roughly four in number. They are mentioned in the order of the frequency of their use: (1) stone and similar substances; (2) plain floor boards; (3) wood blocks; (4) linoleum on top of floor boards or wood blocks. Stone or mosaic floors are seldom found beyond entrance halls and lobbies, or in other parts of buildings where readers do not remain for any considerable time. Floor boards seldom show the wearing qualities required, where hundreds — sometimes thousands — of people walk over them daily. Linoleum cemented to floor boards, wood blocks, or a bed of materials of a stone nature is more common now that it was. The higher-class qualities process great wear resisting properties, more particularly when oiled and dressed, and worn places may be readily made good by the inser-

tion of new pieces. Wood blocks, when rift-sawn and treated with floor dressing instead of being constantly washed, have enormous wear-resisting qualities, and although not so silent as linoleum are, as a rule, sufficiently silent when the chairs in the rooms are fitted with pads or domes. Rubber flooring has superb qualities, but it has had no test in this country in connection with Public Library wear.

10. Point Lighting is the term applied to an arrangement of lights at the points requires; as for instance, a point of light — consisting of one or more lamps — over a single table or a newspaper stand close to the surface to be illuminated. General Lighting is the direct antithesis of point lighting, being in general a few large lamps or clusters of small lamps distributed at comparatively wide intervals, at a height sufficient to throw the rays of light a considerable distance laterally; while the shades, which in point lighting are opaque and concentrate the beams on the point of illumination, are so arranged that a considerable percentage of the illumination is allowed to escape in other directions than a downward one. Diffused Lighting is sometimes described as reflected light. Although there are variations in the method, the general one is a large number of lights quite close together, shaded from the room and throwing the rays of light on to a white wall or ceiling from which they are reflected back into the room.

11. A judicious combination of point and general lighting would appear to be the best method of illuminating reading rooms (including in the term, newsrooms) and lending libraries on the open access plan; and point lighting alone for reference room use. There is no doubt that shaded or softened light is best for long sustained reading of comparatively small and solid type. General lighting of sufficient power for general reading rooms is very much more costly than point lighting, while point lighting with the points only a few inches above the eye level produces a dim appearance over the upper portions of the rooms.

Interested in Becoming a Librarian?

Now that you've seen the fun and interesting side of librarians, are you thinking about becoming one? Or do you think your child would make a wonderful librarian? If so, you may want to peruse one or more of the following books about library careers.

You'll notice that there are significantly more children's books about library careers than adult books. This is no surprise since studies have shown that career decisions are made early in life. The items listed below are just a sample of the many career books and other information available. Be sure to visit your local library and ask the librarian for additional resources about library careers. And while you're there, take a moment to talk to the librarian about his or her job and career.

FOR ADULTS:

Career Opportunities in Library and Information Science, by Linda P. Carvell. Checkmark Books, 2005.

Careers for Bookworms & Other Literary Types, by Marjorie Eberts, Margaret Gisler. McGraw Hill, 2002.

Jump Start Your Career in Library and Information Science, by Priscilla K. Shontz, Steven Oberg, Robert Newlen. Scarecrow, 2002.

The Librarian's Career Guide Book, by Priscilla K. Shontz. Scarecrow, 2004.

Opportunities in Library and Information Science Careers, by Kathleen de la Pena McCook. McGraw Hill, 2001.

Straight from the Stacks: A First-Hand Guide to Careers in Library and Information Science, by Laura Townsend Kane. American Library Association, 2003.

Current information on librarianship, including average salaries and career outlook, can be found in the *Occupational Outlook Handbook* issued by the U.S. Bureau of Labor Statistics. You can read the information online at www.bls.gov/oco.home.htm.

The American Library Association provides information about library careers on their website. Go to www.ala.org and click on "Education and Careers."

FOR CHILDREN:

A Day in the Life of a Librarian, by Liza Burby. PowerKids Press, 1999.

I Can Be a Librarian, by Carol Greene. Children's Press, 1988.

I Want to Be a Librarian, by Donna Baker. Children's Press, 1978.

Librarian, by Heather Miller. Heinemann Library, 2002.

Librarians, by Charnan Simon. Child's World, 2003.

Librarians, by Judith Jango-Cohen. Lerner Publications, 2004.

Meet the Librarian, by Elizabeth Vogel. PowerKids Press, 2002.

That's Our Librarian! By Ann Morris. Millbrook Press, 2003.

We Need Librarians, by Jane Scoggins Bauld and Gail Saunders-Smith. Capstone Press, 2000.

11

Interesting Bits About Libraries and Library History

Now that you've seen the interesting side of librarians, it's time to take a quick look at some interesting aspects of library history and libraries of today. These bits of information will also help you understand the many conditions that librarians have or are currently working under. And if you're a trivia fan, don't overlook this chapter.

Ancient Libraries Had No Books

Libraries in ancient times did not house books like they do today. Mesopotamian libraries back in the seventh century BC housed clay tablets of information. In the Roman Empire, great libraries like the Library of Alexandria housed papyrus scrolls of information. And during the Han Dynasty in China, libraries housed pieces of bamboo that had lines of Chinese characters inscribed on them. A few "books" were also carved in stone.

Bound in Leather and Chained

In the fifteenth, sixteenth and seventeenth centuries, it was often common for libraries to bind their books in leather and chain them to a fixture in the library. From the library at the Sorbonne in Paris to the Vatican Library and the Library at Trinity College in Cambridge, this practice was used to safeguard the collection.

Camel Libraries

If you thought getting library service from a bookmobile was nifty, take a look at how services are provided in Kenya. In 1996 the Kenya National Library Service began its Camel Library Service in the isolated North Eastern Province of the country. About 300 books, a table, and chairs are loaded onto three camels. Then a librarian and helpers head to one of the designated Camel library service points in a caravan. Once there, they set up the tent, unpack the books, and establish a temporary library service point. Once the day is over, they pack everything up and head back to the library.

You can read more about this Camel Library Service on the web at the Kenya National Library Services website, www.knls.or.ke/camel.htm.

Curses Preventing Book Theft and Mutilation

At one point in history, libraries used curses to prevent the theft and mutilation of library materials. Some examples of these curses, which appear in J.W. Clark's *The Care of Books* (1901) follow:

> Should anyone by craft or any device whatever abstract this book from this place [Jumieges] may his soul suffer, in retribution for what he as done, and may his name be erased from the book of the living and not recorded among the Blessed.

This next curse appeared in a manuscript held at Christ Church in Canterbury.

> May whoever destroys this title, or by gift or sale or loan or exchange or theft or by any other device knowingly alienates this book from the aforesaid Christ Church, incur in this life the malediction of Jesus Christ and of the most glorious Virgin His Mother, and of Blessed Thomas, Martyr. Should however it please Christ, who is patron of Christ Church, may his soul be saved in the Day of Judgment.

And just in case the library user was not worried about his immortal soul, Mr. Clark also presents "a specimen in verse, from at breviary now in the library of Gonville and Caius College, Cambridge":

> Wher so ever y be come over all
> I belonge to the Chapell of gunvylle hall;
> He shal be cursed by the grate sentens
> The felonsly faryth and berith me thens.
> And whether he bere me in poke or sekke,
> For me he shall be hanged by the nekke,
> (I am so well beknown of diverse men)
> But I be restored theder agen.

Largest Library in the World

The Library of Congress is said to be the largest library in the world. Its collection consists of more than 130 million items on approximately 530 miles of bookshelves. To put those 530 miles of bookshelves in perspective, the distance from one end of Texas to the other (east-west) is 773 miles.

Library Bookcases Set Against the Wall an Innovation

It wasn't until 1563, with the building of the Escorial Library in Spain, that placing bookcases against the wall became a new library system of arrangement. John Willis Clark states in his 1901 book *The Care of Books*:

> While in England we were struggling with the difficulties of adapting medieval forms of libraries and bookcases to the ever-increasing number of volumes, a new system was initiated on the continent, which I propose to case the wall system.... I do not mean by this sentence that nobody ever set bookshelves against a wall before the third quarter of the sixteenth century.... What I wish to enforce is that before the Escorial was built, no important library was fitted up in that manner from the beginning by the architect.

Library Services by Boat

Camels are not the only means of providing library services. In Bangladesh, some residents receive library services from a boat library. A large number of the residents work and live in flood prone areas. During monsoon season, the Shidhulai Swanirvar Sangstha, a nongovernmental entity uses indigenous boats loaded with books and a computer to provide library services to remote communities in flood prone areas. The boats dock at riverside communities and bring library services to those areas that are cut off from traditional libraries during the rainy season.

Library Staff Were Slaves

If you work in a library and sometimes feel like a slave, there's a historical reason behind that feeling. In the Roman Empire most libraries were staffed by slaves. According to Lionel Casson's book, *Libraries in the Ancient World,* "In the Roman as in the Greek world, white-collar work, like so many other forms of labor, was done by slaves. Cicero and Atticus used highly trained Greek slaves for their library personnel ... they took care of the day-to-day tasks — reshelving rolls, repairing damaged rolls, keeping the catalogue up to date, and so on."

Mercantile Library Pays Librarian Less Than French Cooks

The Mercantile Library was a popular subscription library in the United States in the 1800s. According to an article in the January 1898 issue of the *Bookman*, "It is not so old as the Philadelphia Library Company, it having originated in 1821 from a notice inviting the merchants and merchants' clerks, and those friendly to the formation of a Mercantile Library Association, to meet in the Mayor's Court Room; and in January of the following year, the rooms of the second story at 100 Chestnut Street were engaged at a rental of $130 per year, and a librarian at a salary of $100 per year, from which it will be seen that the public estimate of the value of a librarian's services has risen somewhat in seventy years, though the highest rewards of the profession are still inferior to those of the best class of French cooks."

If you think that was a sad statement as to how libraries paid their librarians, Fred Lerner's book *The Story of Libraries* states that in the Arab world in the thirteenth century "at the Ahmadiyya in Aleppo the librarian received the same pay as did the porter and the sweeper...."

New Hampshire First State Library

According to Edward Edwards' *Memoirs of Libraries* (1859), the New Hampshire State Library was the earliest state library, "founded at Concord, about 1770. The best furnished is that of New York, which was not commenced until 1818, but is rapidly taking rank amongst the most important of American Libraries. During the long interval which elapsed between the establishment of these two Libraries, only two others of the same kind were formed — that of Pennsylvania, at Harrisburg, in 1816, and that of Ohio, at Columbus, in the following year."

Pillaging for Library Materials

In today's tight budget times, librarians may want to take a cue from the actions of Ptolemies as they developed the Library of Alexandria. "They confiscated any books found on ships unloading at Alexandria; the owners were given copies..." according in Lionel Casson's book, *Libraries in the Ancient World*.

Presidential Libraries for Only 12 Presidents

Only 12 past presidents of the United States have presidential libraries administered by the U.S. National Archives and Records Administration. Those libraries are: Hoover Library (West Branch, IA), Nixon Presidential Materials (College Park, MD), Roosevelt Library (Hyde Park, NY), Ford Library (Ann Arbor, MI), Truman Library (Independence, MO), Carter Library (Atlanta, GA), Eisenhower Library (Abilene, KS), Reagan Library (Simi Valley, CA), Kennedy Library (Boston, MA),

Bush Library (College Station, TX), Johnson Library (Austin, TX), Clinton Library (Little Rock, AR).

Recycling Old Card Catalogs

Did you ever wonder what happened to all those old card catalogs that used to be in libraries? Many libraries have found ways to recycle those old card catalogs. Some libraries have found other uses for the catalog cabinets, like storing slides or cassette tapes in them. On the Librariana Listserv, members were asked to contribute ideas for using the old catalog cabinets. Many members came up with the idea of using them as storage devices for items ranging from pens and envelopes to Barbie dolls. The entire list can be viewed on the Library History Buff website (www.libraryhistorybuff.com/cardcatalog.htm).

In 1982 *American Libraries* also asked their readers to put on their thinking caps to come up clever uses for old card catalogs. Readers came up with a variety of creative ideas such as using them as kitty hotels and in fundraisers where folks buy tickets to open one of the drawers and win a prize. You can read all the winning ideas readers came up with in the November 1982 issue of *American Libraries*.

As far as the old catalog cards are concerned, using them for art projects seems to be one of the most common methods of recycling them. For example, a July 5, 2005, press release from the University of Iowa Library states that as part of their 150th anniversary, the library distributed their old cards to folks across the state and invited them to create a work of art on the card. The cards were then used as part of a public art project.

Bibliography

Battles, Matthew. *Library: An Unquiet History*. New York: W.W. Norton, 2003.

Birrell, Augustin. *In the Name of the Bodleian and Other Essays*. New York: Charles Scribner's Sons, 1905.

Carvell, Linda P. *Career Opportunities in Library and Information Science*. New York: Checkmark, 2005.

Casson, Lionel. *Libraries in the Ancient World*. New Haven: Yale University Press, 2001.

Clark, John Willis. *The Care of Books: An Essay on the Development of Libraries and Their Fittings, from the Earliest Times to the End of the Eighteenth Century*. Cambridge, MA: Cambridge University Press, 1901.

Coutts, Henry Thomas. *Library Jokes and Jottings: A Collection of Stories Partly Wise But Otherwise*. White Plains, NY: H.W. Wilson, 1914.

Dana, John Cotton. *Suggestions*. Boston: F.W. Faxon, 1921.

de la Peña McCook, Kathleen. *Opportunities in Library and Information Science Careers*. Lincolnwood, IL: NTC., 2001.

Drake, David. *Each of Us Is a Book*. Jefferson, NC: McFarland, 2003.

_____. *Overdue Notice: Poems from the Library*. Jefferson, NC: McFarland, 1995.

Eberts, Marjorie, and Gisler, Margaret. *Careers for Bookworms and Other Literary Types*. Chicago: VGM Career Horizons, 2003.

Edwards, Edward. *Memoirs of Libraries: Including a Handbook of Library Economy*. London: Trubner, 1859.

Foss, Sam Walter. *Song of the Library Staff*. New York: John A. Anderson, 1906. Reprint, Berkeley, CA: Peacock Press, 1965.

Gorman, Michael. *Our Own Selves: More Meditations for Librarians*. Chicago: American Library Association, 2005.

_____. *Our Singular Strengths: Meditations for Librarians*. Chicago: American Library Association, 1998.

Hessel, Alfred. *A History of Libraries: Translated, with Supplementary Material by Reuben Peiss*. Washington, DC: Scarecrow, 1950.

Kane, Laura Townsend. *Straight from the Stacks: A First-Hand Guide to Careers in Library and Information Science*. Chicago: American Library Association, 2003.

Lerner, Fred. *Libraries Through the Ages*. New York: Continuum, 1999.

_____. *The Story of Libraries: From the Invention of Writing to the Computer Age*. New York: Continuum, 1998.

Meir, Golda. *My Life*. New York: Putnam, 1975.

Pearson, Edmund Lester. *The Librarian at Play*. Boston: Small, Maynard, 1911.

_____. *The Library and the Librarian: A Selection of Articles from the* Boston Evening Transcript *and Other Sources.* Woodstock, VT: Elm Tree, 1910.

_____. *The Old Librarian's Almanack.* Woodstock, VT: Elm Tree, 1909.

_____. *The Secret Book.* New York: Macmillan, 1914.

Petroski, Henry. *The Book on the Bookshelf.* New York: Alfred A. Knopf, 1999.

Richardson, Ernest Cushing. *Biblical Libraries: A Sketch of Library History from 3400 B.C. to A.D. 150.* Princeton, NJ: Princeton University Press, 1914.

Shontz, Priscilla K. *The Librarian's Career Guide Book.* Lanham, MD: Scarecrow, 2004.

_____, Steven Oberg, and Robert Newlen. *Jump Start Your Career in Library and Information Science.* Lanham, MD: Scarecrow, 2002.

Wheatley, H.B. *How to Form a Library.* 2nd ed. New York: Armstrong, 1886.

Index

Index

Index